Values and Social Change in Ireland

Edited by
Christopher T. Whelan

GILL & MACMILLAN

For Yvonne

Published in Ireland by
Gill & Macmillan Ltd
Goldenbridge
Dublin 8
with associated companies throughout the world

© Tony Fahey, Niamh Hardiman, Michael P. Hornsby-Smith,
Christopher T. Whelan 1994
0 7171 1947 5
Print origination by Seton Music Graphics Ltd, Bantry, Co. Cork
Printed in Ireland by ColourBooks Ltd, Dublin

A catalogue record for this book is available from the British Library.

Contents

List of Tables   *vii*

Acknowledgments   *xi*

1. Values and Social Change
   Christopher T. Whelan   1

2. Religious and Moral Values
   Michael P. Hornsby-Smith and Christopher T. Whelan   7

3. Marriage and the Family
   Christopher T. Whelan and Tony Fahey   45

4. Work Values
   Christopher T. Whelan   82

5. Politics and Democratic Values
   Niamh Hardiman and Christopher T. Whelan   100

6. Values and Political Partisanship
   Niamh Hardiman and Christopher T. Whelan   136

7. Values and Psychological Well-Being
   Christopher T. Whelan   187

8. Irish Social Values: Traditional or Modern?
   Christopher T. Whelan   212

References   216

List of Tables

2.1 Frequency of church attendance: a comparison, 1981 and 1990   21
2.2 Trends in frequency of church attendance   23
2.3 Weekly or more frequent church attendance, by sex, employment status, and location, 1990   24
2.4 Weekly or more frequent church attendance, by age and employment status, distinguishing between urban and rural location, 1990   25
2.5 Impact of class on church attendance, by age: percentage attending weekly or more often, 1990   28
2.6 Weekly or more frequent church attendance, by education and age: percentage attending weekly or more often   28
2.7 Religious and moral values: a comparison, 1981 and 1990   31
2.8 Religious and moral values, by age group   32
2.9 Traditional religious values, by age group   33
2.10 Percentage drawing comfort and strength from prayer, by age group and time of survey   34
2.11 Views on God, by age group and time of survey   35
2.12 Average scores on extent to which divorce and abortion can ever be justified, by time of survey   35
2.13 Circumstances under which abortion is approved of: comparison of Irish and European views   36
2.14 Values that it is important to learn: a comparison, 1981 and 1990   38
2.15 Percentage holding traditional religious beliefs among Catholics, by country   39
2.16 Percentage of Catholics considering that the church gives adequate answers to problems, by country   41
2.17 Views among Catholics regarding issues on which it is proper for the church to speak out   42
3.1 'Traditional' sex role attitudes: Ireland and Europe compared   51
3.2 'Traditional' sex role dimensions: comparison of Irish and European average scores   52
3.3 'Traditional' sex role attitudes, by sex   53
3.4 'Traditional' sex role attitudes, by age group   54
3.5 'Traditional' sex role attitudes, by level of educational qualification   55
3.6 'Traditional' sex role attitudes: comparison of women in paid employment and in home duties   56

3.7 'Traditional' sex role attitudes: comparison of educational and age extremes — 57

3.8 'Traditional' sex role attitudes to career cost: differences by sex, 18–29 age group — 58

3.9 Ideal family size, by age group: Ireland and Europe compared — 61

3.10 Ideal family size, by age group and urban v. rural location — 61

3.11 Percentage agreeing with the view that parents' duty is to do the best for their children even at the expense of their own well-being, by age and date of survey — 63

3.12 Percentage agreeing with the view that parents' duty is to do the best for their children even at the expense of their own well-being, by age and education — 64

3.13 Percentage agreeing that regardless of one's parents' qualities and faults one must always love and respect them — 65

3.14 Extent of shared attitudes with parents, by age group and time of survey — 67

3.15 Approval of abortion under particular circumstances, by age group and time of survey — 71

3.16 Attitudes to abortion, by age group — 72

3.17 A. Extent to which abortion can ever be justified
B. Approval of abortion where mother's health is at risk from pregnancy (percentage approving)
C. Approval of abortion where it is likely that child would be born physically handicapped (percentage approving) — 72

3.18 Extent to which divorce can ever be justified (average scores) — 73

3.19 Percentages agreeing that marriage is an outdated institution, by age, sex, location, and class — 75

3.20 Views on sexual freedom, by age — 76

3.21 Attitudes to traditional family patterns: comparison of Ireland and Europe — 77

3.22 Attitudes to traditional family patterns, by age group — 77

3.23 Important factors contributing to a successful marriage: comparison of Irish and European scores — 79

3.24 Things that make for a successful marriage — 80

4.1 Importance of different areas of life, by sex, controlling for marital status: percentage considering each area to be very important — 86

4.2 Job importance dimensions, by sex and marital status for full-time employees — 88

4.3 Job importance dimensions, by class — 89

4.4 Percentage considering particular job characteristics important, by class — 89

4.5 Meaning of work for employees, by sex and marital status — 91

4.6 Percentage who agree that men have more right to a job than women when jobs are scarce — 92

4.7 Percentage who agree that men have more right to a job than women when jobs are scarce, by age group and educational level — 92

4.8 Meaning of work, by age group — 93

4.9 Meaning of work, by class — 94

4.10 Impact of unemployment on the meaning of work — 96

5.1 Confidence in public institutions — 103

5.2 Importance in life of different areas: Ireland and Europe compared (percentage considering each area important) — 105

5.3 Role of politics in everyday life: Ireland and Europe compared 105
5.4 Role of politics in everyday life, by social class 106
5.5 Role of politics in everyday life, by education 107
5.6 Role of politics in everyday life, by sex 108
5.7 Cumulative effect of social background on role of politics in everyday life 108
5.8 Membership of selected voluntary organisations, by sex 109
5.9 Percentage who agree there is nothing they could do if an unjust law were passed 110
5.10 Percentage who agree there is nothing they could do if an unjust law were passed: impact of social class and education (percentage by column) 111
5.11 Proneness to conventional forms of political protest: Ireland and Europe compared 113
5.12 Proneness to unconventional forms of political protest: Ireland and Europe compared 113
5.13 Proneness to conventional forms of political participation, by education (percentage by column) 114
5.14 Probability of having engaged in conventional forms of participation, by priority given to protecting freedom of speech 117
5.15 Role of politics in everyday life: comparison of unemployed and employees 119
5.16 Protest proneness: comparison of unemployed and employees 120
5.17 Political and social conservatism: Ireland and Europe compared 123
5.18 Political and social conservatism, by age group 124
5.19 Political and social conservatism, by educational level 124
5.20 Authoritarianism: Ireland and Europe compared 127
5.21 Authoritarianism, by age group 128
5.22 Authoritarianism, by educational level 128
5.23 Confidence in establishment institutions, by authoritarianism 129
5.24 Confidence in institutions: comparison of unemployed and employees 130
5.25 Pride in nationality among those considering themselves to be Irish compared with the European average 131
5.26 Localism versus cosmopolitanism (primary identification with geographical groups): Ireland and Europe compared 131
5.27 Localism v. cosmopolitanism, by educational qualification 132
6.1 Party preference, by class 143
6.2 Percentage voting Fine Gael or Progressive Democrats and Labour or Workers' Party, by class 144
6.3 Party preference, by farm status of chief earner 145
6.4 Party preference, by urban v. rural location 146
6.5 Party preference, by age 147
6.6 Party preference, by education 147
6.7 Party preference, by age and education 148
6.8 Probability of supporting Fianna Fáil, by class origins, controlling for class 150
6.9 Distribution of self-assignment to the left or right: comparison of Irish and European distributions 153
6.10 Percentage assigning themselves to the left, by age group 154
6.11 Percentage assigning themselves to the left, by party preference 155

6.12 Left-wing economic attitudes, by educational qualification and
      age: percentage left   159
6.13 Left-wing economic values and liberalism on sexual morality,
      by class   161
6.14 Left-wing on sexual morality, by age group (percentage scoring
      left)   161
6.15 Relationship between left-right self-assignment and left-right
      values: matrix of correlations   162
6.16 Extent of left-wing values: Ireland and Europe compared   163
6.17 Postmaterialism, by age group and educational qualification   167
6.18 Postmaterialism, by age group: Ireland and Netherlands compared 168
6.19 Relationship of postmaterialism to left-right dimensions   169
6.20 Support for civil rights and environmental movement,
      by 'postmaterialism'   169
6.21 Style of life items, by postmaterialism   170
6.22 Willingness to bear costs in order to protect environment, by
      postmaterialism   171
6.23 Percentage giving priority to economic stability and progress
      towards a society in which ideas count more than money, by
      class and age   173
6.24 Composition of party support in terms of left-wing
      economic attitudes and liberalism on sexual morality   174
6.25 Party preference, by left-wing economic attitudes   176
6.26 Party preference, by left-wing economic attitudes and liberalism
      on sexual morality   176
6.27 Party preference, by 'postmaterialism' and confidence in
      establishment institutions   177
6.28 Fianna Fáil or Fine Gael and left-wing or Green support, by
      left-wing value dimensions   179
6.29 Cumulative effect of lack of confidence in establishment
      institutions, left-right self-assignment, left-wing economic attitudes
      and liberalism on support for Fianna Fáil and left/Green Party 179
6.30 Left-wing economic values: comparison of unemployed
      and employees   181
6.31 Party support: comparison of unemployed and employees   181
6.32 Party preference, by economic values and class (percentage by
      column)   184
7.1   International variations in psychological well-being   190
7.2   International variations in interpersonal trust and happiness   191
7.3   Factors affecting variation in life satisfaction and happiness 194
7.4   Variation in positive and negative feelings, by state of health 198
7.5   Variation in positive and negative feelings, by socio-
      demographic situation   199
7.6   Variation in positive and negative feelings, by life-style deprivation 202
7.7   Impact of being in full-time unpaid home duties on positive affect 204
7.8   Subjective well-being and satisfaction with different areas of life 205
7.9   Affect balance score, by pride in nationality   207
7.10 Affect balance score, by trust responses   208
7.11 Negative affect score, by religious and racial prejudice   208
7.12 Affect balance score, by importance in life of different areas 209

Acknowledgments

The research reported in this book has been made possible by the contribution to its funding made by the European Value System Study Group. In addition Dr David Barker has provided support and encouragement throughout the project.

We are grateful to our colleagues at the Economic and Social Research Institute, economists and sociologists, for the support they have consistently provided throughout this and other projects. Brendan Whelan, Mary Lou O'Kennedy and the staff of the ESRI's Survey Unit were responsible for the collection and processing of the Irish survey data, and we are most grateful for the efficient manner in which the operation was conducted.

Mary Cleary and her colleagues have borne the brunt of the demands arising from the preparation of this manuscript with their usual efficiency and good humour. Finally we would like to thank Maura Rohan for providing a comprehensive library service and Pat Hopkins for her efficient response to photocopying demands.

1 Values and Social Change

CHRISTOPHER T. WHELAN

THE EUROPEAN VALUES SURVEY

In this volume we report on the results of our analysis of the 1990 European Values Survey. This survey was conducted in a range of European countries, and the results are available to us for:

> France
> Great Britain
> West Germany
> Italy
> Spain
> Portugal
> The Netherlands
> Belgium
> Northern Ireland
> Republic of Ireland

The results we report in relation to the Republic of Ireland are based on a nationally representative sample of 1,000 respondents. In each of these countries—with the exception of Northern Ireland, where the figure was 312—at least 1,000 respondents, representing a cross-section of the adult population, were interviewed. In reporting overall European results we have weighted the results to allow for variations in adult population size.

The main focus of our discussion and analysis is the Republic of Ireland. Where the name 'Ireland' appears in the text it is to be taken to refer to the Republic, except where it is otherwise indicated or where the context makes clear that the reference is to the island as a whole. North-South comparisons are obviously of particular interest.

1

The European Values Study questionnaire was designed to measure values in important domains of life such as religion and morality, politics, work, and marriage and the family. The selection of items was determined by a steering committee to ensure that the content of the questionnaire was identical in the different countries. The selection of items to be included in the study was mainly guided by broad ideas on the impact of modernisation. A substantial proportion of the items had also been included in the 1981 European Values Study, allowing for the possibilities of comparison across time. The sample size in Ireland in 1981 was 1,217. The under-25 age group was deliberately over-sampled in the 1981 survey, and we have weighted the results in order to take this into account.

Given the focus on change, questions were selected that could reveal traditional values, stressing order and authority, and modern values, characterised by an emphasis on the importance of self-determination (Ester et al., 1993, 23).

One of the difficulties involved in discussing values is that the definition of the term varies substantially between disciplines. In philosophy or aesthetics the concept is used in a normative sense to discriminate between good and bad, beautiful and ugly. This principle is also captured in colloquial usage, as in 'decline of values' and 'value crisis'. In the social sciences the term is used in a rather different sense to convey the notion of a disposition or propensity to respond, or act, in a certain way.

The notion of values employed in this study is of a very general kind. A distinction is frequently made between values, beliefs, and attitudes, with beliefs relating to cognition and values to motivational content and with values being viewed as more encompassing than attitudes. However, in the European Values Study the true content of the questionnaire is such as to make it unhelpful to attempt to distinguish rigorously between beliefs, attitudes, and values. Most of the questions are pitched at a relatively general level, and for convenience of presentation we will tend to use the term 'values' in an inclusive fashion.

MODERNISATION, INDIVIDUALISATION, AND CONVERGENCE

A comparative analysis of the 1990 European Values Study material by Ester et al. (1993) had as its central working hypothesis the notion that as countries advance economically, their populations increasingly shift in the direction of individualisation. This process is seen to involve growing autonomy of individuals in developing their own values and norms and to be part of a wide-ranging modernisation process.

Modernisation is understood to involve the interaction of a number of different processes over varying historical time scales. It involves interdependent fundamental change in the economic, technological, socio-cultural and political domains. At the economic level it involves the emergence of a monetarised exchange economy based on large-scale production and consumption of goods through the market, industrialisation, commercialisation, and decline in the agricultural sector. At a technological level it involves a range of developments that have to do with increased control of the environment, through technology and knowledge. Within the political domain, modernisation means the dominance of secular forms of power and authority and conceptions of sovereignty and legitimacy characteristic of the modern nation-state. In social terms, the decline of fixed social hierarchies and overlapping allegiances is central. Such structural modernisation is hypothesised to be accompanied by cultural modernisation, involving the decline of the religious world view typical of traditional societies and the emergence of secularised, and individualised, religious and moral values and the instrumental impulses characteristic of a consumer culture.

The process of individualisation is seen by Ester et al. (1993) to involve a number of inter-related developments. Within the religious domain it is associated with secularisation, involving the declining social significance of religious institutions, activities, and consciousness. Once religion is seen as a 'private affair', the individual may choose from an assortment of ultimate meanings. With the decline of the role of ideology and traditional class influences, political orientations may come to be seen as a 'political menu' from which ideas and concepts are selected 'à la carte'. Individualisation in the domain of primary relationships puts increasing pressure on the traditional role patterns and on work relationships between men and women. In relation to marriage and the family, it appears that there is greater tolerance of individualistic values, but this is not quite the same as saying that all members of societies actively embrace these values.

The second hypothesis guiding the Ester et al. (1993) analysis of the European Values Study material was that, in the long run, modern societies will converge in the direction of individualised value systems in religion, morality, politics, primary relationships, and work—although they acknowledge that this notion of cultural convergence has been the subject of heated debate in the social sciences.

General notions of individualisation and convergence have played a central role in comparative sociology in generating propositions about change that are open to empirical examination. This has been true whether they be associated with general theories of modernisation or with more specific variants, such as the liberal theory of industrialisation. The latter approach argues that a logic of industrialism constrains social structure and processes, and ultimately requires the emergence of value systems that are consistent with the functional exigencies of an industrial society.

In interpreting the Irish material from the European Values Study we will, as we have done elsewhere (Goldthorpe and Whelan, 1992), treat ideas of a logic of development, or societal convergence, with a considerable degree of scepticism. In part our position is influenced by the task we have set ourselves. This is less a systematic cross-national comparison of values than an attempt to situate value change in Ireland in the context of important social structural developments, while highlighting what is distinctive about the Irish case through the use of comparative material.

Our approach is also influenced by the desire to exploit the heuristic value of modernisation theory while at the same time avoiding its social-evolutionary implications. Indeed, following Bendix (1967), we would hold that there is an important sense in which, as a consequence of the importance of timing and sequence, modernisation cannot occur in the same way twice. The path taken by latecomers is crucially influenced by the presence of the earlier developers. This arises because of the possibility of learning from their experience and as a consequence of relationships between countries at different levels of development.

It is also necessary to take into account the specific social structural context of societal transitions. Here it is important to distinguish between modernisation and industrialisation. Many attributes of modernisation have been adopted in isolation from other aspects of modernity. The Irish case provides a particularly good example of such sequencing, in that modernisation of the society ran well ahead of its industrial development. Under British rule, Ireland acquired a modern state apparatus and a modern financial system. Furthermore, the Catholic Church in the nineteenth century developed as a highly bureaucratic modern organisation and played a critical role in the creation of a modern education system that ensured virtually universal literacy (Goldthorpe, 1992; Fahey, 1992).

Goldthorpe (1992, 417) notes that the Irish case fits rather well Wrigley's (1979) suggestion that industrialisation might best be understood as a possible solution to problems of population pressure created by prior modernisation, with mass emigration being an important alternative. The availability of such an alternative undermines any notion of an inevitable course of development. The Irish experience of emigration, as has been widely recognised, has had pervasive consequences for the development path that ensued, the shape of the class structure, family relations, and the formation of national culture and identity (Breen et al., 1990; Mjøset, 1992; Lee, 1989). The impact of emigration in Ireland provides an example of the importance of external relations as well as internal development. Taken together with the evidence relating to the importance of timing and sequencing of modernisation processes, such considerations lead us to be sceptical of the operation of any logic of industrialism in the Irish case. It follows that in attempting to understand the nature and consequences of modernisation in Ireland, 'history must carry at least as great a weight as theory' (Goldthorpe, 1992, 414).

Relying on notions of unfolding sequences of modernisation is also likely to be unhelpful, because of what Giddens (1990, 36) has termed the 'reflexivity of modernity'. In traditional cultures the past is honoured, while in modern social life social practices are constantly re-examined. Such examination encompasses postmodernist challenges to Enlightenment notions of progress and cumulative knowledge. Enlightenment conceptions of progress and, indeed, the view of Europe as the cradle of progress in the world were shattered by the rise of Nazism and the Holocaust. It is possible, however, to develop a perspective on the Enlightenment that does not see it as involving the substitution of secular providence for religious certainty but as involving a critical questioning of all faiths, including faith in reason (McLennan, 1992).

Thus Giddens (1990, 38–9) sees modernity as being associated not so much with conviction regarding progress as with puzzlement and existential doubt—an outlook that is unsettling to a degree to which we have only recently come to fully appreciate. The risks and dangers of the modern world, including that of nuclear confrontation, lead Giddens (1990, 139) to draw on the image of a juggernaut rather than the 'train of history' to convey what is involved in living in such a world.

Since the outcome of historical and social research is absorbed into the general body of knowledge, such critical examination of modern social life is not restricted to sociologists. Important ideas in social science generally arise as a consequence of reflection on social trends and, in turn, are fed back in a way that influences the response to such trends. As the example of debates on marriage, divorce and sexuality in Ireland demonstrates, in an important sense, the social scientist is only one step ahead of the enlightened practitioner (Dillon, 1992). Marriage and the family, Giddens notes (1990, 43), would not be what they are today if they were not thoroughly 'sociologised' and 'psychologised'.

It should have become clear by now that in this volume we will make no attempt to specify a general theory of value change; instead we will seek, within each of the substantive areas with which we deal, to offer an interpretation of the evidence available to us in the light of our understanding of the nature of the processes of social change impinging on values in that particular domain.

This approach, which we have adopted from the outset in attempting to come to grips with the Irish material, is supported by the findings of the Dutch team, who have brought a modernisation perspective to bear on the European data as a whole. They found that while we are increasingly confronted with a plurality of value orientations, 'stage of economic advance' was not a crucial explanatory factor. Neither was any coherent pattern of either traditional or individualised values found. 'Only the hypothesis that individual value systems in modern society tend to be fragmented remained plausible' (de Moor, 1993, 232). The authors of the Dutch study were led to the conclusion that modernisation theory is far too general to explain the dynamics of change in the various value domains and the changes in each domain in individual countries. Fragmentation, they argue, is likely to be rooted in the structure of particular societies, and what is required is an examination of the manner in which country-specific factors interact with the globalisation of values through mobility and the mass media. In this volume we hope to make a contribution to the process of 'generating empirically founded partial theories' (de Moor, 1993, 232) through an examination of the Irish case.

2 Religious and Moral Values
MICHAEL P. HORNSBY-SMITH AND
CHRISTOPHER T. WHELAN

INTRODUCTION

In this chapter we will be looking at the evidence of behavioural and value changes in relation to religion and morality and will compare the results of the 1990 survey with those obtained nine years previously. At the beginning of the 1980s what was particularly noticeable was 'the shift across generations from stronger to weaker acceptance of orthodox beliefs and practice and of the authority of the Church.' Even so, Ireland (North and South) retained a far more traditional religious character than the rest of Europe (Fogarty et al., 1984, 12, 125–8). Similarly, when considering moral principles, people in the Republic were twice as likely as those in the North, or in the rest of western Europe, to take the optimistic view that 'everyone is basically good.' They were also tougher than the rest of Europe on the issues of euthanasia and abortion, while respondents from Northern Ireland took a less permissive stance on matters of honesty, drugs, sex, and violence (Fogarty et al., 1984, 21, 137–9).

Irish people generally stressed the importance of God in their lives and were more strict morally than people in eight other countries of western Europe. Similarly, their adherence to the Ten Commandments was higher and their tolerance of 'morally debatable' behaviour lower than in these countries (Harding and Phillips, 1986, 18, 60). In sum, on the wide range of indicators considered, both parts of Ireland were far less secularised than any of the countries of western Europe, although there was some evidence that generational change might be reducing the differences. The 1990 survey data enables us to explore the nature and extent of any changes in the religious character and moral values of the people of Ireland throughout the 1980s as well as to evaluate the evidence of normative convergence with the people of western Europe generally.

SOCIAL CHANGE AND SECULARISATION

In discussions relating to the impact of social change on religious and moral values, the model most frequently referred to in popular and academic debate is that of 'secularisation'. Secularisation has been defined as 'the process by which sectors of society and culture are removed from the domination of religious institutions and symbols' (Berger, 1973, 113). Ireland, which has experienced significant processes of social and economic transformation since the 1950s (Goldthorpe and Whelan, 1992), provides a particularly interesting test case for the generally hypothesised relationship between industrialisation, modernisation, and religious transformation.

For Berger 'it is industrial society in itself that is secularising,' even though he grants that monocausal explanations are incomplete (1973, 115–16). Luckmann (1970, 30) hypothesises that 'the degree of involvement in the work processes of modern industrial society correlates negatively with the degree of involvement in church-oriented religion.' Wilson (1982) claims that industrial society does not need local religion and that 'secularisation is intimately related to the decline of community, to increased social mobility, and to the impersonality of role-relationships.' Such claims can be tested and explored in the present study.

Irish society has experienced significant economic transformations in recent decades, with attendant occupational shifts from agricultural employment into manufacturing and services, steady increases in the levels of educational attainment, a growth in professional and technical occupations, the increasing involvement of women in employment in place of their traditional domestic roles, mobility from rural to urban locations, and the replacement of tightly knit rural communities with urban 'anomie' exacerbated by high levels of unemployment and signs of urban deprivation and alienation. In this context, secularisation theory would lead one to make a number of specific predictions about differences of religious behaviour and moral values for groups differing by age, sex, education, occupation, location and mobility experiences that can be tested with the European Values Survey data.

One might expect that younger age groups, which had been exposed more comprehensively to modern, 'secular' influences, such as television, in their formative years, would be less completely socialised to church-oriented religion and official standards of personal and social morality. Similarly, one would expect women to be more 'religious' and traditional in their moral values than men but for these differences to decline the more integrated they are with industrial and commercial employment. Those with longer educational exposure to rationalising influences would similarly be expected to diverge more from traditional values and behaviour. Those who had left agricultural employment or moved to the urban areas in search of alternative types of employment would no longer be subject to the reinforcing influences of local community social and religious life.

All these variables serve as proxies for the length and type of exposure to particular kinds of experiences that reinforce or retard the development of meaning systems or 'plausibility structures' for a Christian world view. As Berger (1973, 55) has argued,

> the reality of the Christian world depends upon the presence of social structures within which this reality is taken for granted and within which successive generations of individuals are socialized in such a way that this world will be real *to them*. When this plausibility structure loses its intactness or continuity, the Christian world begins to totter and its reality ceases to impose itself as self-evident truth.

We would expect interactions between the variables. For example, in so far as age is a proxy for length of exposure, we would expect it to have different effects in rural areas, characterised by traditional values, and in urban areas, subject more to modernising influences.

While it is convenient for our purposes to use secularisation theory as a focus for our analysis of religious practice and moral values in Ireland in the 1990s, it is important to recognise that secularisation theory is strongly contested (Bruce, 1992; Hornsby-Smith, 1992a, 1992b). In the first place it is necessary not to 'confuse the evaluative and the analytic' and to distinguish the thesis of secularisation, which is empirically testable, and the notion of secularism, 'the ideology of those who wish to promote the decline of religion and hasten the process of secularisation' (Wilson, 1985, 11; Martin, 1965). We wish to take seriously Dobbelaere's requirement that 'we should be ready to falsify our theories on the basis of new empirical material' (1989, 28).

Secondly, since an evaluation of the process of secularisation requires comparisons across two points in time, the choice of the earlier point may always be contested. Hornsby-Smith (1987, 1991) in his studies of English Catholicism has found striking similarities between the responses of grass-roots Catholics in London at the turn of the century and the 'customary' religion of 'ordinary' Catholics in the 1970s and 1980s. In the case of Ireland, an 'alternative popular culture' existed in pre-Famine days, and regular Mass attendance would have been possible for, at most, only 42 per cent of Catholics as late as 1840 (Kirby, 1984; Larkin, 1976). There never was a 'golden age' of religion in Ireland. While we do not wish to exclude from consideration changes that have occurred over a longer time span, for example since the period of major economic restructuring was initiated in the 1950s, in the main we will be comparing responses to identical question wordings in the 1981 and 1990 European Values Surveys.

Thirdly, in spite of the fact that, among social scientists generally, the secularisation thesis in an age of industrialisation, modernisation, rationalisation, bureaucratisation and urbanisation is 'the conventional wisdom' (Hammond, 1985, 1), there is plenty of contrary evidence. The proliferation of 'new religious movements', the evident strength of an aggressive conservative Christianity and the 'religious right', the resurgence of fundamentalist Islamic movements and the power of the basic Christian community movement legitimated by 'Third World' liberation theologies should all give empirically oriented sociologists grounds for reappraisal (Hadden and Shupe, 1985; Hornsby-Smith, 1992a, 1992b).

Fourthly, it is necessary to allow for contingencies such as the close relationship between religious commitment and nationalist sentiment at times of oppression or ethnic and political domination. Poland and Northern Ireland are evident examples of the role played by religion in the 'politics of cultural defence'. Where culture, identity and sense of worth are threatened by an alien religion, secularisation will be inhibited (Wallis and Bruce, 1992; Martin, 1978). There are, then, good reasons to be wary of any uncritical assumption of an inevitable process of secularisation resulting from processes of social and economic change, such as industrialisation and urbanisation.

In order to explore the nature and significance of the changes in religious practice and moral values in recent years, it is necessary to recognise the complexity of these changes and identify appropriate criteria for monitoring them. The longitudinal nature of the European Values Surveys is a major contribution to this end.

Dobbelaere (1981, 1985) argues that secularisation is a multidimensional concept. In particular, he has distinguished three dimensions: (*a*) laicisation at the macro or societal level, the process of structural differentiation whereby 'institutions are developed that perform different functions and are structurally different'; (*b*) religious involvement at the micro or individual level, which refers to individual behaviour and measures the degree of normative integration in religious bodies; and (*c*) religious change at the sub-system or organisational level, which 'expresses change occurring in the nature of religious organisation . . . in matters of beliefs, morals, and rituals, and implies also a study of the decline and emergence of religious groups.' While Dobbelaere postulates 'an underlying modernisation process' involving the 'disengagement of modern man from religious bodies,' he also allows for contrary processes of de-laicisation and de-secularisation. 'Secularisation is not a mechanical process, and it allows for religious groups to react' (1989, 37).

This framework provides the possibility of overcoming some of the difficulties that secularisation theory has had in explaining particular developments (Hornsby-Smith, 1992a, 1992b). Thus, any evaluation of Irish Catholicism requires an appreciation of the fact that 'with the loss of the Irish language the Catholic Church became the single most important mark of [Irish] separate identity' (Kirby, 1984, 62). The development of the Catholic Church in Ireland in the nineteenth century was the outcome of a complex interaction between social, political and religious change.

CHURCH-STATE RELATIONS IN IRELAND

The basis for church and state partnership dates back to the middle of the nineteenth century, when the church, in close co-operation with Catholic political movements, had successive battles with the UK government to gain control over schools for Catholic children. It also developed a substantial role in the provision of hospital facilities. So when the new southern state gained independence, the Catholic Church could build on its base as the 'church of the people' and on the shared experience of the long struggle against a foreign oppressive power (Breen et al., 1990, 107).

Institutional developments relating to education, health care and child care services and farm inheritance contributed to the consolidation of the Catholic Church. The outcome of these processes in Ireland clearly presents a case of 'Catholic monopoly'. Inglis, in his review of the situation in the early 1980s, documents the scale of the Catholic Church's physical and bureaucratic organisation and notes that for an estimated Catholic population of 3.7 million there were 1,322 parishes, 2,639 churches, 591 Catholic charitable institutions, including hospitals, homes for the deaf and blind, and reformatories, and 3,844 primary and 900 secondary schools (Inglis, 1987, 33–62). It is the sheer scale of such resources that enables the Catholic Church 'to control the moral discourse and practice of the Irish people' and maintain a 'moral monopoly' (Inglis, 1987, 33).

As Breen et al. (1990, 107) note,

> the original 1922 Constitution of the Free State, which was agreed in negotiations with the UK government, contained no explicit religious or moral overtones. The 1937 Constitution, however, was explicitly ethnic and religious in its overtones and in some of its provisions. It formally affirmed the 'special position' of the Catholic Church in Article 44 (removed in 1972) as 'the guardian of the faith of the great majority of the citizens' and in other 'moral' and institutional provisions supported that position.

In his recent analysis of the normative character of the Constitution, Basil Chubb (1991, 7) has observed that it reflected the three great formative influences on Irish society:

— the great legacy of the British connection that both geography and history made inevitable;
— nationalism, for it was enacted only sixteen years after the treaty that gave the twenty-six counties their independence and bequeathed Ireland as a whole its major problem;
— the Roman Catholic social teaching of the inter-war years, which the Catholic population (then 93 per cent of the total) were conditioned to accept without question.

Whyte, in his review of the evidence of church-state relations, concluded that there were only sixteen measures out of about 1,800 statutes enacted between 1923 and 1970 where there was clear evidence that one or more bishops had been consulted or had made representations (1980, 363–4). This led him to reject any suggestions that Ireland was a theocratic state. He also rejected the alternative view that the Catholic hierarchy was simply one interest group among many, and, following the suggestion of Ryan (1979), concluded that 'the best model to use for the hierarchy's current role is to see it as seeking to be the conscience of society' (1980, 416).

Fulton (1991, 134–5), while conceding that the state apparatus is certainly secular, points out that this

> was not to signify an absence of Roman Catholic power in the construction of public morality but rather an indirect recognition of the sovereignty of the Church in most areas of moral concern besides education . . . [Indeed] Roman Catholic power was to be accepted as normative in an entirely natural way by the Catholic-nationalist population . . . [and its] hegemonic role can be seen in the translation of religious preoccupations into law via the concept of natural law.

He has traced the influence of the papal social teaching of the 1930s on the 'special position' of the Roman Catholic Church, the recognition of the family as the primary unit of society with rights in education as interpreted by the church, the obligation of the state to protect marriage and the family, the right to the private ownership of property, the invocation of the principle of subsidiarity to control the growth of state power and its extension into welfare provision, the importance of voluntary organisation, and so on. De Valera consulted theologians on church-state relations in the drafting of the Constitution to ensure what Fulton refers to as the 'shoring up [of] monopoly Catholicism'.

THE SOCIAL CONTEXT OF RELIGIOUS CHANGE

It is in this social and religious context that we must consider the implications of the economic transformations of recent decades. Few societies have changed so rapidly or so radically as Ireland since 1960. The resulting transformation is, as Breen et al. (1990, 1) emphasise, particularly striking given Ireland's image as a 'rural conservative and Catholic backwater of post-war Europe.'

As one of the first nations to achieve independence from a colonial power in the twentieth century, Ireland seemed destined to mark out a new course. The Irish Free State, however, was characterised by stability and continuity. De Valera's Ireland was dominated by a reawakened search for economic and cultural sovereignty (Breen et al., 1990, 3). In a famous broadcast for St Patrick's Day in 1943 de Valera expressed the dominant and 'stifling Catholic nationalist orthodoxy' (Kirby, 1984, 18) in his 'unworldly vision' (Murphy, 1975, 84) of the good society:

The Ireland which we have dreamed of would be the home of a people who valued material wealth only as a basis of right living, of a people who were satisfied with frugal comfort and devoted their leisure to things of the spirit; a land whose countryside would be bright with cosy homesteads, whose fields and villages would be joyous with the sounds of industry, with the rompings of sturdy children, the contests of athletic youths and the laughter of happy maidens, whose firesides would be forums for the wisdom of serene old age. It would, in a word, be the home of a people living the life that God desires that man should live. (Lee, 1989, 334)

Critics have suggested that this dream was unrealistic, 'bore no relationship' to people's material and spiritual lives (Kirby, 1984, 18), and was a totally unsuitable basis for the construction of national economic policy (Lee, 1989, 334). Nevertheless it does illustrate a strong Catholic suspicion of industrial capitalism and its attendant materialism and consumerism.

The war years demonstrated possibilities beyond a nationalism based on impoverished self-sufficiency, and the values underlying de Valera's Ireland were subjected to sceptical scrutiny and found wanting by a new generation of intellectuals and civil servants. The 1950s marked the end of a post-independence search for a national identity and economy rooted in conceptions of traditional rural Ireland.

After four decades of independence, Ireland in 1960 could be characterised economically as one of the peripheral regions of the British Isles (Hechter, 1975). Entry into the labour market for each new generation often meant emigration to Britain. For the one-half of new workers who remained in Ireland, their main expectation was inheriting a family business. It is in this context that 1958 has a claim to be one of the milestones in the evolution of Irish society. With the publication of the Programme for Economic Expansion in that year, the primary objective of national policy became to reap full benefit from participation in the world economy. It marked the formal recognition that the old agenda was no longer tenable. Within a ten-year period, state-induced economic development industrialised Irish society.

The immediate consequence of the drive for industrialisation in the 1960s was that the international migration flow was reversed in the 1970s, and the population of the Republic, which had reached a nadir at the beginning of the 1960s, increased by one-quarter over the next twenty-five years (Kennedy et al., 1988, 140). With the dash for growth, agriculture declined in importance and a major process of urbanisation was generated by the migration of workers from peripheral regions to the towns. The population of Dublin increased by one-sixth between 1971 and 1978 (Whyte, 1980, 381), faster than any other western European capital (Lee, 1989, 605). The result is that around one-third of the population now lives in the greater Dublin area. The new economic strategies resulted in a significant shift of employment from agriculture to manufacturing and services. There was a steady increase in the female labour force participation rate. This was especially striking for married women and increased from one in twenty in 1961 to one in five in 1987 (Breen et al., 1990, 101, 117).

The swiftness of its class transformation sets Ireland apart from the experience of most other countries. We can identify three periods of rapid dislocation. First, during the 1950s many positions in self-employment and in low-skill labouring ceased to be viable. There was no countervailing process creating new opportunities within the class structure in that period. Second, during the 1960s and 1970s the class structure was reconstructed around those positions that were created through industrialisation and economic expansion. That did not synchronise with the change process involved in class transformation, as the new positions were largely beyond the reach of occupants whose viability had been undermined. This is reflected in the extent to which relative mobility rates in Ireland are more unequal than in countries like France, Great Britain, and Sweden (Erikson and Goldthorpe, 1992; Hout, 1989; Whelan et al., 1992). Third, as economic expansion gave way to prolonged recession, the new class structure became firmly implanted. The rate of expansion of new middle-range positions in secure, well-paid occupations slowed considerably, and working-class categories experienced high rates of unemployment. However, the class position of most families had already been established in the 1960s and 1970s. This depended, by and large, on the ability to take advantage of the opportunities for education opened up in those decades and, consequently, to secure access to a favoured location in the class system.

The intensity of change was such that it is easy to overlook its incompleteness. A large part of the labour force was stranded in the cause of industrial development, especially farmers on marginal holdings and labourers without skills. So at the beginning of the 1990s the class structure contains a substantial number of positions that are viable only in so far as they are underwritten by state social welfare programmes and from which, especially given present economic circumstances, there appears to be no exit. Such positions currently account for more than one-quarter of what is ironically termed the 'gainfully occupied labour force'. This reflects the dark side of the progress that class transformation generally brought to Irish society. For those families unable to achieve upward mobility, the cost was severe. Emigration was no longer an attractive alternative, and there were no opportunities in the traditional forms of employment in which previous generations of their families had been engaged (Breen et al., 1990; Whelan et al., 1992).

In sum, the economic transformations of the past three decades have been uneven. While some class fractions have been favoured, others have increasingly become marginalised. It is now possible to identify a marginalised working class characterised by long-term and persistent unemployment and associated with poverty and fatalism (Whelan, 1993). In an increasingly polarised society, secularising tendencies might be expected not only among the economically successful, highly educated and upwardly mobile but also among the 'rootless' migrants and unemployed in the anomic areas of recent urban development.

THE POST-VATICAN PERIOD

Any description of religious change in Ireland must take into account not only the impact of economic development but also the consequences of the renewal processes within Roman Catholicism set in motion by the Second Vatican Council. The pre-Vatican church stressed the virtues of loyalty, the certainty of answers, strict discipline, and unquestioning obedience. In a stable, unchanging world the church manifested the characteristics of a 'mechanistic' organisation, such as a distinct hierarchical structure of control, authority, and communication, and the tendency for interaction between superiors and subordinates to be vertical and for normal behaviour in the institution to be governed by instructions and decisions issued by superiors (Burns and Stalker, 1966). The hierarchical authority structures were seen as mediating grace and truth to the laity, and there was a marked tendency for the institution to be concerned with its own maintenance and survival (Winter, 1973).

However, it was becoming increasingly clear that this model of the church was inadequate in the postwar, postcolonial world with its democratic imperative, in the Cold War world of the nuclear threat, the world of new contraceptive technology and mass communications. The strategy of suppression or intransigence (Berger, 1973, 156) that had been ruthlessly followed for over half a century since the condemnation of modernism was beginning to break down. The Vatican Council's emphasis on collegiality and participation by all the 'people of God' can be interpreted as a shift to an 'organic' management structure in a changing world, with far more emphasis on lateral consultation than on vertical command (Burns and Stalker, 1966). The church was to be transformed from a pyramid of organisation and power into a community of service and mission on the move (Moore, 1975, 34–5). Alternative 'community', 'sacrament', 'herald' and 'servant' models of the church were to be given increasing emphasis (Dulles, 1976).

Irish Catholicism was seriously unprepared for the Vatican Council, but its liturgical reforms and new ecumenical openness were dutifully adopted, according to the letter, if not the spirit, of the Council (McRedmond, 1980, 42; Nic Giolla Phádraig, 1988, 209). All the same, the European Value Systems Study Group noted a decade ago that there was clear evidence that Vatican II had influenced Irish Catholics in three ways:

> It revealed to many Catholics the possibility of a private world of conscience and behaviour; it stressed that the Church was not merely the pope and bishops but the entire people of God whose common convictions carry an inner truth of their own; and it transformed religious thinking from being introverted and pessimistic to be outward-looking and optimistic. (Fogarty et al., 1984, 104)

Mention must also be made of the undoubted impact of the mass media in opening up the Irish consciousness to the social and cultural changes that were taking place elsewhere, and especially in Britain. The proclivity to censorship in Roman Catholic Ireland collapsed in the face of the range of developments in mass communications in recent years and especially television, pirate radio, video recorders, and satellite broadcasting (Farrell, 1984, 115). As a result of these developments, free discussion of formerly prohibited moral and social issues was increasingly tolerated. Kirby, for example (1984, 20), notes that the Saturday night, 'Late Late Show' on television became, in the late 1960s and early 1970s, something akin to an alternative teaching authority to that of the Church, systematically stimulating discussion and dissent on issues of moral and religious belief which most Irish Catholics had previously never questioned.

A greater openness to external influences also resulted from membership of the EC and the influence of equality legislation and the judgments of the European Court (Nic Giolla Phádraig, 1988, 213).

SECULARISING TENDENCIES AND RELIGIOUS REVITALISATION

In a review of available evidence, Hornsby-Smith (1992c) has recently used Dobbelaere's three levels to evaluate the evidence for secularisation or religious revitalisation in Ireland. Focusing first on the societal level, evidence of processes of structural differentiation in recent decades and particularly developments in health, education and law has been taken to indicate a gradual secularisation deriving more from the complexity of Irish society than direct ideological pressures.

> The expansion in educational provision led to a corresponding decline in the proportion of the teaching force belonging to religious orders—from over one half of the second level total in 1961 to a mere 16 per cent in 1983. A similar pattern occurred in health care. As hospital services mushroomed, the dominance of religious orders in hospital administration and staffing dwindled. (Breen et al., 1990, 108–9)

These developments were related to significant falls in the number of church personnel available to serve the growing population (Kirby, 1984). More generally, as the logic of industrial capitalism overflowed from the industrial and commercial sectors into all aspects of society, non-scientific and religious interpretations and legitimations lost their pre-eminence.

Secularisation meant that the various state functions became removed from the religious domain, while the political system lessened its close alliance with the Catholic Church. This has been viewed as a gradual and initially amicable adjustment, 'not of conflict but of consensus' in Whyte's view (1980, 388). There is certainly evidence for such a characterisation in the removal by referendum in 1972 of the Constitution's recognition of the 'special position' of the Catholic Church, the move to a more restricted church role in the control over second-level education, changes in the legal status of children, and the 1979 amendments to laws governing the sale and distribution of contraceptives. In its language and its actions, the Catholic Church throughout the 1970s drew clear and explicit distinctions between the religious and the civil role of citizens. Moreover, a number of prominent bishops, sensitive to the nuances of the Northern Ireland problem, argued for a greater separation of church and state, articulating the view that legislators are free to form their own opinions about the balance of social advantage on most moral issues and that if they came to the conclusion that the law need no longer prohibit what was condemned by the church they were entitled to act accordingly (Whyte, 1980, 407–8). This episcopal policy, however, did not outlast the 1970s.

Despite the scale of the evidence relating to secularising tendencies, Hornsby-Smith (1992a) has argued that there are clear signs of religious revitalisation and counter-secularising tendencies, which cannot be discounted. In reviewing the role of the Catholic Church in Ireland, Peillon (1982) has argued that it abandoned its former vision of a society constructed on corporatist principles, which provided an alternative to both capitalism and communism. Hornsby-Smith, however, questions whether it is right to view acceptance of policies of economic growth as implying a process of secularisation. He notes that in recent times the hierarchy has been seen less in the role of close collaborator of the state and more in that of social critic. Such a role can be viewed as part of a process of revitalisation rather than secularisation. Seeds of a transformed Catholicism are also found in the success and international recognition of Trócaire, the Third World development organisation, and in the growing number of organisations working in inner-city areas or with deprived groups and attempting to raise awareness of some of the social injustices associated with uncontrolled forms of western capitalism.

While the 'option for the poor' developments provide evidence of revitalisation that takes a left-wing or prophetic form, the emergence of lay-initiated and lay-run organisations, which were enormously successful in motivating Catholics in defence of traditional positions regarding divorce and abortion in two referendums in the 1980s, provided evidence of revitalisation of a rather different form.

Finally, we wish to review the evidence to date regarding secularisation understood in terms of individual religious involvement. The general picture, as Ryan (1983) concluded on the basis of the 1981 European Values Study, is one of solidity, with adherence to the faith remaining strong. Evidence from a number of surveys in the 1980s provides indications of trends consistent with secularisation theory. All the same, church attendance remains remarkably high, although there has been a substantial decline in attendance at Confession (Mac Gréil, 1991).

There is, however, evidence of significant socio-demographic variation. The lowest levels of adherence are among the more 'modern' sections of society: men, the young, the more educated, and those living in urban areas (Nic Giolla Phádraig, 1988). There is also frequent reference to the fact that the unemployed appear to be a particularly alienated group, though whether this is a consequence of modernisation processes or not is unclear.

Such, then, is the context of our analysis of the findings from the 1990 European Values study. In a recent review of secularisation theory, Martin (1991) has drawn attention to the contingent nature of secularisation. Ireland provides an important test case for the thesis, since in many respects it appears to be a deviant case in the context of the battle between the church and the Enlightenment in western Europe over the past two centuries. We have in the 1981 and 1990 surveys the opportunity to investigate in some detail evidence relating to changes in individual religious involvement over the past decade. In so doing we will be in a better position to test the conventional wisdom that modernisation processes inevitably bring in their train processes of secularisation.

EVIDENCE FROM THE EUROPEAN VALUES SURVEY

In the remainder of this chapter we will draw on the European Values Surveys of 1981 and 1990 to examine changes and continuity in religious and moral values in Ireland. Such changes will be contrasted with the results from Northern Ireland and, more generally, placed in the context of the overall pattern of the European results.

The starting point for our analysis is denominational affiliation. During the 1980s the proportion of respondents identifying themselves as belonging to a religious denomination declined very slightly, from 98 to 96 per cent. The corresponding figure for Northern Ireland in 1991 was 91 per cent. Both parts of Ireland showed much higher levels of affiliation than Great Britain (58 per cent) and the European average (75 per cent). In Ireland the long-term trend towards religious homogeneity continued, and the proportion of those who expressed a denominational affiliation who are Roman Catholics increased to 97 per cent.

CHURCH ATTENDANCE

Whyte has noted that 'Ireland is unusual in having a large majority, not just of Catholics, but of committed and practising Catholics' (1980, 4). In table 2.1 we set out the pattern of church attendance for both parts of Ireland and for Europe as a whole. During the 1980s the proportion attending church (usually Catholics attending Mass) more than weekly in the Republic declined by about one-fifth. On the other hand, the proportion attending church at least weekly declined much less sharply, from 83 to 81 per cent. The corresponding proportions of at least weekly attenders are one-half for Northern Ireland, which has changed little over the past decade, and three out of ten for Europe as a whole. The contrast in terms of non-attendance is even more dramatic, with almost one out of two of the European sample as a whole recording attendance less often than at Christmas or Easter, compared with one in fourteen of the sample in the Republic and one-quarter in Northern Ireland.

TABLE 2.1 *Frequency of church attendance: a comparison, 1981 and 1990*

	Republic of Ireland		Northern Ireland		European average
	1981 %	1990 %	1981 %	1990 %	1990 %
More than once a week	28(30)	22(24)	18	12(14)	7(10)
Once a week	55(57)	59(61)	34	38(71)	23(32)
Once a month	6(5)	7(7)	15	19(4)	11(12)
Christmas or Easter	3(2)	5(5)	4	3(2)	8(9)
Less often	9(6)	7(4)	29	28(9)	51(37)

Figures in parentheses relate to Mass attendance for Catholics.

Such differences are not entirely explained by different proportions of Roman Catholics in the populations of the different countries. Although there is a norm of weekly Mass attendance for

Catholics, significant variations of practice can be discerned in different European countries. Whereas the proportion of weekly Mass attenders in the Republic declined from 87 per cent in 1980 to 85 per cent in 1990, the corresponding figures for Catholics in Northern Ireland fell from 93 per cent in 1981 to 85 per cent in 1990, while for Europe as a whole the figure in 1990 was 42 per cent. All these comparisons point to the distinctiveness of the Irish situation, as Whyte noted.

While the differences in attendance between 1981 and 1990 are relatively modest, the possibility exists that the overall figures may conceal more substantial variations among particular groups. In order to test hypotheses deriving from the secularisation thesis, we will look in particular at the effect of four variables that, as we previously noted, can be regarded as indicators of the modernisation process: age, sex, education, and location.

In table 2.2 two measures of attendance have been broken down by age group. Since there is close to a nine-year gap between the two surveys, our age-group breakdown has been chosen to facilitate comparisons between cohorts as well as between age groups. It can be seen that at both times, attendance increases significantly with age. Thus, in 1990 the proportion attending weekly or more often rises from 71 per cent in the 18–26 category to 92 per cent in the 71 and over age group. These figures are very similar to those reported by Mac Gréil (1991, 11) on the basis of his survey of religious practice and attitudes among a representative sample of the adult population in 1988/89; differences between the two sets of data are well within sampling error. (See also Weafer, 1986, 1993.) During the 1980s there is strong evidence for a decline in church attendance in all but the oldest age group. These trends are even more striking when considering attendance more often than weekly, which, for the two youngest age groups, has declined by one-half over the period. The pattern for Mass attendance in the case of the Roman Catholics is rather similar.

If, however, we follow through over time the cohorts for which we have presented data, i.e. if we compare the results for the 18–26 cohort in 1981 with those for the 27–35 cohort in 1990, and so on, the results are surprising. For the youngest cohorts, those aged 18–35 in 1980, there is evidence of a decline in attendance more than weekly. This is consistent with increasing domestic obligations at this stage of the life cycle. For the other cohorts, though, there is no evidence of a decline in attendance. The results for aggregate weekly

TABLE 2.2 *Trends in frequency of church attendance*

| | Attending more often than weekly | | Attending weekly or more often | |
	1981 %	1990 %	1981 %	1990 %
18–26	16(17)	8(9)	75(79)	71(76)
27–35	19(20)	10(11)	75(77)	68(74)
36–44	23(25)	14(15)	82(87)	79(85)
45–53	41(42)	24(25)	95(97)	87(89)
54–62	34(35)	39(41)	91(92)	91(93)
71+	46(48)	42(44)	90(93)	92(93)
Total	28(29)	22(24)	83(88)	81(85)

attendance are also striking. Decline in church attendance over the life cycle is observed only in those cohorts aged 18–26 and 45–53 in 1981. The latter is a cohort that is likely to have been particularly adversely affected by increased unemployment. For those aged 27–44 at that time, church attendance increased over the 1980s.

What overall decline has occurred in the average figures can therefore be attributed not so much to an inevitable process of secularisation, affecting individuals in all generations, but to a decline in attachment on the part of the youngest adult groups, which, to some extent, they carry forward with them as they grow older. A number of factors are likely to have contributed to this, but their net effect seems likely to have been less successful processes of social-isation to the norms of institutional religion as Ireland has moved from a position of 'moral monopoly' (Inglis, 1987) to de facto plural-ism, where there is ready access to multiple media sources, values, and life-styles. The data suggest that a significant cultural shift (Inglehart, 1990) occurred for those under the age of thirty-five in 1990, that is, among those cohorts born since the mid-1950s. These cohorts will have grown up since the modernisation and indus-trialisation policies were initiated in Ireland. Thus while there is no evidence to support claims for secularisation as far as changes throughout the 1980s are concerned, there are indications that a major cultural shift may have occurred for those born in recent decades. In particular, the trend for the youngest cohort in 1981 is one that gives some cause for concern for the Catholic Church, since it is by no means certain that the shift towards increased attendance over the life cycle observed among the earlier groups will hold for this cohort. Even if it does, the base from which it occurs will be lower than heretofore.

The second independent variable that may affect church attendance is sex, but its effect is likely to be mediated through urban or rural location and also by employment status. Our findings are summarised in table 2.3, where it can be seen that, as expected, women are more likely than men to attend church weekly. As we have noted, however, secularisation theory would lead us to expect that the church-oriented religion of women would converge towards that of men the more completely they were integrated into the economic system of capitalist industrial society. The data do in fact give support to this, and there is a significant decline in the weekly attendance of women from those in unpaid domestic home-making roles (93 per cent) to those in full-time employment (78 per cent). This indicates convergence towards the figure for men in full-time employment (75 per cent). Strikingly, only 61 per cent of women who are unemployed attend weekly. This compares with 52 per cent for unemployed men and indicates that both sex and employment status are explanatory variables in the determination of religious practice.

TABLE 2.3   *Weekly or more frequent church attendance, by sex, employment status, and location, 1990*

	Employment status				Location	
Sex %	Full-time %	Part-time %	In full-time unpaid home duties %	Unemployed %	Urban %	Rural %
Male	75	63	—	52	65	87
Female	78	81	93	61	80	91

Apart from employment status, the data clearly indicate the importance of location. We have collapsed our data to distinguish rural from urban locations and are able to test the hypothesis that cultural expectations in rural areas ensure higher levels of church attendance than in the more anomic situation in urban areas. This is likely to be the case particularly where rural migrants have been unable to develop appropriate support mechanisms, but unfortunately we do not have any information on where people spent their childhood years. The major contrast emerges between those in towns of 2,000 or less-populated areas and all others. The findings presented in table 2.3 are consistent with the notion that for both men and women the movement from rural to urban areas is likely to result in a decline in the level of church attendance. Whereas in rural areas around nine in every ten people, both men and women, attend church weekly, in urban areas only two in every three men and four in every five women do so.

Urban versus rural location turns out to have a critical impact on church attendance, not only through its direct effect but also by the manner in which it mediates the impact of age, sex, unemployment, and life-style deprivation.

Table 2.4 presents some of the relevant findings. It can be seen that while age differences do not entirely explain the lower religious practice in urban areas, the effect is much stronger for those born since the Second World War or reaching their teens since the 1960s. Another way of viewing this finding is to focus on the fact that age differences are much more substantial in urban as opposed to rural areas. In the former there is a difference of almost 30 per cent between the youngest and the oldest age group, while for the latter it falls to 10 per cent.

TABLE 2.4 *Weekly or more frequent church attendance, by age and employment status, distinguishing between urban and rural location, 1990*

				Age				Employment status	
									Not
Location	All	18–26	27–35	36–44	45–53	54–62	62+	Unemployed	unemployed
	%	%	%	%	%	%	%	%	%
Urban	73	62	56	70	81	89	90	40	76
Rural	89	83	82	90	93	94	93	73	90

The impact of unemployment is also clearly mediated by location. In rural areas, where there is likely to be stronger community support as well as stronger expectations of church attendance than in urban areas, three-quarters of the unemployed practise regularly, com- pared with nine-tenths of those who are not unemployed. In urban areas, however, where social integration is likely to be weaker, unemployment almost halves weekly church attendance, from three-quarters of those not unemployed to only two-fifths of the unemployed.

Another measure that interacts with location in this way is what we refer to as primary life-style deprivation. This measure derives from the analysis of dimensions of life-style deprivation that was carried out as part of the Economic and Social Research Institute poverty project (Whelan et al., 1991; Callan et al., 1993). In the course of this project a set of basic items relating to food, clothing and heating, whose enforced absence constituted an important component of what was defined as poverty, was identified. The enforced absence of such items has been shown to be strongly related to psychological distress (Whelan et al., 1991). A comparable set of items was included in the 1990 European Values Study. In fact there is no difference in the frequency of church attendance in rural areas between those experiencing such deprivation and other people. In urban areas, on the other hand, church attendance is substantially reduced by such deprivation, with a difference of fifteen percentage points emerging in relation to weekly or more frequent attendance.

Apart from the provision of financial rewards, employment provides access to a variety of important categories of experience that are crucial for maintaining self-esteem and facilitating a wide range of social activities. The results of the ESRI Poverty Survey show that the unemployed are substantially more likely to think of themselves as worthless and less likely to feel that they are playing a useful part in things (Whelan et al., 1991). In view of such findings, it is hardly surprising that the unemployed are less likely to participate in community rituals such as church attendance. It might also be noted that such findings lend no support to the compensatory view of religion (Stark and Bainbridge, 1985).

Exclusion from ordinary living patterns, customs and activities is a standard way of defining poverty (Townsend, 1979; Mack and Lansley, 1980). The life-style measure of deprivation provides an indicator of such exclusion, and consequently we would expect it to be related to lower levels of participation in community rituals. In fact, as we have noted, this holds only for those in urban areas. Furthermore, no effect is observed among the unskilled manual class, where such deprivation is not unusual. The impact is concentrated among the other classes, where it is less usual.

These results suggest the possibility that unemployment and deprivation affect church attendance through the impact they have on an individual's self-esteem rather than through the estrangement of significant segments of the working class from Catholicism per se. As we shall see in a later section, the results of our analysis of religious and moral values tend to support this conclusion. It also seems likely that the stronger impact of unemployment in urban areas is due to a combination of (*a*) the fact that unemployment is more likely to lead to deprivation in urban areas and (*b*) the fact that the consequences of deprivation for church attendance are stronger in urban than in rural areas.

In the 1990 European Values Study, six social classes were distinguished, with married women being allocated to the class of their husband, in the absence of information which would allow us to implement alternative satisfactory procedures (Breen and Whelan, forthcoming). The data show remarkably little variation in weekly church attendance by social class. Average attendances ranged from 77 per cent for those in the higher professional and managerial occupations to 84 per cent in unskilled manual occupations. The weakness of the social class effect is also contributed to by the fact that primary life-style deprivation makes its strongest impact outside the unskilled manual class. Thus, while the enforced absence of one or more primary life-style items has no effect on weekly church attendance for the unskilled manual class, for all other classes it reduces attendance from 82 per cent where there is no deprivation to 69 per cent where there is (Whelan et al., 1991).

There is, however, a significant interaction between social class and age in their effect on church attendance, as shown in table 2.5. For those aged forty or over, the non-manual respondents are more likely to attend church, with 94 per cent attending weekly or more often, compared with 84 per cent of the manual group. For those under forty, on the other hand, the pattern is reversed, with 78 per cent of the manual class attending weekly or more often, compared with 64 per cent of the non-manual category. Thus differences in church attendance by age are largely concentrated among non-manual respondents.

Not surprisingly, a similar type of interaction is observed between age and highest level of education. The effect of highest educational level on church attendance is summarised in table 2.6. While on average only two-thirds of those with third-level education attended weekly, compared with over four-fifths of those with lower levels of education, the effect is almost entirely to be found among those born since the early 1950s. Once again it is apparent that significant cultural shifts can be dated from around the 1960s. Of course, another way in which this finding can be expressed is by focusing on the fact that age differences are most substantial among those with higher levels of education.

TABLE 2.5   *Impact of class on church attendance, by age: percentage attending weekly or more often, 1990*

	Under 40 %	40 or over %
Non-manual	64	94
Manual	78	84

Multivariate analysis shows age, third-level education, sex, unemployment, primary life-style depreciation and being in full-time unpaid home duties to have independent effects on frequency of church attendance. If we focus on the extremes, the following comparisons illustrate the cumulative impact of these variables. A 65-year-old woman in full-time unpaid home duties has a 0.98 probability of attending church weekly or more often, while for a twenty-year-old urban unemployed male the probability falls to 0.32. If, on the other hand, we drop the assumption of unemployment, the probability is 0.46.

TABLE 2.6   *Weekly or more frequent church attendance, by education and age: percentage attending weekly or more often*

Education level	Under 40 %	40 or over %
Primary Cert. or less	71	88
Intermediate or Group Cert.	77	88
Leaving Cert.	73	91
Third level	57	86

To summarise the evidence for secularising tendencies as far as church attendance measures are concerned:

1. The impact of modernisation influences can be seen in the lower levels of church attendance displayed by men, the young, those in urban areas, and those with third-level education.
2. Age and sex are more powerful predictors of church attendance in urban than rural areas.

3. Unemployment is negatively associated with church attendance in both urban and rural areas, although its effect is stronger in urban areas.
4. Social class appears to have no overall impact, but this arises because a higher social class position reduces the probability of attendance for those under forty but increases it for those over forty.
5. The foregoing finding is related to the fact that third-level education has a striking negative impact among those under forty but none at all for those over forty. These findings clearly suggest the possibility that over time, social class will come to have an unambiguously negative effect.
6. Our multivariate analysis demonstrates the cumulative impact of social-demographic influences on church attendance, with age and urban versus rural location having the strongest effects, followed by third-level education, unemployment, being a housewife, sex, and poverty.

Finally, before proceeding to an examination of the dimensions of religious and moral values, the importance attached to religious rites of passage might be noted. Well over 90 per cent of our respondents considered it important to hold a religious service for births, marriage, and death. In each case the figure was at least 20 per cent higher than the European average. It is also striking that there was only a very modest variation by age, with the averages remaining above 90 per cent even for the youngest age group. These figures on rites of passage are once again consistent with Mac Gréil's findings and, as Nic Giolla Phádraig notes, may be connected with the continuing importance of kinship ties.

DIMENSIONS OF RELIGIOUS AND MORAL VALUES

In order to deal with the mass of material available to us on religious and moral values, it is necessary to impose some structure on the data through the identification of distinguishable dimensions. Here we are fortunate in being able to draw on the work of the group of researchers at the University of Tilburg (Ester et al., 1993) who have devoted substantial resources to the analysis of such dimensions, making use of the overall European data set. In the area of religious and moral values they have identified five dimensions that are of particular importance to us:

1. Traditional Christian beliefs
   —God
   —life after death
   —a soul
   —the Devil
   —Hell
   —Heaven
   —sin
2. Religiosity
   —importance of God in one's life
   —thinking of oneself as a religious person
   —belief in a personal God, in some spirit or life force
   —taking comfort and strength from religion
   —taking some moments for prayer
3. Confidence in the ministry of the church
   —adequacy of the church's answers to moral problems
   —adequacy of the church's answers to family problems
   —adequacy of the church's answers to spiritual needs
4. Permissiveness
   —married men or women having an affair
   —sexual relations under the legal age of consent
   —homosexuality
   —prostitution
   —abortion
   —divorce
   —euthanasia
   —suicide
5. Civic morality
   —claiming state benefits illegally
   —avoiding a fare on public transport
   —cheating
   —buying something knowing that it was stolen
   —taking a car that is not one's own
   —taking marijuana or hashish
   —keeping money that one has found
   —lying in one's own interest
   —accepting a bribe in the course of one's duties
   —fighting with the police
   —failing to report damage done accidentally to a vehicle
   —threatening workers who refuse to join a strike
   —killing in self-defence
   —political assassination

For both 1981 and 1990 these scales proved to be highly reliable, with the alpha coefficient (which provides an indication of whether items are tapping the same underlying dimension) varying from 0.67 to 0.81. The items forming the religious dimensions are all in a dichotomous form, and a respondent's score is simply the number of items agreed with. For the permissiveness scale, each item is scored from 1 (never justified) to 10 (always justified), while for the civic morality dimension this pattern of scoring is reversed, so that a high score implies stricter standards of morality. The scale scores are the average score on the items included in the index.

Although five separate dimensions have been identified, they are clearly not independent. While all the indices are interrelated, traditional religious values and religiosity are particularly highly correlated, as are permissiveness and civic morality, with the correlation in each case being 0.6. Church attendance and confidence in the church are more evenly correlated with the other variables.

A comparison of scores on the religious and moral dimensions is set out in table 2.7. The results show that there has been no overall change in the level of belief in traditional Christian values or religiosity, a modest decline in confidence in the church, a significant increase in permissiveness, and a modest strengthening of civic morality. A comparison with the scores for the European countries as a whole shows that the Irish respondents' scores on the religious dimensions are far above those for the other countries; they also display lower levels of permissiveness and a slightly more absolutist view on civic morality.

TABLE 2.7 *Religious and moral values: a comparison, 1981 and 1990*

	Traditional religious values	Religiosity	Confidence in the church	Permissiveness	Civic morality
	Average	Average	Average	Average	Average
1981	5.36	3.60	1.65	2.09	8.11
1990	5.30	3.63	1.45	2.49	8.46
European average, 1990	3.18	2.57	1.21	3.81	8.27

In table 2.8 we show the distribution of such scores across age groups for both 1981 and 1990. It is clear that the age effects are a good deal more substantial than the period effects. Both for traditional Christian values and religiosity, those respondents aged under thirty-five display significantly less likelihood of adhering to traditional values and substantially lower levels of religiosity. Confidence in the church shows a more gradual decline across age. Permissiveness and civic morality are also systematically related to age, although the shift during the 1980s towards greater permissiveness and higher standards of civic morality is evident in all age groups.

TABLE 2.8 *Religious and moral values, by age group*

	Traditional religious values		Religiosity		Confidence in the church		Permissiveness		Civic morality	
	1981	1990	1981	1990	1981	1990	1981	1990	1981	1990
	Average	Average	Average	Average	Average	Average	Average	Average	Average	Average
18–26	4.7	4.7	3.0	2.9	1.1	1.1	2.8	3.1	7.6	7.9
27–35	4.9	5.0	3.3	3.4	1.3	1.4	2.3	2.7	8.1	8.4
36–44	5.5	5.0	3.7	3.6	1.6	1.3	2.1	2.8	8.2	8.3
45–53	5.9	5.6	4.0	3.8	1.9	1.5	1.7	2.3	8.5	8.6
54–62	5.8	5.8	3.9	4.0	1.9	1.6	1.6	2.2	8.4	8.7
63+	5.9	5.9	4.2	4.3	2.3	1.9	1.5	1.7	8.2	8.8

While the scores on the dimensions allow us to summarise a great deal of information, it is still of considerable interest to look at the patterns relating to the individual items. In table 2.9 we present the breakdown of the individual items relating to traditional religious values by age group. Once again comparison with the European figures shows how exceptional the Irish results are, with the Irish twice as likely to believe in Hell, the Devil and Heaven and substantially more likely to believe in God, life after death, and sin. There has been no change over the 1980s in the proportion believing in God: it ranges from 92 per cent in the younger age group to close to 100 per cent in the older group. There are very slight increases in the percentages believing in life after death, a soul, and Heaven, and comparable slight decreases in the levels of belief in Hell, the Devil, and sin. Thus, while the overall picture of no great change is confirmed, the results do support the hypothesis of a move towards a more optimistic interpretation of religion. With the exception of God and sin, age variations are quite pronounced on all the items. On average, over 70 per cent of the youngest group believe in life after death, a soul, and Heaven, compared with in excess of 90 per cent of the oldest group. Similarly, while over 60 per cent of the latter believe in Hell and the Devil, this falls to 40 per cent among the younger age groups. An examination of the pattern of results by cohort gives no indication that these views alter simply as a consequence of age.

TABLE 2.9 *Traditional religious values, by age group*

Percentage believing

	God			Life after death			A soul			Heaven			Hell			The Devil			Sin		
	Ireland	Ireland	Europe	Ireland	Ireland	Europe	Ireland	Ireland	Europe	Ireland	Ireland	Europe	Ireland	Ireland	Europe	Ireland	Ireland	Europe	Ireland	Ireland	Europe
	1981	1990	1990	1981	1990	1990	1981	1990	1990	1981	1990	1990	1981	1990	1990	1981	1990	1990	1981	1990	1990
18–26	92	92	62	67	69	39	74	75	56	72	78	36	41	39	18	45	41	20	80	79	47
27–35	93	96	67	69	76	39	74	79	55	79	82	34	46	40	18	51	43	21	81	84	49
36–44	97	93	73	75	68	41	86	81	59	86	80	41	57	48	22	60	49	24	86	83	55
45–53	98	97	78	87	84	45	90	90	66	93	87	45	66	53	25	68	58	27	90	88	62
54–62	98	97	81	83	88	50	90	91	68	92	92	52	65	60	30	67	63	32	91	87	66
63+	96	100	85	84	85	52	91	94	71	92	95	58	66	62	33	67	64	35	91	87	69
Total	95	96	73	76	78	44	83	85	62	84	85	44	55	50	24	58	53	26	86	84	57

In tables 2.10 and 2.11 we break down the individual items of religiosity by age group. The proportion taking comfort from prayer increases between 1981 and 1990 from 80 to 82 per cent. There is a sharp variation across age groups, with two-thirds of the youngest group taking such comfort but over nine out of ten in the oldest group. The evidence clearly supports the view that the extent to which people draw comfort from prayer increases with age.

TABLE 2.10 *Percentage drawing comfort and strength from prayer, by age group and time of survey*

	1981 %	1990 %
18–26	66	64
27–35	69	72
36–44	85	82
45–53	91	89
54–62	91	95
63+	93	92
Total	80	82

From table 2.11 we can see that there has been a significant shift in views regarding the nature of God. Between 1981 and 1990 the proportion believing in a personal God fell from 77 to 67 per cent, while there was a corresponding increase from 15 to 24 per cent in the number whose notion of God was closest to 'some sort of spirit or life force'. Not surprisingly, older respondents are more likely to have an idea of God that conforms to that of a personal God, with eight out of ten of them holding such a view, compared with fewer than six in ten of those in the youngest age group. However, what is striking is that the shift in opinion has occurred in all age groups; in fact for those aged thirty-five or over the percentage choosing the 'spirit or life force' option doubles in the period between the two surveys. Thus the evidence suggests that the shift in views is quite general. Finally, the proportion thinking of themselves as religious people actually increased between 1981 and 1990, from 67 to 72 per cent. The figures range from 63 per cent of those aged twenty-five or less to 85 per cent of those seventy or over.

TABLE 2.11 *Views on God, by age group and time of survey*

	Percentage by column												
	18–26		27–35		36–44		45–53		54–62		63+		Total	
	1981	1990	1981	1990	1981	1990	1981	1990	1981	1990	1981	1990	1981	1990
	%	%	%	%	%	%	%	%	%	%	%	%	%	%
There is a personal God	65	56	68	64	81	60	85	67	83	77	90	83	77	67
There is some sort of spirit or life force	22	32	20	28	16	32	10	22	10	18	7	12	15	24
Don't really know what to think	10	10	9	8	2	6	5	9	7	5	2	5	6	7
Don't really think there is any sort of spirit, God, or life force	3	2	3	0	1	3	0	1	1	0	1	0	2	1

Turning our attention to the increase in permissiveness, as shown in table 2.12, we can see that by 1990 respondents were significantly less likely to think that there were no circumstances under which divorce and abortion could be justified. The range of scores runs from 1 (never justified) to 10 (always justified). Once again this shift was observed in all age groups, although substantial differences in levels of support registered are observed by age group. Irish respondents remain strikingly less willing than their European counterparts to accept that divorce and abortion can be justified. On divorce the Irish score is half the European average, while for abortion it is just above one-third the European figures.

TABLE 2.12 *Average scores on extent to which divorce and abortion can ever be justified, by time of survey*

	Divorce Average	Abortion Average
1981	3.3	1.7
1990	4.1	2.4
European average, 1990	8.3	7.0

Table 2.13 provides a more detailed breakdown of views on abortion. (In looking at these views it should be remembered that events since 1990 have indicated continuing substantial change in attitudes to abortion.) Respondents were asked to indicate whether they approved or disapproved of abortion under the following circumstances: (*a*) where the mother's health is at risk by pregnancy, (*b*) where the child is likely to be physically handicapped, (*c*) where the woman is not married, and (*d*) where a married couple do not want to have any more children. The only circumstance in which a majority of Irish respondents are willing to approve of abortion is when the mother's health is at risk. Even in this case, though, only two-thirds approve of abortion, compared with nine out of ten of the European respondents as a whole. In no other case does the Irish figure come near to a majority, even though four-fifths of the European sample are willing to accept the risk of physical handicap as a justification. Further analysis of this issue will be deferred until chapter 3.

TABLE 2.13 *Circumstances under which abortion is approved of: comparison of Irish and European views*

	Percentage approving	
	Ireland %	Europe %
A. When the mother's health is at risk by the pregnancy	65	92
B. Where is it likely that the child would be physically handicapped	32	79
C. Where the mother is not married	8	27
D. Where a married couple do not want to have any more children	8	34

At this point we draw on the results of our multivariate analysis to assess the impact of socio-demographic background on religious and moral values. Traditional beliefs and religiosity, age, sex, urban versus rural location and religious upbringing are the only background factors to have a significant influence. They explain approximately 9 per cent of the variance in the former factor and 18 per cent of the variance in the latter. Unemployment and lifestyle deprivation have no significant influence: in fact the deprived have slightly higher religiosity scores. The major influences on religious values appear to be those associated with modernisation rather than class divisions and their consequences.

The tendency of the unemployed and deprived to participate less frequently in the ritual of church attendance does not form part of general disenchantment with, or alienation from, religion. In this case behaviour is more radically affected than beliefs. In the case of church confidence, age, unemployment and religious upbringing are the main predictors, explaining 9 per cent of the variance. In this case, though, unemployment actually has a positive effect, with the unemployed displaying a higher level of confidence in the church.

Similarly, while the young and those in urban areas and those with third-level education are likely to be somewhat more permissive, the unemployed are actually less rather than more permissive. The significant impact unemployment and deprivation have in relation to the religious and moral dimensions is that together with being young, female and urban they tend to lower scores on the civic morality dimension.

While the Irish respondents are substantially more likely than their European counterparts to condemn absolutely divorce and abortion, the percentage agreeing that 'there can never be absolutely clear guidelines about what is good and evil' is identical with the European average of 55 per cent. The strength of religious values is shown, perhaps, by the fact that such uncompromising positions on divorce and abortion can coexist with such general beliefs that reject the possibility of making absolute judgments of right or wrong.

The increasing importance of individual judgment is shown in a shift in the type of values it is considered important for children to learn. Here again we draw on the work of the Tilburg research group (Halman, 1991) in order to distinguish the following dimensions.

1. Social conformity
   —emphasis on obedience
   —good manners
   —no emphasis on feelings of responsibility
2. Individualism
   —emphasis on imagination
   —independence
   —perseverance
3. Success orientation
   —emphasis on hard work
   —thrift

—no emphasis on tolerance
—unselfishness

From table 2.14 we can see that between 1981 and 1990 there has been an increase in the emphasis put on individualism and a decrease in the emphasis on conformity. The tendency to stress the importance of orientation to success has also increased. With regard to the individual items, in 1990 43 per cent considered independence to be an important value to be encouraged, compared with 30 per cent in 1981; for imagination the respective percentages are 22 and 14, for determination and perseverance 26 and 10, while for feelings of responsibility the figures are 61 and 22 per cent.

TABLE 2.14 *Values that it is important to learn: a comparison, 1981 and 1990*

	Success orientation Average	Individualism Average	Social conformity Average
1981	1.0	0.5	1.8
1990	1.3	0.8	1.5

COMPARISONS BETWEEN EUROPEAN CATHOLICS

There were significant variations in the religiosity of Catholics in different countries in western Europe, which point to the importance of contextual factors. Interestingly, Catholics in both parts of Ireland are almost identical in their beliefs and practices and retain, to a much greater extent than Catholics elsewhere in Europe, a traditional approach.

Eighty-five per cent of Catholics in Ireland attend Mass weekly or more often, compared with just less than one-half in Spain and Italy, approximately a third in most other countries, and less than one in eight in France. In spite of the low Mass attendance rates reported for many other countries, substantial proportions of Catholics in all countries derive comfort and strength from their religion. The proportion is greatest for Ireland, North and South, where the figure is 85 per cent; this compares with Great Britain, at

73 per cent, and West Germany, where the figure is at its lowest at 46 per cent.

In table 2.15 we report the range of traditional beliefs among Catholics in European countries. Ninety-eight per cent of Catholics in Ireland believe in God, compared with a minimum of 74 per cent in West Germany. Similarly, 80 per cent believe in life after death, while in only three other countries does this figure rise above 60 per cent and in Portugal it drops to less than 40 per cent. Traditional beliefs in the Devil and Hell are much lower among Catholics in the Netherlands than among other Catholics. It is noticeable that there are significantly lower attachments to such beliefs in the Republic than in Northern Ireland. Fifty-four per cent of Catholics in the South believe in the Devil, compared with 18 per cent in the Netherlands, and 86 per cent believe in sin, compared with 54 per cent in the Netherlands. Finally, 72 per cent of Catholics in the Republic believe in the resurrection of the dead, compared with only 35 per cent in Spain, and 88 per cent believe in Heaven, compared with 38 per cent of West German Catholics.

TABLE 2.15 *Percentage holding traditional religious beliefs among Catholics, by country*

	God	Life after death	A soul	The Devil	Hell	Sin	Resurrection of the dead	Heaven
				Percentage believing				
	%	%	%	%	%	%	%	%
France	82	48	63	27	24	57	39	43
Great Britain	89	67	87	60	60	87	61	75
West Germany	74	49	69	21	18	63	42	38
Italy	90	60	73	39	39	72	50	51
Spain	88	45	64	29	29	61	35	52
Portugal	94	39	72	28	29	76	43	64
Netherlands	91	46	73	18	12	54	37	46
Belgium	86	46	66	22	20	55	38	40
Northern Ireland	99	69	90	75	70	92	77	89
Republic of Ireland	98	80	87	54	52	86	72	88

These results are striking and show how exceptional Irish Catholics, North and South, are in their attachment to traditional orthodox beliefs in comparison with Catholics elsewhere in western Europe. Nevertheless there are indications in the lower levels of belief in the Devil, Hell and sin of the emergence of a more optimistic interpretation of religion on the part of Catholics in the South. It remains true, though, that the magnitude of the variations between Catholics in different countries indicates clearly that no assumption of homogeneity of belief system can be made on behalf of Catholics in Europe and points to the importance of cultural and contextual effects.

The level of belief in a personal God, at 69 per cent, is slightly lower than for Portugal, Italy and Northern Ireland but substantially higher than for France and West Germany, where it barely rises above 30 per cent. Our two measures of private devotionalism behave somewhat differently. First of all, just over one-half of Catholics in both parts of Ireland claim to pray often outside of religious services, compared with a minimum of only 18 per cent among French Catholics. The second measure of taking some moments of prayer, meditation or contemplation again reaches its highest among Irish Catholics, where it reaches 86 per cent, but the range of responses is lower, reaching a minimum of 59 per cent among French Catholics.

Finally, we wish to consider the extent to which Catholics feel that the church gives adequate answers to a range of different contemporary problems. The evidence relating to this is set out in table 2.16. It is clear that Irish Catholics are much less distinctive in relation to such confidence in the church than in their religious behaviour or beliefs. Forty-two per cent of Catholics in the Republic have confidence in the church's ability to meet the moral problems of the individual. Only for the Netherlands, where the figure falls to 29 per cent, do we observe a substantially lower figure. A similar situation pertains in relation to problems of family life, where only 35 per cent express such confidence. Here the highest levels of confidence are expressed in Northern Ireland, Portugal, and Great Britain. These countries also lead the way when the issue is the social problems facing the countries. The figure for Ireland, on the other hand, is not significantly higher, at 34 per cent, than for any of the other countries. Only in relation to the spiritual needs of the individual does Ireland score relatively highly, reaching 71 per cent. On this issue Catholics in Northern Ireland express the highest level of confidence, while the Dutch once again occupy the bottom position in the confidence league.

TABLE 2.16 *Percentage of Catholics considering that the church gives adequate answers to problems, by country*

	Moral problems & needs of the individual %	Problems of family life %	People's spiritual needs %	Social problems facing the country %
France	46	35	67	32
Great Britain	49	51	73	50
West Germany	38	32	63	36
Italy	51	44	66	45
Spain	41	40	53	37
Portugal	55	54	56	52
Netherlands	29	24	45	29
Belgium	41	37	57	31
Northern Ireland	44	54	81	49
Republic of Ireland	42	35	71	34

There was little change between 1981 and 1990 in the extent to which Catholics felt that the church was giving adequate answers to people's spiritual needs. In fact the relevant proportion rose from 66 to 71 per cent. In relation to family life, however, there was a decline from 48 to 35 per cent, and with regard to the moral problems and needs of the individual the drop was from 53 to 42 per cent. These figures seem to support the view that there has been a general collapse in the 'moral monopoly' of the church, or, at a minimum, a loss of at least some moral authority. However, if the Catholic Church in Ireland is no longer automatically thought to have the right answers, this should not be taken to mean that there is a desire that it should restrict its attention to strictly religious matters.

In table 2.17 we set out our respondents' views on the range of issues on which it is appropriate for the church to speak out. The nine specific issues covered range from Third World problems, racial discrimination and unemployment to disarmament and environmental issues. An additional question referred more generally to 'Government policy'. For each of the specific issues a clear majority considers it proper for the church to speak out. The level of support ranges from over nine out of ten in the case of Third World problems to six out of ten in relation to environmental issues, and finally drops to just above one-third for Government policy. It seems that it is perfectly proper for the Catholic Church in Ireland to express its views on a wide range of issues. In every case the Irish figure is substantially higher than the European average. However, it also appears to be an increasingly held view that it is proper for Irish Catholics to make their own assessments of the adequacy of the responses offered by the church.

TABLE 2.17 *Views among Catholics regarding issues on which it is proper for the church to speak out*

Rank		Percentage considering it proper
1	Third World problems	94
2	Racial discrimination	84
3	Abortion	82
4	Euthanasia	80
5	Unemployment	78
6	Extramarital affairs	73
7	Disarmament	68
8	Homosexuality	61
9	Ecology & environmental issues	59
10	Government policy	36

Furthermore, a relatively clear distinction seems to be drawn by many respondents between the general moral influence that the church can legitimately have and more specific attempts to influence Government policy. Thus, while almost eight out of ten consider it proper for the church to speak out on unemployment, only just over one-third consider it proper in the case of Government policy.

CONCLUSIONS

Church attendance in Ireland, adherence to traditional religious values and levels of religiosity remain remarkably high by western European standards. This conclusion holds even if we restrict our comparisons to Catholics.

The results we have presented provide no evidence of a general process of secularisation operating throughout the 1980s. Instead what we find are suggestions of a significant cultural shift among those cohorts born since the 1950s.

Both church attendance and religious and moral values are, rather predictably, affected by those factors that serve as indicators of modernisation: age, education, sex, urban versus rural location, and labour force participation. The extent of such change will be over-estimated if we simply rely on age comparisons, because such differences may also reflect life cycle effects that ensure that people become more religious as they get older. Thus, despite significant age differences in the percentage taking comfort from prayer, the overall level actually increased during the 1980s. However, consideration of the results relating to both 1981 and 1990 does support the view of significant behavioural and cultural shifts among selected groups. It is by no means inevitable that the trend towards return to Mass attendance at later stages of the life cycle found for older cohorts will hold for the younger ones. The impact of third-level education is strikingly different among the younger cohorts compared with the older ones. A clear possibility exists that, over time, class differences, which have not been apparent up to this point, will emerge. The extent to which age differences in urban areas are substantially greater than in rural areas also suggests that something more than life cycle effects is involved here.

A rather different set of factors was also found to be related to church attendance. The crucial influences were unemployment and relatively extreme life-style deprivation. The impact of these factors is not mediated by any shift in religious and moral values. It is more credibly interpreted as being related to the consequences of social marginalisation for self-esteem and involvement in communal activities rather than estrangement from Catholicism.

Indeed, the Catholic Church can take satisfaction from the extent to which Irish society has remained insulated from secularisation influences. It does, however, face problems, if of rather different kinds, at both ends of the class hierarchy and among the younger cohorts. It also has to confront the fact that confidence in its ability to provide solutions to problems in a variety of areas is relatively low and has declined over the past decade. At the same time there is clear majority support for the view that it is appropriate for the church to speak out on a wide range of social and moral issues. The evidence relating to the younger cohorts does suggest the possibility that, after a time lag of some decades, Irish Catholics will be seen to come significantly closer to western European norms. Such a trend is not inevitable but will be, to some degree, determined by the extent to which counter-socialising tendencies, or renewal of the Catholic

Church, or religious revitalisation, are actively and effectively pursued. If, however, we concentrate on the overall pattern of results what is noticeable is the extent to which they are consistent with Ryan's observation (1983, 6) that what is striking about Ireland is not so much secularisation as the emergence of the 'new Catholic'. Among the characteristics that distinguish such 'new Catholics' our evidence provides substantial confirmation of the following:

1. An informed appreciation of the value of the supernatural and sacramental life of the church, including an increasing tendency to think in terms of a spirit or life force rather than a personal God.
2. An outlook that questions the church's right to speak with absolute authority on matters of personal morality or to speak out on Government policy while at the same time considering it appropriate that the church should be outspoken on social issues.
3. A liberal attitude on sexual matters, which can be coupled with an adamant rejection of abortion except in circumstances where the mother's health is at risk.
4. An optimistic interpretation of religion, one's standing before God and the world; Hell, the Devil, sin and doom-and-gloom fears of damnation have all taken a bad beating.

The extent to which such evidence will be taken to support the secularisation thesis is, to an important degree, dependent on the theoretical perspective that one brings to bear on the data. Thus even proponents of the thesis do not argue that religion will disappear from the modern world. The contrast they wish to draw is between the public role of religion and privatised belief and practice (Wallis and Bruce, 1992, 11). A rather different perspective is provided by those such as Hornsby-Smith (1992b) who argue that the loss of nominal adherence, social performance of religious rites, shallow acceptance of prevailing dominant ideas and unnecessary entanglement of religious roles and institutions with secular matters may leave behind a firm, or even firmer, religiosity in those who continue to practise. It is not a view to which those Catholic lay groups that have sought to provide absolute safeguards for traditional values through legislative and constitutional measures are likely to be persuaded. However, we will defer further consideration of these issues until chapter 3.

3 Marriage and the Family

CHRISTOPHER T. WHELAN AND TONY FAHEY

INTRODUCTION

The density, complexity and elusiveness of cultural values and their uncertain relationship with economic development are particularly well illustrated in Ireland in connection with issues of marriage and the family. On a number of occasions since the early 1980s, such as the abortion referendum of 1983, the divorce referendum of 1986, and the further three-part referendum on abortion in 1992, public debate has been convulsed by controversy over the 'politics of the family'. On the surface, the dominant outcome of this conflict has been to reaffirm traditional approaches to family matters. The first two referendums just mentioned, for example, rejected any lessening of the prohibition of divorce in Irish law and installed an anti-abortion clause in the Constitution, thus placing Ireland in an exceptionally conservative position on these matters by comparison with other western countries.

However, this surface adherence to tradition belies the shifts and uncertainties that have emerged beneath. Both before and after the divorce referendum in 1986, for example, opinion polls showed substantial majority support for allowing divorce (Dillon, 1993). In the event, the defeat of the referendum measure that would have enabled that to happen by a margin of almost two to one could be read simply as an illustration of human (or Irish) perversity. But it could equally be seen as a sign of uncertainty in views on the law of marital breakdown and of the complexity and volatility in public discourse on that issue (Dillon, 1993). The same is true of abortion: a strong and apparently unshakable anti-abortion consensus prevailed during the 1980s, yet in 1992 this consensus was thrown into turmoil by the details of the 'X' case, which came before the Supreme Court early in that year. The court ruled that a fourteen-

year-old girl who was the victim of an alleged rape had a constitutional right to an abortion on the grounds that her life was
threatened by the suicidal tendencies arising from her pregnancy.
Given the dramatic circumstances of the girl's plight, the court's
finding in favour of her right to have an abortion was greeted with
widespread relief and led in turn to a new openness to pro-choice
points of view in public debate (Kennelly and Ward, 1993). In the
three-part referendum held later that year to deal with the unsettled
constitutional questions concerning abortion arising from the
Supreme Court's ruling, the electorate showed a significant shift in
a liberal direction. The right to travel abroad to have an abortion
and to disseminate information in Ireland on legal abortion services
abroad were affirmed, while a proposed new and more restrictive
wording for the 1983 anti-abortion clause in the Constitution was
rejected. The wider significance of this shift is still difficult to interpret. At the time of writing, while a new referendum on divorce is
proposed for late in 1994, commentators are uncertain if the liberal
swing has been strong enough to ensure that the electorate will
remove the constitutional ban.

One could list many other instances of complexity and internal
contradiction in cultural attitudes towards family matters. As noted
in the previous chapter, for example, strong adherence to traditional
religious belief and practice among Irish Catholics has proved no
obstacle to the widespread practice (and, it would seem, moral acceptance) of contraception and of sexual activity before marriage (issues
referred to again below). Likewise, a conservative approach to many
aspects of women's position (Pyle, 1990) sits side by side with the
Irish electorate's claim to have been the first country in the world to
elect a feminist (in the person of Mary Robinson) as head of state. In
the legal field, strong support in statute and constitutional law for the
'traditional' family has coexisted with decisive moves away from
traditional legal concepts in order to accommodate to new patterns
of behaviour in family life. Thus the Status of Children Act, 1987,
was aimed at abolishing the traditional legal disabilities suffered by
non-marital children. It thereby greatly weakened the traditional role
of marriage as a means of distinguishing the claims of 'legitimate'
and 'illegitimate' children yet nevertheless passed into law without
any great controversy. Similarly, the Judicial Separation and Family
Law Reform Act, 1989, introduced what is in effect a liberal, no-fault
regime regarding judicial separations. While it carried strong echoes
of liberal divorce law in other western countries (short of allowing

re-marriage) and revolutionised family law in Ireland, it too met with little popular resistance.

Even from these general indications, therefore, one can see that as far as family values are concerned there is striking change in some areas and equally striking lack of change in others, along with considerable flux and uncertainty on many issues. This mixed picture makes it difficult to rely on a simple overarching distinction between tradition and modernity as a means of making overall sense of what is happening. It may be reasonable and useful to resort to such a distinction when talking in a circumscribed way about individual questions; but in bringing individual items together in the larger picture, the idea of unilinear movement from an integrated, coherent starting point labelled 'tradition' to an equally integrated and internationally standard end-point labelled 'modernity' is too simplistic. It may be more useful to consider, as Dillon (1993) does, that emerging Irish patterns of family values represent a 'pick-and-mix' approach, which blends a variety of traditional and modern value positions together to form a distinctive alternative. This alternative may not so much occupy a particular place on the tradition–modernity continuum as represent one of the many possible departures from it. This suggestion is in keeping with a more general view of social change as contingent and diverse and so conforming to no single underlying model of modernisation. In looking at family values in Ireland in these terms, therefore, it may make some sense to ask of attitudes on individual items how 'advanced' or 'backward' they are as far as movement along the path to modernity is concerned. But we should not be entirely surprised if the overall package of values does not sit easily with the image of 'progressive' change towards a standard 'modern' end-point.

The findings of the European Values Survey on issues concerning marriage and the family can offer some insight into these questions. Before looking at those findings we should remind ourselves of the limits of the kind of information the data to hand offers. As the instances already mentioned suggest, people's judgments on what is valuable or acceptable in family matters are far from clear and fixed. Rather they are fluid, very much influenced by context, and thus difficult to identify and pin down in any consistent form. It is clear from the 1986 divorce referendum, for example, that many people expressed a willingness in opinion polls to allow divorce legislation but at the same time rejected the step in that direction offered by the referendum. Likewise there was a great deal of inconsistency between opinion poll findings and actual voting in the 1992 abortion referendum, along with considerable evidence of volatility in public opinion during the accompanying public debate (Kennelly and Ward, 1993). Exploring the nuances and uncertainty of feeling suggested by such variability can best be dealt with by drawing on a number of different forms of research. However, the material available here does at least indicate some of the general contours of the value landscape and some of the important sources of tension. It is with that broad objective in mind that the findings of the European Values Study on family values are explored here. Three main issues are looked at: women's role in the family and economy, family size and parent-child relationships, and various aspects of what might loosely be called sexual morality (for example divorce, abortion, sexual freedom, and the status of marriage).

WOMEN'S ROLE IN THE FAMILY AND ECONOMY

In most western countries after the Second World War the majority of married women spent their lives at home looking after children, husbands, and homes. Today the conventional view is that that pattern has been stood on its head, as married women have entered the paid labour force in large numbers. As a result, married women in most western countries engage in full-time housework either not at all or only for short periods when their children are small. This transformation in women's economic roles is often regarded as one of the key 'modernising' transitions in family life: it gives women a measure of economic independence vis-à-vis their husbands, reduces their willingness to have a large number of children (or, in many cases, any children at all), and helps them break out of a limiting confinement to the narrow sphere of home and family. Because of the importance of these changes for attitudes and behaviour patterns in family life, labour force participation rates among women (especially married women) are often taken as a good indicator of how far traditionalism in family matters, and indeed in society as a whole, has waned.

On this count, Ireland is in an uncertain position. On the one hand, married women's labour force rates are generally judged to have increased by more than four times since the 1960s (Callan and Farrell, 1992), indicating a rapid rate of 'modernisation' in women's economic roles. On the other hand, the present rate is still often presented as one of the lowest in the western world, so that Ireland has been characterised as particularly backward in this area and as uniquely conservative and patriarchal among western countries in its treatment of women (Pyle, 1990). The issue is complicated by questions of definition and measurement. It is not at all clear how extensive women's labour force participation is, how it has changed over time, or how it compares with patterns in other countries, simply because accurate, comprehensive and readily comparable statistics in this area are much harder to come by than is often realised (Fahey, 1990, 1993). There has also been much questioning, particularly by feminist scholars, of the supposed transformation in women's family and economic roles in other countries (Hakim, 1993; Jonnung and Persson, 1993). Thus we have to be careful in making assertions about how 'advanced' or otherwise Ireland is in this context, by comparison either with its own past or with the standards now prevailing in other countries.

Against this background of uncertainty about the nature and significance of recent changes in women's roles in Ireland, the European Values Study in 1990 set out to measure attitudes towards the interplay of women's economic and family roles. To that end, respondents were asked to indicate whether they agreed or disagreed with each of the following statements:

Career costs attitudes
　(i) A working mother can establish just as warm and secure a relationship with her children as a mother who does not work.
　(ii) A pre-school child is likely to suffer if his or her mother works.

Pro-homemaker attitudes
　(i) A job is all right, but what most women really want is a home and children.
　(ii) Being a housewife is just as fulfilling as working for pay.

Anti-employment attitudes
　(i) Having a job is the best way for a woman to be an independent person.
　(ii) Both the husband and wife should contribute to household income.

While each of these groups is relatively distinct, they are associated, and it is possible to combine all six items into a measure of 'traditional sex role attitudes'. We will draw on such overall aggregate measures and measures for the three sub-groups in reporting our findings, but will begin by looking at results for the individual items.

IRISH-EUROPEAN COMPARISON OF SEX ROLE ATTITUDES

Our first results will involve a comparison of Irish and European attitudes. In table 3.1 we set out the percentage of respondents giving answers that may be characterised as involving 'traditional sex role' responses to each of the items. The first point to be made is that the Irish responses are by no means uniformly more traditional than the European average. Just over one-third of the Irish respondents do not accept that a working mother can establish just as satisfactory a relationship as a mother who does not work. This figure is almost identical to the European average. While just over half the Irish sample think a pre-school child is likely to suffer if his or her mother works, the corresponding European figure is considerably higher. It comes close to seven out of ten in Europe as a whole, while in Italy, Portugal and West Germany it exceeds 80 per cent. Thus, in their evaluation of career costs the Irish show no evidence of being more traditional than other Europeans.

On the pro-homemaker dimension, the evidence is mixed. Almost six out of ten Irish respondents think that while a job is all right, what a woman really wants is a home; but this figure is extremely close to the European average. Irish people are more likely to agree that being a housewife is just as fulfilling as working for pay. Close to three out of four of those interviewed in Ireland agree with this statement, compared with less than six out of ten in the European countries as a whole.

With regard to anti-employment attitudes, the Irish are somewhat more traditional. The figure representing those thinking that having a job is the best way for a woman to be an independent person reaches six out of ten in Ireland, while the European figure is close to three-quarters. Seven out of ten Irish people think that both the husband and wife should contribute to household income—a figure that is just below the European average of 75 per cent.

The comparison of Irish and European sex role attitudes can be dealt with in a more summarised way by presenting the results in

TABLE 3.1 *'Traditional' sex role attitudes: Ireland and Europe compared*

		Ireland %	European average %
(i)	A working mother can establish just as warm and secure a relationship with her children as a mother who does not work: *percentage disagreeing*	37	36
(ii)	A pre-school child is likely to suffer if his or her mother works: *percentage agreeing*	53	68
(iii)	A job is all right, but what most women really want is a home and children: *percentage agreeing*	59	57
(iv)	Being a housewife is just as fulfilling as working for pay: *percentage agreeing*	72	57
(v)	Having a job is the best way for a woman to be an independent person: *percentage disagreeing*	39	26
(vi)	Both the husband and wife should contribute to household income: *percentage disagreeing*	30	25

terms of average scores for each of the three sub-groups of items referred to earlier. Each of the component scales and the overall scales have a range of scores from 1 (for the least traditional position) to 4 (for the most traditional). In table 3.2 we set out the Ireland-Europe comparison. It is striking just how close the Irish pattern is to the European. The Irish display slightly stronger anti-employment attitudes, but the difference is modest. It is clear that there is no basis for any explanation of distinctive aspects of Irish participation rates, or any other economic aspects of sex roles in Ireland, that relies on the consequences of Irish sex role attitudes. This conclusion is in line with that of Kelley et al. (1991), using almost identical measures but drawing on a different data set. It is also consistent with the conclusion reached by Callan and Farrell (1992) on the basis of their econometric analysis of female labour force participation.

In general, therefore, while Irish attitudes are not significantly more traditional than European views, the pattern of results does

TABLE 3.2   '*Traditional' sex role dimensions: comparison of Irish and Europen average scores*

	Career cost attitudes	Pro-homemaker attitudes	Anti-employment attitudes	Traditional sex-role attitudes
Ireland	2.4	2.7	2.3	2.5
Europe	2.5	2.6	2.1	2.4

Scoring: 1 = least traditional, 4 = most traditional

point to the continuing influence of values that underpin sex role differentiation. Thus while attitudes to women's employment are generally positive, substantial proportions of the adult population consider that there are negative effects for children. Furthermore, significant majorities consider that women can be fulfilled in the role of housewife and indeed that this, rather than jobs outside the home, is what they really want.

Variations in sex role attitudes within Ireland
It is clearly of considerable interest to discover how sex role attitudes vary by socio-demographic background. One obvious possibility is that men and women hold different attitudes. However, as is clear from table 3.3, the hypothesis receives only qualified support. Men do tend to think that career costs, in terms of negative impact on children, are higher, and they are slightly more likely to think that 'what women really want is a home and children.' On the other hand, the differences between the sexes on pro-home and anti-employment attitudes are modest and a good deal less substantial than those produced by other variables.

The most substantial differences occur between age groups. It is useful first to point to a distinction that holds throughout all the socio-demographic variables considered here. Variation is most pronounced for the career costs and pro-home dimensions and is very limited for the employment attitudes scale. With this qualification, age has a consistently substantial impact, as we can see from table 3.4. While only one in four of those between eighteen and twenty-nine think that it is more difficult for a working mother to establish a warm and secure relationship with her children, this figure gradually rises to over one in two for those over sixty. Similarly, while two in

TABLE 3.3 *'Traditional' sex role attitudes, by sex*

		Women	Men
(i)	A working mother can establish just as warm and secure a relationship with her children as a mother who does not work: *percentage disagreeing*	34	41
(ii)	A pre-school child is likely to suffer if his or her mother works: *percentage agreeing*	46	60
(iii)	A job is all right, but what most women really want is a home and children: *percentage agreeing*	55	62
(iv)	Being a housewife is just as fulfilling as working for pay: *percentage agreeing*	71	73
(v)	Having a job is the best way for a woman to be an independent person: *percentage disagreeing*	41	38
(vi)	Both the husband and wife should contribute to household income: *percentage disagreeing*	27	32

five of the younger age group feel that a pre-school child will suffer because of a working mother, this rises to almost seven out of ten for the oldest group. Eight out of ten of the oldest group hold to the view that what most women really want is a home and children, while only four out of ten of those under thirty agree. Similarly, while just over half the latter group think that being a housewife is just as fulfilling as working for pay, this jumps to almost nine out of ten for those aged sixty or over. The differences on the anti-employment dimension are more modest, but it is still true that fewer than one in three people in the youngest age group reject the view that having a job is the best way for a woman to be an independent person. This holds true for just less than one in two of those in the oldest age group.

Not surprisingly in view of the effect of age, traditional attitudes vary sharply across educational level. Thus, as the results set out in table 3.5 show, those with primary education or less are almost three times more likely to think that it is more difficult for a working mother to establish as warm and sincere a relationship with her children as a mother who does not work. They are also twice as likely to

TABLE 3.4 *'Traditional' sex role attitudes, by age group*

		18–29 %	30–44 %	45–59 %	60+ %
(i)	A working mother can establish just as warm and secure a relationship with her children as a mother who does not work: *percentage disagreeing*	23	30	45	54
(ii)	A pre-school child is likely to suffer if his or her mother works: *percentage agreeing*	38	47	61	68
(iii)	A job is all right, but what most women really want is a home and children: *percentage agreeing*	42	54	62	80
(iv)	Being a housewife is just as fulfilling as working for pay: *percentage agreeing*	55	65	73	87
(v)	Having a job is the best way for a woman to be an independent person: *percentage disagreeing*	31	40	42	45
(vi)	Both the husband and wife should contribute to household income: *percentage disagreeing*	24	27	37	31

think that a pre-school child will suffer if its mother works and that what most women really want is a home and children. Finally, they are significantly more likely to think that being a housewife is just as fulfilling as working for pay: over eight out of ten of those with primary education or less take this view, compared with two-thirds of those with third-level education.

Focusing our attention on women for the moment, in table 3.6 we compare the responses of those in paid jobs and those working in the home. The latter are consistently more traditional. Not far short of half of women in the home think that working mothers have difficulty establishing the same quality of relationship with their children as stay-at-home mothers; the corresponding figure for women in paid jobs is one in five. Similarly, close to six out of ten of the former group consider that the pre-school children of a working mother will suffer, compared with one in three of women in employment; while fewer than one in two women who are in employment consider that what a woman really wants is a home and children, compared with

TABLE 3.5 *'Traditional' sex role attitudes, by level of educational qualification*

	Primary or less	Intermediate or Group Cert.	Leaving Cert.	Third level
	%	%	%	%
(i) A working mother can establish just as warm and secure a relationship with her children as a mother who does not work: *percentage disagreeing*	50	37	29	18
(ii) A pre-school child is likely to suffer if his or her mother works: *percentage agreeing*	67	54	43	32
(iii) A job is all right, but what most women really want is a home and children: *percentage agreeing*	75	65	43	37
(iv) Being a housewife is just as fulfilling as working for pay: *percentage agreeing*	84	72	58	66
(v) Having a job is the best way for a woman to be an independent person: *percentage disagreeing*	42	40	37	35
(vi) Both the husband and wife should contribute to household income: *percentage disagreeing*	34	27	24	32

two in three housewives. Eight out of ten of the latter also think that being a housewife is just as fulfilling as working for pay. Women in the home are also less likely to agree that having a job is the best way for a woman to be independent or that both husband and wife should contribute to the household income. Further analysis shows that married women in employment, and indeed married women who are in employment with children in the household, do not differ significantly from other women in employment.

Of course the factors that have been shown to be related to sex role attitudes are in a number of cases related to each other; in particular, level of education is strongly associated with age. However,

TABLE 3.6 *'Traditional' sex role attitudes: comparison of women in paid employment and in home duties*

	Women in employment %	Women in home duties %
(i) A working mother can establish just as warm and secure a relationship with her children as a mother who does not work: *percentage disagreeing*	21	44
(ii) A pre-school child is likely to suffer if his or her mother works: *percentage agreeing*	34	58
(iii) A job is all right, but what most women really want is a home and children: *percentage agreeing*	44	66
(iv) Being a housewife is just as fulfilling as working for pay: *percentage agreeing*	60	81
(v) Having a job is the best way for a woman to be an independent person: *percentage disagreeing*	34	45
(vi) Both the husband and wife should contribute to household income: *percentage disagreeing*	20	33

multivariate statistical analysis shows that each of the factors has an independent influence. If we focus in the first place on the overall measure of traditional sex role attitudes, we find that the most important influences are age and education, followed by sex and being a housewife. For education the crucial distinction is between those with Leaving Certificate or above and all others. When the influence of these variables is taken into account, other factors that might have been expected to have an influence, such as social class and urban versus rural location, have no significant impact.

In table 3.7 we provide a simple illustration of the cumulative impact of socio-demographic influences. This is achieved by contrasting two 'extreme groups': (*a*) men with primary education or less and aged sixty or over, and (*b*) women educated to Leaving Certificate level or above and aged between eighteen and twenty-nine. While well over half such men think that it is not possible for a working mother to have just as satisfactory a relationship with her children as one who does not work, this is true of fewer than one in eight of the younger women. Similarly, while eight out of ten of the former consider that a mother's participation in the labour force has detrimental consequences for pre-school children, the figure drops to just one in four of the latter. Furthermore, while nine out of ten older men are confident that what women themselves really want is a home and children, two out of three younger women offer a dissenting judgment. Finally, while nine out of ten older males think that being a housewife is just as fulfilling as working for pay, younger women seem somewhat less convinced, and the figure drops to six out of ten.

In line with our previous discussion of sex role differences, we wish to draw attention to the fact that, as can be seen from table 3.8, even among the youngest age group there are substantial differences in the evaluation of career costs, with men being almost twice as likely as women to think that pre-school children will suffer and that it is more difficult for a working mother to achieve a warm and sincere relationship with her children.

TABLE 3.7   *'Traditional' sex role attitudes: comparison of educational and age extremes*

		Men, primary education & aged 60 or over %	Women, educated to Leaving Cert. or higher aged 18–29 %
(i)	A working mother can establish just as warm and secure a relationship with her children as a mother who does not work: *percentage disagreeing*	56	13
(ii)	A pre-school child is likely to suffer if his or her mother works	80	28
(iii)	A job is all right, but what most women really want is a home and children	86	33
(iv)	Being a housewife is just as fulfilling as working for pay	87	57
(v)	Having a job is the best way for a woman to be an independent person	39	34
(vi)	Both the husband and wife should contribute to household income	33	23

TABLE 3.8   *'Traditional' sex role attitudes to career cost: differences by sex, 18–29 age group*

		Men %	Women %
(i)	A working mother can establish just as warm and secure a relationship with her children as a mother who does not work: *percentage disagreeing*	30	17
(ii)	A pre-school child is likely to suffer if his or her mother works: *percentage agreeing*	49	28

It is striking that in our analysis so far, age and education are crucial variables. In older age groups the effect of education is much weaker, and this contributes substantially to overall differences between such groups. Thus, the differences we have observed are consistent with the impact of industrialisation and urbanisation, and the transition from a traditional folk structure to the complexity of urban, industrialised societies. Unfortunately our data does not include information on whether the respondents were raised in an urban or rural location. Current location in a rural area is associated with more traditional attitudes, but it does not have a significant independent influence when we control for other factors. While class is not an important determinant of sex role attitudes, the fact that education has a particularly strong influence among the younger age group raises the distinct possibility that this will change over time.

The pattern of attitudes observed in the data suggests that Irish people are not directly hostile to married women's participation in the labour force. However, there is indirect resistance in the form of concern for the effects of such participation on pre-school children and on the relationships mothers have with them. This concern is consistent with the low employment rate in Ireland for mothers with children under five years of age and for mothers with three or more children. It is also consistent with the limited availability of state child care facilities and the absence of tax allowances for child care expenses (McKenna, 1988; Kennedy, 1989). However, recognition of the 'dual burden' carried by working mothers is based on the assumption that women will continue to carry the main burden of homemaking and child care activities.

As Mahon (1991) points out, while equality initiatives initially centre on the equal treatment of men and women in the labour force, they tend to evolve towards ways of facilitating parents who wish to work but also to have time with their children. The initiatives, of course, face the dilemma, to which Mahon refers, of whether to accept the kind of values and attitudes we have been describing and look for ways to modify their marginalising effect on women, or to confront and try to change them, as, for example, through encouraging joint parenting. The sharp variations in traditional sex role attitudes by education are also consistent with the suggestion by Mahon (1991) that formal equality of opportunity is likely to be substantially greater for women in the higher social classes. For all women, however, the fact that men consistently hold more traditional views continues to be an obstacle to equal participation in the labour force.

FAMILY SIZE AND PARENT-CHILD RELATIONSHIPS

Breen et al. (1990, 103) note that in Ireland a moral entente between the church and state consolidated a normative environment in which sexuality was directed into orthodox Christian channels, its active expression being restricted to marriage, and within marriage its enjoyment morally subservient to the procreative function. Marriage was in consequence entered into with an expectation of high fertility.

The components of the distinctive Irish demographic regime were, Coleman notes, formed by the early nineteenth century and included late marriage and low levels of 'illegitimacy' or cohabitation and 'natural' high fertility within marriage. 'The whole system was overshadowed and its particular features made possible by the institutionalization of very high rates of emigration' (Coleman, 1992, 57). Fertility control operated primarily through marriage, and Ireland provided an example of a Malthusian population. At the end of the last century about 30 per cent of Irish men and 23 per cent of Irish women never married. The comparable figures for most of western Europe were about 10 per cent for both sexes. Furthermore, as Breen et al. (1990, 103) note, even these figures understate the uniqueness of the Irish marriage pattern. For those who did marry the average age was nearly six years greater than the average for men in most western European countries.

Recent decades have seen dramatic changes in the Irish demographic pattern. The marriage rate rose sharply in the 1960s and early 1970s but declined to its lowest rate for almost fifty years by the late 1980s. Age at marriage also follows this broad pattern of a sharp decline followed by a subsequent increase. Since the early 1960s a sharp decline in fertility has occurred. Clancy (1992, 166) estimates that marital fertility declined by 37 per cent in the twenty-year period 1961–1981. Attitudes to contraception and contraceptive practices appear to have moved close to European norms (Clancy, 1992; Coleman, 1992). The decline in marital fertility has been accompanied by a rise in fertility outside marriage.

Explanation of the Irish demographic pattern has focused in particular on emigration and the dominance of the Catholic Church. With regard to the latter hypothesis, Coleman (1992, 73) notes that the only circumstances in which Roman Catholic influence was important, over and above the level expected from socio-economic development, were when the religious acquired particular authority through being a focus for the national sentiments of a minority in a larger population. Factors that are considered likely to have contributed to recent changes include the increased cost of children, higher standards of education, particularly among women, knowledge of family planning methods, and the increased participation of married women in the labour force. The decline of large families is evident in fewer higher-order births after 1960. The proportion of fourth and higher-order births to mothers in Ireland fell from just under half to just over a quarter by the late 1970s. Correspondingly, first births increased from about a fifth to almost a third. This proportion was still substantially behind other western societies, where at least 50 per cent of births were first-time births (Coleman, 1992).

In the 1990 survey, respondents were asked to indicate what they thought was the ideal family size. In table 3.9 we compare the results for Ireland and for the European sample as a whole, broken down by age. The pattern of variation can be captured by looking at the numbers opting for two children or fewer and for four or more. Focusing on the latter first, we find that while one-half of the Irish respondents indicate a preference for a family size of four or five, this is true of fewer than one in five of the European respondents as a whole. For a family size of two or fewer the pattern of results is almost exactly reversed. Only Northern Ireland comes in any way close to the pattern for the Republic. The differences between Ireland and Catholic countries such as Italy and Spain are not much different from those relating to other countries. West Germany provides the polar opposite case to Ireland, with 65 per cent stating a preference for a family size of two or less. The pat-

TABLE 3.9 *Ideal family size, by age group: Ireland and Europe compared*

| | Ideal family size | | | |
| | 2 or less | | 4 or more | |
	Ireland %	Europe %	Ireland %	Europe %
18–29	30	59	40	16
30–44	27	60	42	16
45–50	21	56	58	18
60+	10	48	67	22
Overall	22	56	51	18

tern of age variation differs between Ireland and the other countries. For Europe as a whole there is relatively little variation across age groups, while in Ireland age has a significant effect. Thus, 59 per cent of the overall European sample aged 18–29 opt for two or fewer children and 16 per cent for four or five, and almost identical figures are obtained for those aged sixty or over. In Ireland the corresponding figures for the youngest groups are 30 and 40 per cent; among the oldest group, however, the former figure falls to 10 per cent while the latter reaches 67 per cent.

TABLE 3.10 *Ideal family size, by age group and urban v. rural location*

| | Ideal family size | | | |
| | 2 or less | | 4 or more | |
	Rural %	Urban %	Rural %	Urban %
18–29	21	36	48	35
30–44	24	29	52	33
45–59	17	25	67	51
60+	6	16	78	53

Apart from age, the socio-demographic factors that have an influence on ideal family size are urban versus rural location and education. Social class and sex, on the other hand, have no effect. The effect of education turns out to be modest when we allow for the effect of age. Age and urban versus rural location produce the sharpest variation. Rural location has been defined here as living in the countryside or in towns with a population of less than 2,000. In table 3.10 we display the combined effect of age and location. Almost eight out of ten of those aged sixty or more and currently residing in a rural location express a preference for a family size of four or more. For those aged under thirty in urban locations this falls to almost one in three. For a family size of two or less the respective proportions are 6 and 36 per cent.

PARENT-CHILD RELATIONSHIPS

One aspect of economic modernisation that has important effects on family structure is the declining importance of property inheritance and the increasing importance of educational qualifications in determining social and economic position. Breen et al. (1990, 56) illustrate the scale of this transformation by contrasting the occupational outlook of new cohorts of young men (aged 15–19) in the 1920s and 1970s. In the former period, over half the cohort remaining in Ireland would have depended on family employment that would eventually lead to inheritance of the family holding. By the 1970s this was true of less than 15 per cent of the cohort.

Apart from its many other consequences, this shift has had important implications for parent-child relationships. Property inheritance was parent-centred, and the economic demands associated with inheritance were minimised by the lifetime usage obtained from family property by parents (and in particular by fathers) before its eventual transfer. Control over inheritance also gave parents an important instrument of control over their children, even into adult years. In the case of education, by contrast, parents bear the cost of it in the peak years of family formation. The burden it places on parental resources includes not only direct costs but the effect on household income of children remaining at school rather than entering the labour force and of mothers staying at home from work to care for school-going children. The result is to greatly increase the cost of children to parents in terms of effort and commitment as well as money. This in turn is a major contribution to the sharp decline in family size that we have already referred to.

Earlier we looked at some of the socio-demographic aspects of this trend. At this point we will focus on the extent to which changes in these areas are reflected in attitudes towards the nature of parent-child obligations. In both the 1981 and 1990 European Values Study, respondents were asked which of the following two statements they tended to agree with: (*a*) parents' duty is to do the best for their children even at the expense of their own well-being; (*b*) parents have a life of their own and should not be asked to sacrifice their own well-being for the sake of their children.

Irish respondents have a slightly higher than average tendency to accept absolute obligations towards their parents. The proportion adhering to this view is 78 per cent, compared with the European average of 73 per cent. This share has declined slightly from 81 per cent in 1981.

With the exception of the oldest age group, there has been a decline in the percentage adhering to an unqualified view of parental obligations. The general pattern points to generational change: younger age groups do not significantly alter their more individualistic views as they grow older, thus producing a decline in the overall level of population support for the more absolutist position (table 3.11).

TABLE 3.11 *Percentage agreeing with the view that parents' duty is to do the best for their children even at the expense of their own well-being, by age and date of survey*

	1981 %	1990 %
18–27	66	59
28–37	78	66
38–47	84	78
48–57	86	75
58+	84	86

The right of parents to individual fulfilment is thus implicitly given increased emphasis. To date, however, these generational changes are not especially large, so that the traditional position in relation to parental duties still holds among the vast majority. We should note too that both positions are compatible with a desire for smaller families. Precisely because of the unqualified nature of parental obligations, as the cost of children increases dramatically many couples are motivated to control family size. On the other hand, a clear sense of one's right to self-fulfilment may also encourage this tendency.

The other crucial factor influencing views on the nature of parents' obligation is education. However, as we can see from table 3.12, the influence of education is not even across age groups, as it has a substantially stronger effect among those under forty-five. For this group there is a difference of 18 percentage points between those with and without the Leaving Certificate; for those over forty-five this difference is only 6 per cent. Thus rejection of the traditional view on parental obligation is strikingly higher among the young, well-educated group than among any of the others.

TABLE 3.12 *Percentage agreeing with the view that parents' duty is to do the best for their children even at the expense of their own well-being, by age and education*

	Less than Leaving Cert.	Leaving Cert. or more
Under 45	76	59
45 or more	82	77

We also have information from the European Values Study surveys on how children's responsibilities to their parents are viewed. The idea that older people in industrial societies are alienated from their children guided research in social gerontology for most of the postwar period. However, a range of more recent studies has documented the existence of strong social relationships between aging parents and their adult offspring. Not only is contact with children frequent but children are also the most important source of social support. Whelan and Vaughan (1982) in their study of the elderly in Ireland found that in regard to a variety of tasks, if help were to be sought from outside the household, children would be approached most frequently. Research confirms that, while for short-term problems neighbourhood and friendship networks are important sources of assistance, they are supplements to, rather than replacements for, relatives as sources of support. In a study of married women in the city of Cork, Gordon (1977) confirmed findings from the United States and Hungary that for problems of short duration, neighbours were seen as most helpful, followed by kin and friends, whereas for longer-standing problems the ordering was relatives, neighbours, and friends.

Cantor (1979) concludes that kin are clearly considered the primary source of help, regardless of the task. Only to the extent that family, particularly children, are not available, and with respect to certain well-defined tasks, do friends, neighbours and formal organisations become important in the provision of informal support. Even where children were seen infrequently or were no longer in regular contact, they still remained the preferred choice.

As with parents' obligations to their children, the question regarding children's obligations to their parents in the European Values Study survey sought once again to uncover the extent to which they were perceived to be absolute. Thus respondents were asked to choose between the following two options: (*a*) regardless of what the qualities and faults of one's parents are, one must always love and respect them; (*b*) one does not have a duty to respect and love parents who have not earned it by their behaviour and attitude.

Seventy-eight per cent of Irish respondents accept the former proposition, a figure that is five points higher than the European average. The Irish figure has fallen three percentage points during the 1980s. From table 3.13 we find that the change is accounted for by shifts towards less absolute positions among the middle-aged groups. At both points in time almost nine out of ten of the oldest age group and two out of three of the youngest accepted unqualified obligations to their parents. Once again we find that education has a substantially stronger influence among younger than older respondents, the respective differences being 16 and 6 per cent when we take the age of forty-five as a cut-off point. The number adhering to the traditional view among the young well-educated falls to two out of three.

The tendency of the younger, better-educated respondents to reject traditional notions of both parent and child obligations might be taken to imply that in the future family support networks will be undermined among the middle classes. Such an implication might be thought to have particularly detrimental consequences if children are

TABLE 3.13 *Percentage agreeing that regardless of one's parents' qualities and faults one must always love and respect them*

	1981 %	1990 %
18–27	68	68
28–37	82	75
38–47	83	78
48–57	87	77
58+	88	88

seen to be an important part of the 'emotional support system of parents' (Shanas, 1973). However, high rates of interaction between children and parents, and a strong sense of obligation on the part of children towards their parents, do not necessarily lead to higher levels of well-being among parents. A large number of studies have failed to find a positive correlation between interaction with adult children and feelings of well-being among elderly people. Lee (1979), despite a reluctance to accept this counter-intuitive finding, nevertheless found that his own observations were consistent with it. A study of retirement in Ireland by Whelan and Whelan (1988) also pointed in the same direction. In fact 56 per cent of those who had daily contact with their children were enjoying retirement, while this was true of over 70 per cent of those who saw their children fortnightly or less often. Such differences could not be accounted for adequately by factors such as health status.

This is not to suggest that family ties are incidental, or even detrimental, to the well-being of the elderly. But it does suggest that the quality rather than the quantity of family interactions is important and that what counts as 'quality' in this context may vary greatly from case to case. Furthermore, the willingness to invest time and effort in constructing good-quality interactions may not of itself yield positive results, since parents and children may experience difficulty in sharing experiences and may lack common interests, attitudes, and values (Hess and Waring, 1978).

To explore the question of shared attitudes as an aspect of parent-child interactions, the European Values Study respondents in both 1990 and 1981 were asked the extent to which they shared any of the following with their parents:

(i) Attitudes towards religion
(ii) Moral attitudes
(iii) Social attitudes
(iv) Political attitudes
(v) Sexual attitudes

The results, broken down by age group for both years, are set out in table 3.14. The first point to be made is that the extent of intergenerational agreement shows no sign of having declined over the decade. At both points in time there is a fairly high level of agreement on religious and moral attitudes, with the average figure coming close to 70 per cent. The figures for social attitudes tend to be slightly lower. For political and social attitudes, consensus is much less common, with the average figure being close to one-third. Such lack of agreement is not a recent development, since for each dimension the degree of shared attitudes is higher in 1990 than in 1981. Finally, the number of respondents sharing none of these attitudes with their parents is identical in both years, and the distribution across age groups is remarkably similar.

TABLE 3.14 *Extent of shared attitudes with parents, by age group and time of survey*

	Religion		Moral attitudes		Social attitudes		Political attitudes		Sexual attitudes		None	
	1981 %	1990 %	1981 %	1990 %	1981 %	1990 %	1981 %	1990 %	1981 %	1990 %	1981 %	1990 %
18–27	60	63	60	57	55	59	30	42	27	26	14	14
28–37	72	66	69	72	60	67	42	43	32	26	8	9
38–47	77	77	68	70	57	66	35	48	24	27	5	7
48–57	68	78	57	68	49	63	36	46	25	31	8	10
58+	81	92	67	87	56	77	38	63	27	43	4	2
Total	72	76	64	72	55	67	36	49	27	31	8	8

Thus parents and children are close on some attitudes but rather far apart on others, and neither a comparison of the two surveys nor differences across age groups suggest that this is a recent pattern. Given this lack of consistency, it seems unlikely that the character of parent-child interaction can be accounted for by such differences. Thus, other explanations for the effects (or lack of effects) of kin contact on parents' morale need to be sought. A wide range of approaches have been suggested. One such approach is to compare the effects of kinship and friendship on parents' well-being. Adam (1967) sees the ascribed or obligatory character of kinship versus the non-obligatory, consensual nature of friendship as the key issue here. Lee (1979, 350) likewise argues that the critical distinction between friendship and kinship may centre on mutuality or reciprocity of choice.

A related but somewhat different approach is provided by exchange/power analysis, which focuses on those qualitative characteristics of contact between adult children and their parents that are connected with dependence and the absence of mutuality or reciprocity. The effect of this approach is to challenge the 'sentimental' or 'utopian' model of the family as a harmonious, egalitarian retreat from the outside world. It points instead to the inequalities of power and resources within families—particularly, as far as the elderly are concerned, in connection with health and income—and to the dependence and loss of esteem that arise from the resulting unbalanced social exchange between family members (Dowd and La Rossa, 1982, 185–6). The desire of the elderly to live apart from their children and to maintain 'intimacy at a distance' can be interpreted as an attempt to minimise the costs associated with such unbalanced social exchange.

A further concern emphasised by the exchange/power perspective is that support for the elderly is provided not so much by families as by particular members of families, especially middle-aged daughters (Brody, 1981; Lang and Brody, 1983; Stroller, 1982). A recent study confirms that in Ireland, as elsewhere, community care in practice generally means care by a female relative, regardless of social class or rural versus urban background (O'Connor, Smyth, and Whelan, 1988). In addition, it is not always clear that the elderly are at the receiving rather than the giving end of aid. While it is often held that old age is a time of role reversal—elderly parents become dependent and in a certain sense 'child-like' in relation to their adult children (Sussman, 1965)—there is evidence that many parents continue to benefit their children even into advanced old age (Covey, 1981). Cohler (1983, 36) suggests that the real struggle for independence among the elderly is not to continue looking after themselves but to wean their children—that is, to maintain relationships with them but to avoid being overwhelmed by their demands. In Ireland, Whelan and Whelan's study (1988, 66) of retired people found that visits to children were positively associated with enjoyment of retirement, while visits *from* children had a negative effect. They interpreted these results to mean that the ability of parents to choose the conditions under which interaction with relatives took place had a major effect on its benefits for them.

DIVORCE AND ABORTION

In the preceding section we focused on family size and parent-child relations. However, much of the argument about the consequences for family life of social change associated with industrialisation has focused on 'moral' questions connected with marriage and sexual behaviour. Breen et al. (1990, 120–1) have argued that class inequalities, the gradual weakening of religious influence and growing unemployment rates almost inevitably imply increasing strains on conventional institutional arrangements in these areas. The most visible indicators of these strains are such things as increases in the level of sexual activity outside marriage, in the rates of non-marital birth, in the incidence of Irish abortions in Britain, and in the rate of marital breakdown.

Changes in behaviour in these areas can be summed up by saying that the traditional tight sequencing of marriage, entry into sexual activity and procreation has been greatly disrupted, if not entirely abandoned. Sex now typically begins before marriage (probably, in most cases, a long time before marriage, though the evidence on this is scanty). Procreation also often begins before marriage. In 1991, 18 per cent of all births occurred outside marriage (up from about 2 per cent in 1960), though the continuing importance of marriage is suggested by the fact that the majority of single mothers apparently marry within a few years of becoming parents. In most cases also, whether inside or outside marriage, sexual activity is not intended to lead to procreation and does not in fact do so, because of effective contraceptive practice. In addition, the incidence of Irish abortions has risen to around 4,000 per year. As a result, the overall fertility rate in 1989 dropped below the population replacement level for the first time in Irish history. The traditional permanence of marriage has also been diluted, though information on this issue is scanty. The number of persons reporting themselves as 'separated' in any sense (that is, informally separated, legally separated, deserted, divorced in another country, or having the marriage annulled) rose from 37,000 in 1986 to 55,000 in 1991, an increase of just about 50 per cent in five years. But the absolute numbers involved are still quite small, representing about 3.5 per cent of the ever-married population in 1991.

The question raised by all this change for our present concerns is what it suggests about Irish values in these areas. Kennedy (1989, 1) suggests that many of the behavioural changes in marriage and sexuality have occurred 'notwithstanding the fact that some of them conflict with the professed value system of the majority.' However, as mentioned at the beginning of this chapter, professed value systems in this area have lost the stability and homogeneity of the past and are now in a state of uncertainty and flux. There may indeed be a gulf between values and behaviour, but equally there may be a good deal of adjustment and accommodation as people work towards new values to give coherence and meaning to these areas of their lives. The conflict of recent years over public policy in relation to divorce and abortion, and to some extent contraception, is the most obvious sign of this new and uncertain quest.

It is against this background that the 1990 European Values Study examined respondents' attitudes to certain aspects of marriage and sexuality. Comparable findings from the 1981 study make possible some examination of trends over time.

On the controversial issues of divorce and abortion, the findings suggest that Irish respondents have become more tolerant over time but remain quite distinctive in European terms. From table 2.12 in chapter 2 we saw that Irish people in 1990 had become more likely to agree that divorce and abortion are acceptable under some circumstances. On divorce, though, the Irish level of permissiveness was only half that of Europeans as a whole; in the case of abortion it was as low as one-third.

In chapter 2 we also saw that the only circumstance in which Irish respondents are willing to approve of abortion is when the mother's health is at risk. Even in this case only two-thirds approve of abortion, compared with nine out of ten European respondents. In no other case does the Irish figure come near to a majority, even though 80 per cent of the European sample are willing to accept the risk of physical handicap as a justification for abortion. The percentages willing to accept not being married or avoiding having more children as a justification for abortion are extremely small in the Irish case, although for Europe overall they exceed one in four in the former instance and one in three in the latter.

Given that tolerance of abortion in Ireland is significant only where the mother's health is at risk or where the child is likely to be born physically handicapped, we will examine socio-demographic variation in attitudes to abortion only in connection with those two circumstances. Table 3.15 shows the variation across age groups for both 1981 and 1990. While Irish attitudes vary systematically by age, only in the case of risk to mother's health does this have substantive implications: the young are much more likely to approve of abortion in that circumstance than are the old. In the case of likely physical handicap in the child, the age variation is in a similar direction but is much less pronounced. Over time there has been a large increase in willingness to approve of abortion where the mother's health is at risk. The proportion approving goes from 45 per cent in 1981 to 65 per cent in 1990, and this shift is as marked in the older age groups as in the younger.

TABLE 3.15 *Approval of abortion under particular circumstances, by age group and time of survey*

| | Where mother's health is at risk by the pregnancy | | Where it is likely that child would be born physically handicapped | |
	1981 %	1990 %	1981 %	1990 %
18–26	64	80	32	33
27–35	56	80	28	35
36–44	50	72	33	39
45–53	37	60	15	36
54–62	36	52	22	27
63+	16	42	13	22
Total	45	65	25	32
European average		92		79

Over and above the straightforward age effect on attitudes on this item, we find in addition a particular interaction between age, social class, and sex. In table 3.16 we set out these results, first for attitudes to abortion as a whole and then in connection with abortion in the two specific circumstances just mentioned. From panel A of table 3.17 we can see that among respondents of the manual class it is women who are more liberal but among the non-manual it is men. Furthermore, while for each combination of sex and class those under forty-five are more liberal, the difference is least for non-manual men. As a consequence, while manual women over forty-five are slightly more liberal than their non-manual counterparts, in the case of men it is the non-manual group who are significantly more liberal. For those under forty-five we find among the manual class that women are more liberal, but among the non-manual it is men.

These patterns are repeated when we look at the comparable results relating to the issue of risk to the mother's health (table 3.17,

TABLE 3.16 *Attitudes to abortion, by age group*

	Approve of abortion where mother's health is at risk	Approve of abortion where child would be born physically handicapped
	%	%
18–29	79	32
30–44	76	38
45–59	59	34
60+	42	22
Overall	65	32

TABLE 3.17 *A. Extent to which abortion can ever be justified*

	Manual		Non-manual	
	Women	Men	Women	Men
Under 45	2.51	2.29	2.88	3.06
45 or over	1.97	1.64	1.84	2.61
1 = never, 10 = always.				

B. Approval of abortion where mother's health is at risk from pregnancy (percentage approving)

	Manual		Non-manual	
	Women	Men	Women	Men
Under 45	82	74	73	81
45 or over	46	42	45	72

C. Approval of abortion where it is likely that child would be born physically handicapped (percentage approving)

	Manual		Non-manual	
	Women	Men	Women	Men
Under 45	43	35	25	40
45 or over	25	26	22	42

panel B). For those under forty-five the most liberal group are manual women and non-manual men, with the proportions approving of abortion exceeding 80 per cent. For manual males and non-manual females the figure is in each case below 75 per cent. Once again we find consistent age differences but with the effect being at its weakest for non-manual men. As a consequence the non-manual males aged over forty-five display dramatically more liberal views than any of the other members of this cohort. Thus 72 per cent of that group approve of abortion where the mother's health is at risk, compared with 45 per cent of corresponding women.

When we look at attitudes to abortion where the child is likely to be born handicapped (table 3.17, panel C), there is a much lower level of approval overall, but the same peculiar pattern of class and sex differences is again present: older non-manual men and younger manual women have the most liberal attitudes, while non-manual women have the least liberal.

It is worth noting too that somewhat similar class-sex differences carry over into attitudes to divorce (table 3.18). Here, younger people are generally more liberal than older people, but again non-manual men are the most liberal of all.

TABLE 3.18 *Extent to which divorce can ever be justified (average scores)*

| | Manual | | Non-manual | |
	Women	Men	Women	Men
Under 45	4.58	4.13	4.84	5.54
45 or over	3.31	3.03	3.48	4.13
1 = never, 10 always.				

In sum, therefore, while factors such as education and urban versus rural location affect variations in attitudes to abortion, the crucial influences captured in our analysis are the interacting effects of age, class, and sex.

Quite similar effects seem to be present in attitudes to divorce as well. The interactive nature of these effects means that there are no one-dimensional gradients in attitudes to abortion along class, age or sex lines. Rather a multiplicity of lines of cleavage can be detected. The more liberal attitudes of non-manual men are what we would have predicted on the basis of their greater exposure to modernising influences, such as education and affluence. Similarly, increased labour force participation and greater social freedom among non-manual women in the younger age groups, particularly the better educated, would lead us to expect them to be as liberal as men in the same groups. However, this is not the case. Similarly, within the working class the consistently more liberal attitudes of young women compared with young men is not an outcome that we had expected. With hindsight, though, it is precisely this group who bear the costs of absolutist views on sexual morality in the form of unwanted pregnancies. Furthermore, as we shall see, they are the group most directly affected by changing views on marriage as an institution.

At this point we want to consider how such values are related to broader perspectives on traditional marriage and family arrangements. In the 1990 survey, respondents were asked to indicate whether they agreed or disagreed with the view that 'marriage is an outdated institution.' Rather predictably, those under thirty-five are twice as likely to agree with this statement: 15 per cent of that age group agreed, compared with 7 per cent of the over-35s. Similarly, men are more likely to indicate agreement: 12 per cent of men agreed, compared with 8 per cent of women. However, contrary to the expectations of modernisation theory, manual respondents were more in agreement than non-manual. Thus while 13 per cent of the manual group regard marriage as an outdated institution, this falls to 6 per cent for the non-manual group.

Once again, however, we must consider a number of factors in order to understand what is occurring. In table 3.19 we set out the manner in which age, class, urban versus rural location and sex combine to influence views on marriage as an institution. A number of points emerge from this table. First, for both the young and older age groups the manual respondents are more likely to reject the conventional view on marriage, though the class difference is much greater for the older than the younger group. Thus the older non-manual group are the group least likely to question the current relevance of marriage. Among all other groups except one the number adopting a critical position remains close to one in ten. The exception is younger manual men in urban locations, where the figure rises to one in three. Disenchantment with marriage as an institution is heavily concentrated in this group, which in turn reflects the impact of unemployment. Over one in four young unemployed men agree that marriage is an outdated institution.

Rejection of marriage as an institution has fallen from 12 per cent in 1981 to 10 per cent in 1990. This suggests that specific cross-sectional differences are crucial in shaping attitudes in this area rather than a general decline in the popularity of marriage. The Irish figure is significantly below the European average of 19 per cent and lies at the opposite end of the continuum to France, where it reaches 29 per cent.

TABLE 3.19 *Percentages agreeing that marriage is an outdated institution, by age, sex, location, and class*

| | Manual | | | | Non-manual | | | |
| | Rural | | Urban | | Rural | | Urban | |
	Women %	Men %	Women %	Men %	Women %	Men %	Women %	Men %
Less than 35	8	11	11	31	7	7	8	12
35 or over	14	10	11	13	3	3	4	8

The argument for the rather specific consequences of unemployment among young urban respondents is strengthened by the fact that influences on views on sexual freedom are rather different, with age emerging as the decisive influence. In both 1981 and 1990 respondents were asked (a) the extent to which married men or women having an affair could be justified and (b) whether they agreed that individuals should have the chance to enjoy complete sexual freedom without being restricted. Men, those living in urban areas and younger people are more likely to give more permissive responses. In table 3.20 we show the pattern of responses to both questions by age for the 1981 and 1990 surveys. In each year there are sharp differences by age, but on the other hand there is no real evidence of substantial movement over time towards more permissive positions. In the case of extramarital affairs a very modest shift occurs, while on the general issue of sexual freedom, shifts towards permissiveness among the youngest age group are largely cancelled out by contrary tendencies in the next cohort.

The differences in age are quite dramatic: 36 per cent of those in the younger age group are in favour of sexual freedom, compared with 5 per cent in the oldest cohort. However, as the younger age groups grow older, they seem to revert to more restrictive positions. The most striking example of this is that while 28 per cent of the 18–27 group in the 1981 survey agreed with the notion of complete sexual freedom, this was true of only 12 per cent of the 38–47 group in 1990. Thus this age cohort shows no evidence of having maintained their liberal views on sexuality through the 1980s.

The absence of any major shift in permissiveness in the past ten years is reflected in the fact that, while over one in three of the

TABLE 3.20 *Views on sexual freedom, by age*

	Extent to which married people having an affair is justified		Individuals should have the chance to enjoy complete sexual freedom	
	1981 Average	1990 Average	1981 %	1990 %
18–27	2.4	2.3	31	36
28–37	1.8	2.1	28	24
38–47	1.6	1.9	10	12
48–57	1.5	1.8	7	10
58+	1.3	1.4	4	5
Overall	1.7	1.9	16	17

1 = never, 10 = always.

European sample as a whole favour having no restriction on sexual freedom, and the figure rises to over 50 per cent for Spain, the Irish level of support for this view remains at less than half the European figure.

A further element of the traditional versus modern distinction relates to the extent to which traditional family arrangements are valued. This can be assessed by considering responses to the following two questions: (*a*) If someone says a child needs a home with both a father and a mother to grow up happily, would you tend to agree or disagree? (*b*) If a woman wants to have a child as a single parent but she doesn't want to have a stable relationship with a man, do you approve or disapprove? A somewhat mixed picture emerges from responses to these questions, as we can see from table 3.21. Over eight out of ten Irish respondents think that a child needs both a mother and father in order to grow up happy. This figure has actually increased from 76 per cent since 1981 but is still below the European average of 90 per cent. Slight tendencies are observed for men and rural respondents to adopt more conservative positions on this issue. With regard to deliberately chosen single motherhood, just over one in three of the European sample as a whole disapprove, compared with six out of ten Irish respondents. Thus, while Irish respondents may not reject 'accidental' single motherhood, the majority do not approve of it as a deliberate choice.

While men are more insistent on the need for the presence of both a mother and father, no sex differences are observed in attitudes to deliberately chosen single motherhood. Differences by age group, though, are quite dramatic, as shown in table 3.22. The number rejecting deliberate single motherhood rises from one in three of those aged thirty to nine out of ten of those over sixty. Over the 1980s those under thirty have become increasingly less traditional on this issue, with the proportion disapproving falling from 45 to 32 per cent. However, taking all age groups together, there is little change in overall support for the traditional position over time: support remained in the range 61–65 per cent.

TABLE 3.21 *Attitudes to traditional family patterns: comparison of Ireland and Europe*

	Child needs a home with both mother and father to be happy	Woman who wants to have a child without a stable relationship with a man
	Percentage agreeing	*Percentage disapproving*
Ireland	83	61
European average	90	36

TABLE 3.22 *Attitudes to traditional family patterns, by age group*

	Percentage supporting traditional position	
	Child needs a home with both mother and father to be happy	Woman who wants to have a child without a stable relationship with a man
18–29	74	34
30–44	77	53
45–59	87	71
60+	95	89

We extend our analysis of attitudes to marriage by looking at the qualities that people think make for a successful marriage. Statistical analysis of a set of thirteen characteristics revealed the following underlying dimensions:

1. *Cultural equality*
   (i)   Shared religious beliefs
   (ii) Being of the same background

     (iii) Agreement on politics

     (iv) Tastes and interests in common

2. *Material conditions*
   (i)   An adequate income
   (ii)   Housing conditions

3. *Affection*
   (i)   Faithfulness
   (ii)   Marital respect and appreciation
   (iii) Understanding and tolerance

4. *Non-material conditions*
   (i)   Living apart from in-laws
   (ii)   Happy sexual relationship
   (iii) Children
   (iv) Sharing household chores

Responses were scored from 1 (for very important) to 3 (for not very important). The scores for each dimension were averaged so that each scale has a score running from 1 to 3, with a low score indicating high importance and a high score indicating low importance.

Table 3.23 sets out a comparison of the results for Ireland and the European countries as a whole. It is striking how similar the results are. The Irish respondents in 1990 rank the dimensions in order of importance as follows:

1. Affection
2. Material conditions
3. Non-material factors
4. Cultural equalities

The European ordering is very similar, except for the fact that, since the European figure for material conditions is lower than the Irish one, the positions of the material and non-material factors are reversed.

The picture of consensus on the requirements for a successful marriage also extends over time and between the sexes. The scores for 1981 and 1990, both for men and women, are almost identical. The only significant variation in values relating to desirable attitudes occurs between age groups. Again, however, there is no variation in scores for affection and non-material factors, but younger respondents are likely to place less emphasis on cultural equality and material conditions. The absence of any significant changes between 1981 and 1990, though, suggests that those are views that are likely to change over the life cycle.

TABLE 3.23 *Important factors contributing to a successful marriage: comparison of Irish and European scores*

	Irish average	European average
Cultural equality	2.1	2.2
Material conditions	1.5	1.8
Affection	1.2	1.2
Non-material factors	1.6	1.6
Scoring: 1 = very important, 3 = not very important.		

In order to consider the absolute importance of individual items in table 3.24, we set out the percentages considering each characteristic to be very important. Thus, faithfulness is considered very important by over nine out of ten respondents. The next important characteristics—mutual respect and appreciation, and understanding and tolerance—also relate to affection and are considered very important by over eight out of ten people. These are followed in importance by children and a happy sexual relationship, where the relevant figure is approximately two out of three. An adequate income, good housing, living apart from in-laws and tastes and interests in common are considered very important by between 40 and 53 per cent of the sample. This figure drops to about one in three for shared religious beliefs and sharing household chores and to one in four for shared social background. Finally, only 4 per cent of respondents considered shared political views to be very important for a successful marriage.

CONCLUSION

Three general points may be drawn from this examination of Irish values and attitudes regarding family, marriage, sex roles, and related matters. The first is that, as the comparisons with the rest of Europe suggest, Irish values in these areas are not consistently more traditional than those of the economically more advanced countries. On many issues, it is true, Irish values are distinctly conservative—for

TABLE 3.24 *Things that make for a successful marriage*

	Percentage considering each very important
Cultural equality:	
Shared religious beliefs	33
Being of the same background	26
Agreement on politics	4
Tastes & interests in common	40
Material conditions:	
An adequate income	53
Good housing	46
Affection:	
Faithfulness	93
Mutual respect & appreciation	83
Understanding & tolerance	81
Non-material conditions:	
Living apart from in-laws	46
Happy sexual relationship	68
Children	63
Sharing household chores	38

example, as we have seen, on questions of abortion or sexual freedom. On other issues, however, they are quite typical of European patterns, as in the case of attitudes to married women's paid employment or to certain forms of unmarried parenthood. The second point is that Irish values do not form an internally harmonious whole, at least as far as the conventional distinction between traditional and modern stances is concerned. Irish values are 'modern' in some ways and 'traditional' in others, and the precise nature of the resulting blend is not at all easy to comprehend. The third point is that it is somewhat misleading to talk of 'Irish' values as if Ireland itself lacked internal divisions. On some issues there are clear differences in values within Ireland by age, sex, social class, urban versus rural location, and so on, though on other issues such differences are not so obvious. Some of the patterns of internal difference are intriguing and not at all what one would expect, as, for example, the complex interconnected differences by age, sex and social class on attitudes to abortion.

The overall conclusion, therefore, is a reinforcement of the point that is implicit through much of this book: cultural patterns follow a lurching, unpredictable and changing course, at least some of which appear to have little to do with 'modernisation' in any of the usual senses of that term. It is hard enough to account for the pattern of values that has been outlined in the present chapter, or for the changes that have preceded them. Simple schemas of modernisation do not help much in this regard, though if used with appropriate qualifications and restraint, the concept of modernisation is by no means useless in guiding us through the maze. But it is very difficult to say where we are headed or what is pushing us there. As far as family values are concerned, 'modernity' may indeed be pushing its way gradually into the Irish cultural landscape. But modernity is a very uncertain entity, in other countries as much as in Ireland, and we should not be too surprised if Ireland continues to offer its own distinctive, angular variants of modern values for some time in the future.

4 Work Values

CHRISTOPHER T. WHELAN

INTRODUCTION

The term 'work' refers to a variety of rather different activities. It may involve a paid job, voluntary work, or unpaid work in the home. The European Values Survey questions on work were concerned with work defined as 'doing a paid job in the regular manpower system' (Zander, 1993, 129). The survey included questions relating to job satisfaction, general orientation to work, and perceived characteristics of a good job. Our initial focus is on job satisfaction. Given the nature of the themes covered, we will concentrate our attention initially on full-time employees. Subsequently we will address the question of the impact of employment status and, in particular, the extent to which the self-employed and the unemployed present a different picture.

JOB SATISFACTION

We start our analysis of the work attitudes material contained in the European Values Study by examining differences in job satisfaction by sex for both 1981 and 1990. All respondents who were in employment at the time of the survey were asked to rate the level of satisfaction on a ten-point scale representing a continuum from dissatisfaction to satisfaction. Our results are in line with those that have been consistently reported in the literature. In the first place the overall level of satisfaction is high, with average scores of 8.0 in 1981 and 7.7 in 1990. Second, there are no significant differences between men and women across social classes. Finally, changes over time are extremely modest.

There are certain difficulties in interpreting the answers to straightforward job-satisfaction questions, which are reflected in the fact that (*a*) relatively little variation between social classes or between women and men is observed, and (*b*) despite changes in working conditions in the United States, over the fifty years in which job satisfaction questions have been asked, the percentage shown as dissatisfied has remained fairly constant. These findings clearly demonstrate that the reports made by respondents reflect something more than, or something other than, a direct reaction to their working conditions. Most approaches to the problem of job satisfaction recognise that a job is not an entity but a complex interrelationship of tasks, roles, responsibilities, and rewards. It is generally considered possible for individuals to balance specific satisfactions with specific dissatisfactions and consequently arrive at an overall level of satisfaction with the job as a whole.

Within this general framework there have been a number of distinct types of explanations that have been suggested to account for variations in overall job satisfaction and satisfaction with specific job components, such as pay, security, supervision, job content, etc. A great many studies have sought to explain variations in job satisfaction solely by the differences in the nature of the jobs individuals have. The assumption underlying this approach is that there is a difference between the properties of a satisfying and dissatisfying work role. Consequently, most of the studies employing this type of reasoning have dealt with only two sets of variables, one measuring work role characteristics and the other measuring job satisfaction. Those work role variables that are most frequently studied are usually expressed in terms of amounts or probabilities of certain kinds of outcomes. Characteristics frequently employed include wages, security, promotion opportunities, degree of specialisation, control over work methods, and characteristics of organisational structure, such as size, span of control, and technology.

An alternative type of explanation views variations in job satisfaction as arising from differences in individual and social characteristics. People who are satisfied with their jobs are assumed to differ systematically in their characteristics from those who are dissatisfied. Thus numerous studies have been directed towards examination of the relationships between social class, education, age, personality characteristics etc. and satisfaction. Neither of these approaches proves particularly illuminating in terms of their capacity to explain variations in job satisfaction.

It was such difficulties that led to the development of the social action approach to job satisfaction. This approach stresses that a worker's satisfaction with his or her objective situation can be understood only by taking into account the frames of reference employed in evaluating these conditions. The question of satisfaction from work cannot be usefully considered except in relation to the more basic question of orientation to work. The individual's definition of the work situation becomes a key explanatory variable (Goldthorpe et al., 1968; Whelan, 1980).

Orientations to work
The introduction of the social action perspective in the British 'affluent worker studies' of the 1960s allowed the authors to explain the fact that although assembly-line workers disliked the tasks they had to perform, this was not associated with any marked dissatisfaction with the firm as an employer or with the management. These findings were explained as being due to the workers' 'instrumental' orientation to work, seeking a high level of economic rewards at work for expenditure on their homes and families, which were their central interests.

In a similar vein, the absence of differences in levels of job satisfaction between men and women, despite the latter's inferior job conditions, may lead to a focus on explanations concerned with variation in the degree of work commitment. In turn, the presence or absence of such commitment may be seen as linked to norms relating to sex roles and the unequal division of family labour. The extent to which work is a central life goal is a major issue. Within the orientations to work perspective, which emphasises the manner in which individuals make sense of their world, two rather distinct strands can be identified. The first tends to characterise most workers as having an orientation to work that involves clear and dominant priorities. The degree of choice available to workers is emphasised. Thus Hakim (1991) explains the level of job satisfaction displayed by women, despite their concentration in the lowest-status and lowest-paid jobs, by the fact that women's priorities differ from men's, with paid work being accorded less importance than their domestic activities and family life. 'Expectations and aspirations are focused on what has been called the "marriage career" with paid employment taking a back seat' (Hakim 1991, 105).

While this approach emphasises priorities and choice, the alternative perspective emphasises constraints on choice and the manner in which women adjust to the degree of horizontal and vertical labour market segregation imposed on them and thus lower their aspirations and expectations. Such an approach requires that we take into account the standards against which objective job circumstances are evaluated and the process by which some comparisons come to be considered realistic while others are discarded as irrelevant. From this perspective, the meanings that are attributed to work cannot be thought of simply as a question of personal preference; instead we must deal with the issue of how workers come to adapt to the 'inevitable'.

In the 1990 European Values Survey, respondents were asked to indicate how important the following areas were in their lives, on a scale ranging from 'very important' to 'not at all important':

(i)   Work
(ii) Family
(iii) Friends and acquaintances
(iv) Leisure time
(v)   Politics
(vi) Religion

In table 4.1 we set out the proportions considering each area to be very important, broken down by sex and marital status. The figures relate to full-time employees. For men and women the order of importance is identical, and is as follows:

1. Family
2. Work
3. Friends
4. Leisure
5. Religion
6. Politics

In particular, although men are slightly more likely to consider work very important, the difference is modest, the figures for men and women being 72 and 60 per cent, respectively. Not surprisingly, the figure drops to 57 per cent for women in part-time employment. It must be kept in mind that while the majority of part-time workers are women, the great majority of women in employment are full-time workers. In the 1990 European Values Study sample, one in four of the women in employment were part-time workers.

Distinguishing between married and single respondents does not reveal greater differences between men and women. Married people are more likely than single people to think that family and religion

TABLE 4.1 *Importance of different areas of life, by sex, controlling for marital status: percentage considering each area to be very important*

| | Full-time employees | | | |
| | Married | | Single | |
	Women %	Men %	Women %	Men %
Family	99	96	87	80
Work	64	77	67	64
Friends	42	46	59	53
Leisure	34	36	35	30
Religion	39	36	24	19
Politics	5	3	1	1

are most important, while the latter place greater importance on friends than do married people. These differences hold regardless of sex. With regard to the importance of work, the main contrast is between married men, of whom over three-quarters think work is very important, and all other full-time employees, of whom approximately two-thirds hold a similar view.

Irish men and women are significantly more likely than other Europeans to think that both work and family are very important. The interpretation of such findings is not without its difficulties. However, if we are seeking a reference point for the Irish findings, it is striking that the pattern of results is almost identical to that for Britain.

Among all classes we find that work is considered less important by younger than older respondents. Similarly, we find very little difference between manual and non-manual employees in terms of the priority they give to work relative to other areas of their lives. On this count, at least, we find very little support for the notion that we can identify distinctive sex and class orientations to work, involving different priorities arising from variation in central life interests. In the section that follows we will seek to discover whether such evidence can be found in respondents' account of what they personally consider to be important in a good job.

Characteristics of a good job
Each person involved in the 1981 and 1990 surveys was presented with a set of job characteristics and requested to indicate for each aspect if they considered it to be important or not. Three distinct

dimensions emerged in the domain of work, involving the constituent elements set out below.

1. *Personal development*, which entails items referring to expressive aspects of a job, including:
   (i)   An opportunity to use initiative
   (ii) A responsible job
   (iii) A job in which you feel you can achieve something
   (iv) A job that meets your abilities
   (v)   An interesting job

2. *Comfort*, which refers to aspects relating to the importance of secondary working conditions, including:
   (i)   Not too much pressure
   (ii) A job respected by people in general
   (iii) Generous holidays
   (iv) Good hours

3. *Material conditions*
   (i)   Good pay
   (ii) Good security

Among the most important characteristics identified are a mixture of material conditions and personal development opportunities:

Pay: 74 per cent
Security: 64 per cent
An opportunity to use initiative: 65 per cent
A job in which you feel you can achieve something: 58 per cent

Each respondent was given a score of 1 if a particular item was considered important and a score of 0 if it was not. Thus the range of scores runs from zero at a minimum to the number of items tapping that dimension at a maximum. In table 4.2 we show the breakdown of scores on each of these dimensions by sex and marital status for full-time employees. Married women are slightly more likely than their male counterparts to emphasise comfort and slightly less likely to emphasise material conditions. No significant differences exist on the personal development dimension. The pattern for single respondents is rather different, the most outstanding feature of the results being the particularly high score on personal development. However, it is clear from the other scores that this is not being sought at the expense of satisfactory conditions relating to the material conditions and comfort dimensions. Overall it is the similarities between the profiles for men and women that seem more interesting than the differences. A comparison of the 1981 and 1990 results supports this conclusion, the most interesting trend over time being the increased importance of the personal development dimension for both women and men.

TABLE 4.2   *Job importance dimensions, by sex and marital status for full-time employees*

	Personal development		Comfort		Material conditions	
	Married Average	Single Average	Married Average	Single Average	Married Average	Single Average
Female	3.8	4.5	1.8	1.8	1.6	1.9
Male	3.7	3.7	1.4	1.7	1.8	1.7

We do find a more clear-cut pattern of class differences (table 4.3). Manual employees are slightly more likely than non-manual employees to place emphasis on material conditions and comfort. The differences here, however, are not statistically significant. It is in relation to personal development that the most striking difference emerges. In this case it is non-manual employees who are most concerned with such aspects of the job. It is necessary, however, to make clear that there is no suggestion that manual workers are obsessed with material conditions and comfort to the exclusion of all else, or that non-manual employees are entirely indifferent to such factors. In table 4.4 we display the extent to which those groups consider particular job characteristics to be important. In fact the non-manual group are marginally more likely to consider pay important and indeed promotion. However, they are somewhat less concerned with good hours and job security. Similarly, while it is true that over three out of four non-manual employees consider it important that a job should be interesting, the figure for non-manual employees is also in excess of two out of three. The non-manual groups, however, do place greater emphasis on the opportunity to achieve something, to being in a position to use one's initiative and being required to shoulder responsibility. For these characteristics we observe differences that are in the range of 15 to 17 per cent. It is class and related education differences that affect such job priorities rather than age.

TABLE 4.3 *Job importance dimensions, by class*

	Personal development Average	Comfort Average	Material conditions Average
Manual	3.4	1.7	3.4
Non-manual	4.3	1.5	3.2

TABLE 4.4 *Percentage considering particular job characteristics important, by class*

	Manual %	Non-manual %
Pay	72	76
Job security	69	59
Good hours	50	38
Promotion	35	45
A job respected by people	23	33
An opportunity to use initiative	45	69
A job in which you feel you can achieve something	56	72
A responsible job	37	54
A job that is interesting	68	76

THE MEANING OF WORK

At this point we wish to focus on a more general set of questions dealing with the role that work plays in our respondents' lives. Each of the respondents in the 1990 European Values Study survey was asked how much pride they took in their work. They were also presented with a list of reasons why people work and asked to indicate their agreement with them. The list of reasons was as follows:

(i) I enjoy my work; it's the most important thing in my life.
(ii) I enjoy working but I don't let it interfere with the rest of my life.
(iii) I will always do the best I can, regardless of pay.

(iv) Work is like a business transaction: the more I get paid, the more I do; the less I get paid, the less I do.

(v) Working for a living is a necessity. I wouldn't work if I didn't have to do it.

The five options can be seen as representing a continuum from work as extremely desirable to work as extremely undesirable. The first two options reflect a view that sees work less as an obligation than as an invitation or challenge. The first option involves the classic work ethic, in which work is seen as a calling. The third option implies a moral orientation. The source of the moral imperative may be either perceived social obligations or notions of appropriate personal behaviour. The fourth option refers to an instrumental calculating orientation in which work is seen as involving a reward-effort bargain. The final option involves an anti-work ethic (Zander, 1993, 134).

In table 4.5 we show the responses for men and women, distinguishing between single and married respondents. It is clear that women are significantly less likely than men to indicate that work is the most important thing in their life. While one in seven men respond in this fashion, this is true of one in twelve single women and one in twenty married women. Similarly, married women are most likely to say they wouldn't work if they didn't have to: one in three of such respondents indicate this, compared with one in four married men. Age is clearly a factor in accounting for the fact that single respondents are much less likely to answer in this fashion. Women display no greater tendency than men to indicate that while they enjoy work they don't let it interfere with their lives, although the highest figure of 55 per cent does relate to women. Finally, married women are the group most likely to say that they wouldn't work if they didn't have to: almost one in three answer in this fashion. For single women this figure drops to one in four, and for men to less than one in five.

The fact that paid work is not as much of a central life interest for women does not imply that their orientations to work are purely instrumental. In fact it is single men who are most likely to agree that work is like a business transaction, with almost one in four accepting this statement—a figure that is almost three times greater than that for single women. Similar ratios are observed for married people, with the respective figures being 7 and 3 per cent. Similarly, while married men are slightly more likely than married women to say that they would always do their best regardless of

TABLE 4.5 *Meaning of work for employees, by sex and marital status*

| | Percentage agreeing | | | |
| | Married | | Single | |
	Women	Men	Women	Men
Take a great deal of pride in work	82	83	67	67
Work most important thing in life	5	8	14	15
Enjoy working but don't let work interfere with rest of life	55	52	47	50
Always do best regardless of pay	51	60	56	41
Work is like a business transaction	3	7	9	23
Wouldn't work if didn't have to	31	17	24	18

pay, single women are substantially more likely than single men to indicate such a level of commitment, the respective figures being 60 and 40 per cent. These findings are supported by the fact that women are just as likely as men to take a great deal of pride in their work. The main contrast is between married and single employees rather than between the sexes. Over eight out of ten married employees take a great deal of pride in their work, compared with seven out of ten single respondents.

Before looking at the manner in which other factors influence orientations to work, we will look at views on the fundamental issue of the extent to which women think they have a right to work. As the existence of marriage bars and other restrictions on women's participation in the labour force illustrate, such a right could not be taken for granted (Daly, 1978). In the 1990 values survey those interviewed were asked whether they agreed with the statement that 'when jobs are scarce men have more right to a job than a woman.' From table 4.6 we can see that while just over one in three respondents accept this proposition, there is no difference between the attitudes of men and women in this area. Furthermore, Irish attitudes are not distinctive. The figure for Irish men is identical to the European average, while that for Irish women is a modest four percentage points higher.

The major factors determining views relating to the relative rights to employment of men and women are age and education. The proportion considering that women have less right rises from 12 per cent for those under thirty to close to 60 per cent for those aged sixty or over. Similarly, while just less than one in seven of those with

TABLE 4.6 *Percentage who agree that men have more right to a job than women when jobs are scarce*

	Ireland %	European average %
Women	35	31
Men	36	36

third-level education accept that men have superior rights in this area, this rises to one in two for those with primary education or less. While the effect of age and education do overlap, their impact is cumulative, as we illustrate in table 4.7. If we distinguish between those having a Leaving Certificate or higher qualification and all others, we find that at each age level, with the exception of those aged over sixty, the more educated are more likely to reject the idea that women ought to enjoy lesser rights than men. The proportion that asserts the superior rights of men rises from one in ten of those aged under thirty with the Leaving Certificate or higher qualification to close to six out of ten of those aged sixty or over with a Primary Certificate or less.

TABLE 4.7 *Percentage who agree that men have more right to a job than women when jobs are scarce, by age group and educational level*

	Less than Leaving Cert. %	Leaving Cert. or higher %
18–29	17	10
30–44	38	22
45–59	47	36
60+	59	58

As the earlier results relating to the impact of marital status suggest, age is a significant factor in affecting orientations to work. From table 4.8 it is clear that the only item on which age lacks any discriminatory power is that relating to continuing to work if one didn't have to. While one in five of those aged forty-five or over considered work to be the most important thing in their life, this falls to one in ten for those aged between thirty and forty-four and finally to one in twenty for those under thirty. Similarly, two out of three of those over forty-five are significantly more likely to say they would always do their best regardless of pay; below this age the figure falls to less than one in two. Correspondingly, this older group are the least likely to say that they don't let work interfere with their life. In fact they are the only age group where significantly less than half of its members give this response. Those aged under thirty are also substantially more likely to think that work is essentially a business transaction and significantly less likely to affirm that they take a great deal of pride in their work. The figures for these items for the youngest age group are 15 and 67 per cent, respectively, which compare with 6 and 84 per cent, respectively, for those aged over forty-five.

TABLE 4.8 *Meaning of work, by age group*

	Percentage agreeing				
	Take a great deal of pride in work	Work is like a business transaction	Always do best regardless of pay	Wouldn't work if didn't have to	Enjoy work but don't let it interfere with rest of life	Work is the most important thing in life
	%	%	%	%	%	%
18–29	67	15	45	20	59	5
30–44	80	8	45	27	52	10
45+	84	6	67	20	39	21

Work is clearly less central to the lives of those aged less than thirty. Does this reflect a movement from materialist to postmaterialist concerns? If that were the case we might also expect that this younger group would place a lower priority on comfort and material conditions and a great emphasis on opportunities for personal development. They do assign greater importance to personal development than the older groups, but they are no less likely to stress the importance of material conditions. A similar conclusion is suggested by the analysis of trends over time. By 1990 all age groups placed stronger emphasis on personal development, but in no case was this at the expense of material conditions and comfort. This pattern of results would appear to be more parsimoniously interpreted as arising from increasing levels of education than any cultural shift away from materialist preoccupations.

Finally, the manner in which work is understood is significantly influenced by one's class location, but the influence is far from even across the items. Non-manual workers, as can be seen from table 4.9, are substantially more likely to say that they take a great deal of pride in their work: over four out of five respond in this fashion, compared with two out of three manual workers. Similarly, they are a great deal more likely to indicate that they always do their best at work regardless of pay; the figures for manual and non-manual employees are four out of ten and six out of ten, respectively. Finally, while over one in four manual workers say they would not work if it was not a necessity, this is true of less than one in five of the non-manual group.

TABLE 4.9   *Meaning of work, by class*

	Take a great deal of pride in work transaction	Work is like a business	Always do best regardless of pay	Wouldn't work if didn't have to	Enjoy work but don't let it interfere with rest of life	Work is the most important thing in life
	%	%	%	%	%	%
Manual	66	19	38	28	49	12
Non-manual	83	2	61	18	53	11

The pattern of these replies provides consistent evidence that non-manual employees place greater emphasis on the intrinsic value of their work as opposed to the instrumental function of work as a means to the ends of income and security. Replies to the remaining items, however, indicate that they are anxious that such commitment should not be at the expense of fulfilment in other areas of their lives. Only just over one in ten indicate that work is the most important thing in their life, a figure that is almost identical to that for manual employees. Similarly, over one in two indicate that while they enjoy work they don't let it interfere with the rest of their life. Once again little in the way of a significant class difference can be observed.

THE IMPACT OF EMPLOYMENT STATUS

Our analysis up to this point has been confined to full-time employees, because we might expect that at least some of the questions might have rather different meanings for other groups. When we broaden our focus we find that the self-employed have a distinctive profile. They are considerably more likely than employees to consider that work is very important, the respective figures being 70 and 85 per cent. Correspondingly, they are significantly less likely to think that leisure is very important; in this case the relevant figures are 34 and 19 per cent. Not surprisingly, almost nine out of ten indicate that they take a great deal of pride in their work, compared with three out of four employees. Consistent with this, only one in six of the group feel that they wouldn't work if they didn't have to do so out of necessity. Finally, almost one in four of their members hold the view that work is the most important thing in their life, while this holds true for only one in nine employees.

The next group to whom we direct our attention is part-time employees. Six out of ten of such employees are married women. Not surprisingly, this is the group who are least likely to think that work is very important. However, the figure still comes close to six out of ten. Less predictably, though, they are just as likely as other employees to take a great deal of pride in their work, and otherwise do not display a profile in terms of work priorities and general orientation to work that is particularly different from that which we observe for full-time employees. They are slightly more likely to emphasise what we have described as the comfort features of the job situation, but the observed difference is extremely modest.

Finally, we focus on the unemployed. A good deal of the attention that has been directed to the work values of the unemployed has been concerned with employment commitment. Commitment to employment in this sense involves attaching a value to employment that goes beyond earning money. Particular importance is attributed to such commitment because in its absence indefinitely available state income support, which may weaken financial incentives to work, is likely to be viewed with increasing concern. In fact overall the unemployed are marginally more likely than full-time employees to consider work very important, with the figure reaching 74 per cent.

The results relating to more general orientations to work, set out in table 4.10, present a picture that is somewhat more difficult to interpret. Among the unemployed over one in five consider work to be essentially a business transaction, compared with one in ten full-time employees. Similarly, while one in two employees indicate that they would always do their best regardless of pay, this figure falls below four in ten for the unemployed. On the other hand, the unemployed are no more likely to say that they would not work if it was not a necessity, and no less likely to say that it is the most important thing in their life. Finally, they are significantly less likely to say that they don't let work interfere with the rest of their life—although this clearly reflects the manner in which the *absence* of work interferes with the rest of their life.

TABLE 4.10 *Impact of unemployment on the meaning of work*

	Work is like a business transaction	Always do best regardless of pay	Wouldn't work if didn't have to	Don't let work interfere with rest of life	Work is the most important thing in life
	%	%	%	%	%
Full-time employees	10	51	23	51	11
Unemployed	22	38	25	37	13

In interpreting the results relating to the unemployed it must be kept in mind that they are predominantly young, manual workers, and relatively poorly educated; 50 per cent are under thirty, and almost 80 per cent are manual workers, while a similar number possess less than a Leaving Certificate. The results we have observed are generally in line with those we might expect on the basis of the earlier findings relating to the influence of class, education, and age. This conclusion is supported by our analysis of the job characteristics that are deemed to be important by the unemployed in comparison with employees. Here we find that no difference emerges in relation to the importance of extrinsic factors such as pay and security. The unemployed, though, are less likely to emphasise personal development factors, such as using one's initiative and responsibility, and are more likely to place greater weight on comfort factors, such as good hours and generous holidays. However, when we take age, social class and education into account we find that the former difference disappears while the latter, although remaining statistically significant, is of a modest substantive order.

WORK VALUES REASSESSED

The starting point of analysis in this chapter was the fact that women and manual workers, although occupying more poorly rewarded positions than men and non-manual workers, exhibit satisfaction levels that are just as high. The available evidence suggests that this does not arise from ignorance of the rewards available to others but must be understood in the context of respondents' evaluations of what it is 'reasonable' to expect.

Dealing with the sex issue first, we have found that married women are less likely than others to think that work is very important. Furthermore, they are the group most likely to indicate that they wouldn't work if they didn't have to. Can such findings, as Hakim (1991) argues, be explained by the existence of discrete groups of women within the labour force?—

1. A minority of women who are committed to work as a central life goal, achieving jobs at a higher level of status and earnings.
2. The majority of women, who aim for a homemaker career in which hard work is of secondary importance, with their husbands providing strong support for this strategy.

Hakim's argument centres on the fact that convenience factors allowing a job to be fitted in with other life priorities, and the convenience factor of being able to comply with husbands' preferences regarding work, are the two dominant factors explaining women's feelings of satisfaction with their jobs. Hakim accuses social scientists of using a value-laden and biased definition of job quality based on the priorities and preferences of male breadwinners. Women's job preference factors, she argues, emphasise convenience factors over the high pay and security of employment conventionally valued by males.

The results from the European Values Study, however, do not suggest so straightforward a picture. While married women are somewhat less committed to employment, the evidence shows that their degree of pride in their work, and their desire to express themselves, is no less than that of single women and indeed men. The fact that the objective level at which they express satisfaction is significantly below that for males seems most credibly explained in terms of the effect of socialisation experience and the influence of sex role expectations relating to responsibility for domestic and child-rearing tasks.

Hakim wishes to stress women's role as 'self-determining actors and the impact that a woman's desire to work with some degree of long-term commitment can have on her career outcomes.' While we do not wish to deny the potential role of choice, the explanation of job segregation requires reference to much more deeply rooted social structural factors. At a minimum it requires reference to socialisation and the impact of the educational system; but it also requires that one allow for the role of trade unions and employers in perpetuating the traditional division of labour (Hannan, Breen, et al., 1983). One important point, however, on which our results do support Hakim's is that husbands' sex role attitudes are significantly more 'traditional' than those of wives. If, as Hakim concedes, women's high satisfaction with their jobs may be a reflection as much of the patriarchal views of their husbands as of their own attitudes, it is difficult to see why we should focus on choice rather than constraints.

With regard to the absence of substantial differences in job satisfaction between manual and non-manual employees, the most frequently invoked explanation has been one that suggests that these two groups place emphasis on rather different factors in assessing their employment situations. The most overriding distinction is between intrinsic factors (achievement, independence, curiosity) and extrinsic factors (pay, security, working conditions), with manual workers, apparently, responding primarily in extrinsic terms and non-manual workers in intrinsic terms. The calculations of manual workers are frequently perceived to be dominated by economic considerations (Mann, 1973, 40). They are satisfied without being happy, and have 'central life interests' that are outside work.

In fact our results from the 1990 European Values Study survey do show that there is some tendency for manual workers to place less emphasis on personal development characteristics than non-manual workers, and somewhat more on material conditions and comfort. In relation to these final two factors, though, the differences are extremely modest. In the case of personal development, the differences are somewhat more substantial. It remains true, however, that for manual and non-manual workers alike, pay is the most important feature of a job. On the other hand, while manual workers place a somewhat lower priority on personal development characteristics, seven out of ten still consider it important that one have a job that is interesting; over one in two consider it important to be in a job in which one can achieve something; and almost one in two give priority to an opportunity to use one's initiative. Our results provide very little support for the 'happy robot' theory.

For both women and manual workers the values that are expressed must be considered in the context of the opportunities currently available to them. The design of work and the institutional and legal context of work cannot help but express certain values and preferences as against others (Fox, 1974). This raises the question of the number of people who can be said to enjoy even an approximation to a free choice of work values. To a substantial extent workers learn what to expect from their jobs.

One important way in which we learn about the value of paid work is by observing the consequences of its withdrawal when people become unemployed. Employment provides a variety of benefits, both manifest and latent (Jahoda, 1982). The unemployed are substantially more likely than those in employment to suffer psychological distress, even when we control for material conditions. Our evidence relating to the unemployed indicates that, while consistent with the educational and class background, they are somewhat more instrumental than employees; there is no significant evidence of a low level of employment commitment or a decline in the extent to which work is a central life interest.

Observed changes in work value over time appear to be more credibly interpreted as a consequence of rising levels of education and changing patterns of labour force participation than as reflecting any cultural shift in the direction of postmaterialism.

5 Politics and Democratic Values

NIAMH HARDIMAN AND CHRISTOPHER T. WHELAN

INTRODUCTION

In this chapter, and the one that follows, our aim is to chart the main features of Irish political culture. Where relevant we shall trace changes between the two European Values Surveys of 1981 and 1990, since, although we believe that change during this period has been less marked than over the previous decades, we have no reliable data further back than this. We also have the advantage of being able to situate the evidence adduced about Irish political values in a comparative European context. Too often features of Irish political life are noted in isolation and taken as distinctive or unique. In the European data we have a benchmark against which to identify similarities and differences between Ireland and what we might take to be more mainstream political experiences.

Of course every country's experience is unique and is coloured by its peculiar history, institutional inheritance, and internal political conflicts. But there are also many common themes that make international comparison interesting and fruitful. Two broad themes guide our exploration of Irish political culture. The first is that of democratic political values, that is, the attitudes and orientation of citizens towards democratic institutions and democratic participation (see for example the classic studies of Almond and Verba, 1963; Barnes and Kaase, 1979). This is the subject of the present chapter. The second major facet of Irish political culture we wish to investigate is that of political partisanship, its profile and its bases; this is the subject of the following chapter. In both cases the theoretical concerns generated by earlier international comparative studies provide us with our point of departure, and the cross-national evidence from the other countries surveyed in the European Values Study provides us with a basis for locating the facets of Irish political culture that show congruence with or variation upon a generally occurring pattern.

Our first concern, then, is to investigate the values relating to the functioning of democratic institutions and practices. Much of the discussion of Irish political culture to date has tended to concentrate on transition from traditional political culture. There is a well-established body of literature that takes the main characteristics of traditional political culture to be a tendency towards localism and personalism, and a strong reliance on a clientelistic style of politics (e.g. Bax, 1976; Sacks, 1976; Gallagher and Komito, 1992). It has also been argued that 'authoritarianism' has been a central feature of Irish political orientation. In this connection, authoritarianism takes on a rather distinctive meaning. Rather than characterising a style of political leadership, authoritarianism in Irish political culture is said to be manifest in 'a collective disposition to defer to decisions from those in superior positions in a power hierarchy' (Coakley, 1992, 30). This kind of deference has also been associated with hostility to the role of intellectuals in public life and suspicion of the value of independent thought (e.g. Chubb, 1982, 21-3).

However accurate such depictions of Irish political life might once have been, political scientists have also been concerned to suggest that they no longer represent the whole story (cf. Coakley, 1992). Elements of the traditional political culture are seen to be rooted in a distinctive social milieu—in a society that had a strong dependence on agriculture and was dominated by rural and agrarian values, in which the cultural and religious homogeneity of the population could be taken for granted and in which the values of the Roman Catholic church could be assumed to have a major influence. The social structure has been transformed over the past thirty years or so, with the decline of agriculture, the growth of industrial and service sector employment, and the general rise in living standards (see, for example, Breen et al., 1990). While religious practice remains at very high levels in Ireland relative to other developed countries, the role of the Catholic Church in public life has undergone some change (cf. Hornsby-Smith, 1992, and the discussion in chapter 2 of this book). This is not only a matter of the emergence of a previously undeveloped debate about the separation of church and state, as evinced by the changing climate of opinion in relation to legislation on matters of public morality: it is also a consequence of changes within the Catholic Church itself, which have made the imposition of an unquestionable body of doctrine upon its membership more problematic (Inglis, 1987, 217).

In much of the literature on traditional political values the emphasis has been on the distinctive aspects of Ireland's pre-industrial and rather anti-democratic style of politics. This has tended to obscure other important features of political development. Ireland embarked upon independence with an institutional inheritance that was far more developed than its level of industrial development. The modernisation of society had proceeded quite rapidly before independence (Lee, 1973, 1989). A functioning system of local government and administration was in place; commercial and distributive networks, transport and communications systems were also well established. The elementary school system ensured virtually universal literacy. The establishment of the independent state was a violent and divisive affair, and the legitimacy of the state was not fully secured for a number of years after its foundation. However, as political historians have pointed out, the transition to parliamentary democracy was never fundamentally in question. In this respect the Irish experience is very unlike that of many later postcolonial states. The institutions of democratic government, and the values supportive of stable democracy, have proved to be enduring. Similarly, while nationalist separatism provided the basis for the legitimacy of the independent state, and nationalist issues provided the original major cleavage in the party system, successive research reports find minimal support for republican violence in relation to the problems of Northern Ireland.

In this context we would expect to find a profile of political values that, on issues such as respect for the central institutions of the state and the value of political participation, would bear comparison with other European democracies. We are therefore interested in what Ireland shares in common with other European countries as well as in the respects in which Ireland diverges from them.

DEMOCRATIC VALUES

There are several elements in our exploration of attitudes to the structures and processes of political life. We first examine the level of confidence expressed in some major institutions. We then analyse the importance attached to politics in everyday life, and attitudes to political participation. We discuss the respects in which Irish political culture can be said to be conservative; we then investigate the degree to which political values can be characterised as authoritarian.

Finally, we consider the available evidence that localism is a dominant feature of Irish political culture. Throughout this study we are concerned with respondents' attitudes to the political structure and the political process; we are not concerned here with the substance of political decision-making or with the manner in which political institutions actually function.

Confidence in public institutions

We first examine the level of confidence expressed by respondents in a variety of public institutions. This is reported in table 5.1. The evidence of this table reveals that Ireland is comparable to other democratic countries in the level of confidence respondents express in the major public institutions, though in most cases the level of confidence expressed is somewhat greater than the European average. Over half of the Irish respondents had 'a great deal' or 'quite a lot' of confidence in parliament, compared with just over two out of five for the European countries as a whole.

TABLE 5.1   *Confidence in public institutions*

	Ireland 1990 %	Europe 1990 %	Ireland 1981 %
Police	85	65	86
Army	61	51	77
Civil service	59	39	56
Parliament	51	43	53
Legal system	47	51	58
Trade unions	43	34	37
Press	36	35	44

Similarly, three-fifths of Irish people, compared with two-fifths in Europe overall, express confidence in the civil service, and confidence in the police is considerably higher, with 85 per cent of Irish respondents expressing confidence, compared with two-thirds in Europe overall. Not much difference is observed in confidence in the legal system and in the army, and levels of confidence in trade unions and the press are also quite similar.

The fact that Irish respondents evince generally higher levels of confidence in the core institutions of the state might strike some as unexpected, given a widely shared view that many Irish people are rather disillusioned with politicians and the political process and do not have high expectations of what politicians can achieve, particularly in relation to economic performance. However, we believe that what is elicited here is the overall level of confidence people have that the institution in question will function in a fair and efficient manner; satisfaction with outcomes is not explored.

Moreover, we would expect these attitudes to reflect people's actual experiences with the institutions in question. This contrasts with the causal status that authors in the 'civic culture' tradition attributed to attitudes in strengthening or weakening the functioning of public institutions (cf. Barry, 1970; Lijphart, 1980; Pateman, 1980).

This table also reveals relatively little change in confidence in public institutions between 1981 and 1990. Some of the individual items show some change: trade unions attract somewhat higher levels of confidence in 1990, doubtless because of their greater salience in national politics with the revival of a tripartite approach to pay policy; confidence in the army shows a decline, the reason for which is unclear. But these items have a high level of reliability, and we are confident that they are tapping the same underlying dimension. We find that there is very little overall difference over time in the level of confidence in public institutions. We combined the seven items in this table into a single scale, with a score ranging from 1 to 4 for the level of confidence expressed, and we find that the average score for 1981 was virtually identical to that for 1990: 2.51 as against 2.57, which compares with a European average of 2.39. The overall picture is one of strong and enduring levels of confidence in public institutions.

Age is the most important factor affecting confidence in public institutions. The average confidence score increases from 2.5 for those aged between eighteen and twenty-nine to 2.85 for those aged sixty and over. In 1990 only four out of ten respondents in the youngest age group have confidence in parliament, compared with two-thirds of the oldest age group. Over time, though, we observe no significant change. Confidence in public institutions increases with age in both 1981 and 1990; lower levels of confidence are expressed by younger respondents at both dates.

The role of politics in everyday life
The confidence that people express in public institutions is but one aspect of political culture. We need to put the importance people attach to politics into perspective. Doubtless the significance of politics will vary depending on the circumstances, but in general

politics features well below other involvements in people's scale of what is important to them, as is clear from table 5.2. We can see from this table, and from table 5.3, that Irish people are not at all unusual in holding politics to be far less important than family, or work, or religion. On average, other Europeans are only slightly more likely to consider politics important, or discuss it, or have an interest in it. Almost two-fifths of Irish respondents indicated that they were interested in politics, a figure that is slightly below the European average. Nevertheless, as with other Europeans, almost six out of ten confirm that they discuss politics at least occasionally. Furthermore, the proportion doing so rose from 50 per cent in 1981 to 58 per cent in 1990.

TABLE 5.2   *Importance in life of different areas: Ireland and Europe compared (percentage considering each area important)*

	Ireland, 1990 %	European average %
Family	99	97
Work	91	88
Friends	94	90
Religion	84	49
Leisure time	81	84
Politics	28	35

TABLE 5.3   *Role of politics in everyday life: Ireland and Europe compared*

	Ireland %	European average %
Percentage thinking politics is important in their life	28	35
Percentage discussing politics at least occasionally	58	56
Percentage interested in politics	37	44

The restricted role of politics in everyday life is clearly not a recent phenomenon. In both surveys, this tendency is observed in all age groups.

The overall figures also conceal relatively sharp variations by social class, education, and sex. The results set out in table 5.4 show that those in the professional and managerial class are significantly more likely to consider politics important in their life, to be interested in politics, and to discuss politics at least occasionally. Almost four-fifths of those in the highest social class are interested in politics, compared with one in five of those located in the non-skilled manual class. Similarly, they are almost twice as likely to be interested in politics. Finally, while fewer than half of those at the bottom of the class hierarchy discuss politics, this figure rises to over three out of four in the professional and managerial group. Earlier studies found a clear association between class and the level of political interest (e.g. Verba and Nie, 1972) but little difference between countries in the degree to which the higher classes are over-represented (Verba, Nie, and Kim, 1978, 290–1). Similarly, we find that the scale of class differences in Ireland does not deviate significantly from the overall European pattern evident in the European Values Survey.

TABLE 5.4   *Role of politics in everyday life, by social class*

	Consider politics important in their life %	Interested in politics %	Discuss politics at least occasionally %
Higher professional & managerial	39	53	77
Lower professional & managerial	38	53	75
Intermediate non-manual	24	38	57
Skilled manual	25	34	54
Semi-skilled manual	25	26	47
Unskilled manual	23	20	40

The results for education are equally striking, as can be seen from table 5.5. While a mere one in four of those without a Leaving Certificate give politics an important place in their life, this figure rises to over one in three with a third-level education. Well over half this latter group confirm that they are interested in politics, compared with less than one-third of the least-educated group. Finally, eight out of ten of the third-level respondents engaged in discussion of politics, while this figure reaches no higher than half for those without a Leaving Certificate.

Over and above such differences, as set out in table 5.6, women consistently emerge as more weakly oriented to the political system. The difference in relation to the importance of politics is modest, but

TABLE 5.5 *Role of politics in everyday life by education*

	Consider politics important in their life	Interested in politics	Discuss politics at least occasionally
	%	%	%
Third level	36	56	80
Leaving Cert.	31	42	62
Less than Leaving Cert.	25	31	51

men are substantially more likely to be interested in politics and to discuss politics. One in two women are likely to discuss politics at least occasionally, compared with two out of three men. Among full-time employees, we found that all respondents accord greater importance to the role of politics in their lives, though men remain more likely than women to be interested in and discuss politics. But there are substantial differences between women who are full-time employees and women who are in full-time unpaid home duties in the degree of interest in politics and the extent to which it is discussed. In the latter case the relevant figures are 40 and 22 per cent and in the former 60 and 43 per cent. Overall, sex differences in the role of politics in everyday life in Ireland are of broadly comparable magnitude to the overall European differences, although the Irish differentials are consistently higher.

The effects of class, education and sex are cumulative. It is possible therefore to identify groups with radically different cognitive orientations to the political system. In table 5.7 we compare the outcomes for (*a*) professional and managerial men, aged over thirty, with third-level education, and (*b*) non-skilled manual women, aged under thirty, with less than a Leaving Certificate. These are the most and least likely, respectively: the former are twice as likely to consider politics important in their life, four times more likely to discuss politics at least occasionally, and eight times more likely to be interested in politics.

It would be wrong to conclude too quickly from this that educated, upper-class, older men have a monopoly of interest in politics, or that women are excluded from networks of information about politics. But we can point to people's values not only as a determinant of what happens in a democratic country but also as a product of how politics

TABLE 5.6   *Role of politics in everyday life, by sex*

	Consider politics important in their life		Interested in politics		Discuss politics at least occasionally	
	Ireland, 1990 %	European average %	Ireland, 1990 %	European average %	Ireland, 1990 %	European average %
Women	21	28	30	32	50	66
Men	31	35	43	47	68	69

TABLE 5.7   *Cumulative effect of social background on role of politics in everyday life*

	Consider politics important	Interested in politics in their life	Discuss politics at least occasionally
	%	%	%
Male, 30 or over, third-level education, professional & managerial	41	72	92
Female, under 30, less than Leaving Cert., non-skilled manual	23	9	24

is currently organised. An interest in politics, and a sense that it matters to one, is itself a product of political mobilisation, which is mainly undertaken by the political parties. To what extent, then, do people feel able to influence the political process if levels of interest are so clearly distributed along lines of existing social advantage?

Political participation and subjective civic competence
Formal membership of political parties is likely to provide relatively little information about political participation: fewer than 4 per cent of those in the survey were members of political parties, 5 per cent of men and 3 per cent of women. Interestingly, though,

when broadening our conception of political behaviour to include involvement in community development associations or other voluntary groups, we find, as set out in table 5.8, that women have a higher probability of being involved. Eight per cent of women in the Irish survey are also involved in women's groups. The only areas in which involvement is substantially greater for men are trade unions and sports organisations.

TABLE 5.8 *Membership of selected voluntary organisations, by sex*

	Women %	Men %
Local community action on issues like poverty, employment, housing	4	3
Third World development or human rights	2	1
Conservation, the environment, ecology	3	2
Voluntary organisations concerned with health	4	2

We are more interested in respondents' perception of the degree to which they can influence political outcomes, and the channels of activity through which they would be prepared to be politically active. Almond and Verba (1963) argued that while attitudes favourable to political participation form an important part of what they term the 'civic culture', these should also be balanced by what they call 'parochial' values, which maintain the tension between public and private areas of activity and interest. Heath and Topf (1987, 52) summarise this view as follows: 'The ideal citizen in a successful democracy would have "a judicious mixture of respect for authority and sturdy independence" . . . Too much independence would lead to radical "populism" and "ungovernability"; too much respect for authority would lead to the reverse dangers of an author-itarian government unconstrained by fear of public disapproval.'

There is no measure of optimal levels of participation. Fears had been expressed by political scientists that too much democratic partic-ipation might prove unsustainable, even destabilising, as governments would be unable to cope with the 'demand overload' (Britain, 1977; Rose, 1980). Projections of such a crisis of democracy proved to be unfounded; democracies display varying levels of citizen activity, and internal variation over time, without it necessarily signalling any sort of crisis tendency (Schmitter, 1981). We can, however, draw attention to comparisons between Ireland and other European countries, and trace changes over time in Irish responses. The trends are likely to be more illuminating than the absolute figures themselves.

The first aspect of people's approach to political participation concerns their subjective sense of political competence. By this is meant the extent to which a citizen believes he or she can exert influence over a government decision. Respondents were invited to express agreement or disagreement with the statement: 'If an unjust law was passed by the Government I could do nothing about it.' We see from table 5.8 that 44 per cent felt there was nothing they could do. This figure is lower than the overall European figure of 57 per cent. Roughly the same proportion of British as Irish respondents feel powerless according to this question, at 48 per cent, but as many as 70 per cent of French respondents agree with the statement. A substantial proportion of Irish respondents emerge as lacking civic competence, but the Irish are by no means exceptional in this regard and indeed appear to have a somewhat stronger sense of subjective political competence than do other Europeans. Moreover, the level of civic competence appears to have increased over time. Raven and Whelan (1976) asked a similar question, which had featured in the Civic Culture five-country study, in a national survey conducted in the 1970s. They found the level of subjective competence in Ireland to be considerably lower than that found in Britain and the United States and, indeed, almost identical to that found in Mexico. Almost six out of ten Irish respondents felt there was nothing they could do about an unjust or harmful law, compared with one in four in the United States and one in three in Britain.

TABLE 5.9   *Percentage who agree there is nothing they could do if an unjust law were passed*

	%
Ireland 1990	44
European average 1990	57

There has been an increase, therefore, in subjective political competence over time. Why this should be so is unclear, although it is clear that Ireland is far from unique in this regard and that in all the western democracies 'greater public participation in economic and political decision-making has become an important social goal' (Dalton et al., 1984, 4). The international variations in responses may reflect a realistic perception of the probability of achieving a political response: decision-making in France, for example, is often considered to be relatively impervious to most pressure-group or other popular influences (Chafer, 1985; Hall, 1990, 77–8). The institutional configuration of a country may account for a good deal of the variation in people's perceptions of the degree of influence they could exercise over the decision-making process. It is not immediately apparent why subjective perceptions of civic competence should have grown in Ireland during the 1980s. The explanation may be political: the

TABLE 5.10 *Percentage who agree there is nothing they could do if an unjust law were passed: impact of social class and education (percentage by column)*

Social class		Education		Cumulative effects of education & social class	
	%		%		%
Professional & managerial	35	Third level	30	Professional & managerial with third-level education	27
Intermediate non-manual & skilled manual	44	Leaving Cert.	42	Semi-skilled & unskilled manual with less than Leaving Cert.	54
Semi-skilled & unskilled manual	52	Less than Leaving Cert.	48		

end of an era of continuous single-party government may increase people's sense of the political efficacy of opposition parties. It may also have a sociological aspect to it: it may be, for example, that increasing levels of education result in higher levels of confidence about political influence. Certainly we find substantial variation by social class and by education, which is summarised in table 5.10.

Non-skilled manual respondents with less than a Leaving Certificate are twice as likely as those from the professional and managerial class who have enjoyed a third-level education to perceive themselves as politically powerless.

Protest activities

We can now move on from people's general perception of their ability to influence political decisions to the specific manner in which they would be prepared to act. We expect that people's actual involvement in protest activities may not be very extensive, because the occasion may not have arisen. The experience of political involvement is likely to be prompted by concern over specific issues or exposure to a specific context. But in common with earlier researchers we would expect to find that 'the potential to participate, the individual readiness to be mobilized, is an abiding property of a wide sector of the whole political community, whether currently active or not' (Marsh and Kaase, 1979, 58).

Unfortunately, many of the actions that might come most naturally to Irish citizens are nowhere considered in the present survey. Activities such as contacting constituency TDs, in person or in writing, or lodging a protest with the relevant minister or department, are not considered. Extensive use is made of contact with local politicians for a whole variety of objectives, arguably to a greater degree than in most democratic polities—an aspect of what has been taken to be the 'localism' of Irish politics (Chubb, 1962; Hazelkorn, 1986; Sacks, 1976; Bax, 1976; Gallagher and Komito, 1992). The importance of this contact is reinforced by the operation of the electoral system, which increases the incentives to politicians to cultivate popular support and to be attuned to local feelings, not only on account of competition from opposition parties but also because of rivalry from candidates from their own party (Carty, 1981). But although many forms of Irish political activity are not surveyed here, and the level of political activity is therefore underestimated, we can gain additional information from the items asked about.

The political activities that respondents were asked to consider were:

(i)   signing a petition,
(ii) attending a lawful demonstration,
(iii) joining unofficial strikes, and
(iv) occupying buildings or factories;
      and they were asked whether they
(i)   had done so,
(ii) might do so, or
(iii) would do so.

If we focus on the first two activities, what we might call conventional forms of protest, we find, as shown in table 5.11, that respondents' attitudes are very similar to the European average. Irish respondents are slightly less likely to have engaged in such activities but slightly more likely to indicate that they would do so, leaving the Irish figures for those who would never act in this way almost identical to the European average. Just over two in five of the Irish sample had signed a petition, compared with just over one-half of the European respondents as a whole and just about three-quarters of those in Britain. Fewer than one in five absolutely rule out the possibility. The proportion of Irish respondents who had attended demonstrations is below one in five, compared with one in four in the European sample as a whole and more than one in three in Italy and France. But the proportion who would consider taking such action is very similar for Ireland and Europe overall, with just about two-fifths considering they might do so, and an equal number ruling out the possibility.

TABLE 5.11 *Proneness to conventional forms of political protest: Ireland and Europe compared*

| | Signing a petition | | Attending lawful demonstrations | |
| | Ireland | European average | Ireland | European average |
	%	%	%	%
Have done	42	53	17	25
Might do	40	30	41	38
Would never do	18	17	42	42

TABLE 5.12 *Proneness to unconventional forms of political protest: Ireland and Europe compared*

| | Unofficial strikes | | Occupying building or factories | |
| | Ireland | European average | Ireland | European average |
	%	%	%	%
Have done	4	7	2	4
Might do	23	19	19	17
Would never do	73	73	79	79

In Ireland, the figures for unofficial strikes and occupation of buildings are particularly low (table 5.12). Four per cent had been involved in unofficial strikes, compared with the European average of 7 per cent, with even lower numbers engaged in occupying buildings. The Irish and European levels for those who rule out such action are identical: 73 per cent for unofficial strikes and 79 per cent for occupation.

The major factors influencing propensity to engage in conventional political protest are education and sex. Table 5.13 sets out the results for education. Two-thirds of those with third-level education had at some point signed a petition, compared with fewer than one-third of those with a Primary Certificate or less. Correspondingly, while only one in twenty of the former group ruled out the possibility of engaging in such action, the figure rises to over one in four for the latter. Similarly, the figures for having engaged in a lawful demonstration vary from three out of ten of the most highly educated group to one in ten of the least advantaged. The corresponding figures for those who are unwilling to consider the possibility of such action range from one in six to over half.

TABLE 5.13 *Proneness to conventional forms of political participation, by education (percentage by column)*

	Primary Cert.		Intermediate or less		Leaving Cert.		Third level or Group Cert.	
	Signing a petition %	Lawful protest %	Signing a petition %	Lawful protest %	Signing a petition %	Lawful protest %	Signing a petition %	Lawful protest %
Have done	30	11	38	14	50	19	64	30
Might do	43	34	42	40	38	47	31	54
Would never do	27	55	20	46	12	34	5	16

In addition to the education effect, we also find substantial differences between men and women in the likelihood of their having been involved, or being willing to consider being involved, in a lawful demonstration. Men are twice as likely as women to have been involved, with the respective figures being one in five and one in ten. Correspondingly, while just over one-third of our male respondents indicate that they would never engage in such action, the figure rises to one in two for women. No comparable differences arise in relation to signing a petition, although the figures for men are slightly higher.

When we focus attention on unconventional forms of political protest, the major discriminating factors are age and sex. Almost eight out of ten women rule out involvement in an unofficial strike, and nine out of ten adopt this position in relation to occupation. For men the corresponding figures are just under two-thirds and eight out of ten, respectively. The variation by age is somewhat sharper. For both types of action the proportion who would consider such involvement declines across age group, reaching a figure of nine out of ten for those over sixty; in the under-thirty age group, by way of contrast, only two-thirds entirely reject the occupation option and one-half the unofficial strike course of action.

The relevance of sex in accounting for these variations is very much in line with other research on women's political participation. In a seven-country comparative study, Nie, Verba and Kim (1978, 234–68) found that the gap observed between men and women in their knowledge of and participation in politics was, in the main, a function of differences between their respective 'institutional resources', especially their employment situation. Our analysis confirms that differences in political participation between men and women in Ireland are indeed in large part accounted for by the low levels of participation by women in the labour force. When we compare men and women who are in employment we find very little difference in relation to the conventional protest items, although we find some support for the earlier finding that 'being female—even if one has the same educational level, as much affiliation with political institutions, and as much concern about political matters—implies a lower rate of political activity' (Nie, Verba, and Kim, 1978, 268). Differences persist in relation to having actually engaged in unconventional forms of protest. This is not surprising, since the particular items included in the survey are far more likely to be relevant to male industrial employees than to any other sector of the work force.

Referring back to the item concerning the level of confidence in democratic institutions, we find that those who express least confidence in democratic institutions are also those who are most predisposed to engage in political protest. Young people, the better-educated and men rather more than women are the least likely to express unreserved confidence in such institutions; these are also the groups that tend to be the most politically active.

But what is perhaps most striking is that in all categories there is relatively little support for unconventional forms of protest. Irish respondents are very like the British in displaying relatively high levels of support for orderly and conventional forms of protest, but this support declines sharply as one moves on to forms of direct or potentially violent action. In Ireland, as in other countries, involvement in orderly forms of protest activities seems to be seen as an extension of conventional political participation rather than as an alternative to it (Barnes and Kaase, 1979, 93–4). We noted earlier, though, that quite a high proportion of respondents believed that they have no political influence. We find, as Topf (1989, 65) notes, that citizens 'say they would act, and say in ever increasing numbers, and to a much more limited extent they say that they have acted, even though they do not believe they have influence.' However, we need not understand people's actions in purely instrumental terms. They should be interpreted rather as expressions of what people feel they ought to do: they should be seen as evidence of a sense of moral obligation. Thus, signing a petition is meaningful, irrespective of its effectiveness, for those citizens who identify such behaviour as appropriate or required by the situation. We have explored this possibility by looking at the relationship between perceived ability to influence an unjust law and propensity to engage in conventional forms of political protest. Those who have signed or would sign a petition or participate in a lawful demonstration are less likely to feel that they could have no influence on an unjust law. Nevertheless, almost four out of ten of the potentially active group hold the view that they are relatively powerless. A deep value commitment appears to be involved here, which people will act on even if they do not necessarily believe it is an effective means of changing things.

This impression is strengthened by the fact that people who attach a high priority to the value of freedom of speech are also the ones who are most likely to engage in (conventional) political protest, as table 5.14 indicates. Respondents were asked to choose their first and second priority from the following set of desirable goals:

(i)   maintaining order in the nation;
(ii) giving people more say in important government decisions;
(iii) fighting rising prices;
(iv) protecting freedom of speech.

Those choosing 'protecting freedom of speech' as either a first or second choice were contrasted with all others. Those who accord a priority to freedom of speech are significantly more likely to have signed a petition and to have attended lawful demonstrations.

TABLE 5.14 *Probability of having engaged in conventional forms of
participation, by priority given to protecting freedom of speech*

Protecting freedom of speech	Have signed a petition %	Have attended lawful demonstrations %
A priority	51	22
Not a priority	35	13

This finding seems to indicate that whether or not people believe
their involvement will have an influence on political outcomes may
not be the most important consideration for them. Their protest
activities are likely to be regarded as an expression of a broader
value commitment.

Unemployment and political alienation

It has sometimes been suggested that the experience of unemployment, particularly long-term unemployment, produces changes in
people's political values and orientations.

Some project the emergence of greater social unrest, particularly
if unemployment continues to increase, as the unemployed lose their
sense of having a vested interest in conventional social and political
institutions. Thus, quite apart from concern about increasing levels
of crime against property or the spread of drug addiction or other
indices of a decaying social fabric, attention has focused on the
danger of an underclass revolt. This concern has been expressed not
just by right-wing commentators but by those whose political and
philosophical positions are quite obviously ones involving sympathy
with marginalised groups. Thus Healy and Reynolds (1992, 29)
follow Galbraith (1992) in stressing that the exclusion of such groups
can have very serious implications for social stability. Citing
Galbraith's view that the possibility of an underclass revolt has
grown stronger in the United States, Healy and Reynolds point to
the parallels with Ireland. They note (1992, 29) 'widespread anger
and resentment in many areas where poor people are suffering,' and
argue that 'to ensure stability and to prevent the "evolution" of an
"underclass revolt" it is essential to develop participative structures
which give all people access to decision-making processes.' It must
be stressed that Healy and Reynolds base their case for participation on a wide-ranging consideration of the principles that should

underlie a just process of decision-making rather than simply the consequences of such disruption. Inevitably, though, media attention has tended to focus on the underclass issue.

There is substantial evidence demonstrating the degree of hurt, pain and anger associated with marginalisation (Schlossman and Verba, 1979; Whelan et al., 1991). However, the evidence in relation to political alienation is less clear-cut. Heath (1992), in a British study that used a definition of the underclass based on household labour market experience, found that once education had been controlled for there was no evidence that the unemployed were more likely to be non-participants in the political process or that they displayed a lower level of political efficacy.

Similarly, the evidence available from the European Values Survey also provides no support for the notion of an underclass revolt. The number of unemployed in the Irish sample (only thirty-eight) is too small to permit us to distinguish between short-term and long-term unemployment so as to adequately identify an underclass. However, detachment from the labour market is the crucial structural process in the potential emergence of such a class (Jencks, 1992; Whelan, 1993). What we can do therefore is provide a comparison of the unemployed with what appear to be the most appropriate reference groups.

We are aware of the danger of turning merely descriptive findings into conclusions about causal relationships (Heath, 1992, 37). Even if the unemployed were to differ in terms of political values from employees, there may still be no legitimate grounds for assuming that such differences are a consequence of unemployment per se. The unemployed differ from employees in a number of ways. In general they are younger, and they are more likely to be from the non-skilled manual class. In order to bring out in a relatively simple fashion the conclusions arising from our more elaborate statistical analysis, we have used as comparator groups those aged under thirty, and employees in non-skilled manual occupations, to situate the responses of our unskilled respondents in a broader socio-economic context.

In table 5.15 we look at the role of politics in the everyday life of the unemployed. Over one-third of them consider politics not at all important in their lives, compared with a quarter of employees. Over half of the unemployed group indicate that they never discuss politics with friends, while this is true of just over one-third of employees. However, when we compare these results with those of others aged under thirty and those in non-skilled manual occupations it becomes very difficult to argue that this detachment from the political process is actually caused by unemployment. In no case does the figure for the unemployed exceed the overall figures for the age and class sub-groups. The results are entirely consistent with an interpretation that suggests that politics is peripheral to the lives of both the young and the lower working class.

TABLE 5.15 *Role of politics in everyday life: comparison of unemployed and employees*

	Unemployed %	Employees %	Under 30 %	Non-skilled manual %
Consider politics not at all important in their lives	36	26	34	42
Not at all interested in politics	37	24	34	37
Never discuss politics with friends	54	35	52	57

In table 5.16 we address the question of whether the unemployed are more or less protest-prone than employees. We do so by discussing the percentages who indicate that they would never engage in specific forms of political protest. Looking at conventional forms of protest, the figures are identical as regards signing petitions. The only difference between employees and the unemployed is that unemployed people are slightly more likely to indicate that they would never attend lawful demonstrations: 40 per cent, compared with 32 per cent. In both cases the figures for the unemployed are between the overall figures for the young and the non-skilled manual.

The picture for unconventional political protest is somewhat different. In the case of boycotts, unofficial strikes and occupying buildings and factories the unemployed are less likely to rule out the possibility of engaging in such action—particularly the latter two options, where roughly seven out of ten employees reject both, while for the unemployed the figures are one-half and six out of ten, respectively. The contrast between the unemployed and those under thirty or in the lower working class are more modest but still significant.

Finally, almost half of the unemployed feel that there is little they could do to influence an unjust law. Once again, though, this

TABLE 5.16 *Protest proneness: comparison of unemployed and employees*

	Unemployed %	Employees %	Under 30 %	Non-skilled manual %
Would never—				
Sign a petition	13	13	10	25
Attend lawful				
demonstrations	40	32	31	50
Join in boycotts	42	47	41	61
Join unofficial				
strikes	48	67	53	68
Occupy buildings				
or factories	58	74	66	66

figure is similar to that for respondents aged under thirty and that for the non-skilled manual class.

We do not find evidence to support any of the claims that the political values of the unemployed are radically at odds with those of comparable groups in the overall population. We do find evidence of a degree of detachment from the political process, at least as measured by the confidence they express in establishment institutions, and their sense of political efficacy. But, as we shall see later, this does not translate in any straightforward way into political partisanship: the unemployed are not politically mobilised around a distinctive set of values that makes the experience of unemployment their dominant concern (Gallie, 1988).

A CONSERVATIVE POLITICAL CULTURE?

One of the claims sometimes made about Irish political culture is that it is imbued with the values of conservatism across a range of value dimensions. We shall explore a number of facets of conservative values in chapter 6, when we set out several sorts of values relevant to the distinction between right and left. Here, though, we consider whether, arising from our discussion of political participation, we can find evidence of a strong conservative trait in Irish political culture.

We have five measures of conservatism on matters of general political disposition, two of which deal with attitudes towards the pace of political change, one with attitudes to establishment institutions, and two with aspects of traditional morality. While representing distinct dimensions, these measures are interrelated in a manner that is consistent with the notion that they are tapping different aspects of a single dimension of conservatism.

The first measure of conservatism concerns attitudes towards political change. Our respondents were faced with the following three options and asked to indicate which best described their own opinion:

(i) The entire way our society is organised must be radically changed by revolutionary action.

(ii) Our society must gradually be improved by reforms.

(iii) Our present society must be valiantly defended against all subversive forces.

The phrasing of this last item is not entirely satisfactory, since the term 'subversive' may lend itself to very different interpretations in different countries. Nevertheless it does seem to be tapping consistent preferences concerning the pace of social change. In our analysis we focus on the percentage choosing the final option. The second measure is based on whether or not respondents felt that the pace of political reform is moving too rapidly in the country. The third measure is based on the degree of respondents' confidence in establishment institutions, a measure we have discussed earlier in relation to the idea of a 'civic culture'. Respondents were asked to indicate whether or not they had confidence in the following institutions: the church, the armed forces, the legal system, the police, parliament, and the civil service. The scale, running from 0 to 6, displayed almost perfect reliability.

Our fourth and fifth measures are concerned with a more general social conservatism. The first of these relates to the priority attributed to traditional child-rearing values, in particular the extent to which it was felt important to impart the following values:

(i) obedience;

(ii) hard work;

(iii) good manners;

(iv) thrift;

(v) religious faith.

The scale score indicates the number of such values that are considered important.

The final measure involves a sub-set of the items included in the permissiveness scale employed in chapter 2. Respondents were asked the extent to which the following could be justified, on a scale ranging from 1 (never) to 10 (always):

(i)   married men or women having an affair;
(ii) sex under the legal age of consent;
(iii) homosexuality;
(iv) divorce;
(v)   abortion.

An average of these items was taken in order to construct a measure of the extent to which respondents were conservative or liberal on issues relating to sexual morality.

The items used are not the best for our purposes. Attitudes to sex under the legal age of consent, for example, are likely to have been strongly coloured in recent years by greater awareness of sexual abuse, in a manner that might eclipse the earlier focus of the question, that is, tolerance towards early sexual experimentation. In some cases the focus is on the respondent's own attitude to a type of behaviour; in others it is likely to be on the respondent's attitude to public regulation of an issue rather than their personal moral stance. Nevertheless the scale has a highly satisfactory reliability coefficient of 0.70: the item is measuring a consistent set of values.

In table 5.17 we show how the Irish results compare with the European outcomes for this set of indicators. The pattern is not a uniform one. Only one in five chose the conservative option, stressing that 'our present society must be valiantly defended against all subversive forces,' a figure that is not significantly different from the European average. On the other hand, while a similar number of Irish respondents, about one-fifth, think that political reform is moving too rapidly, the overall European figure reaches three out of ten. It is, of course, a possibility that political reforms in the Irish context were in any case occurring at a slower pace than in many other countries in the survey. The Irish profile is more conservative in terms of degree of confidence in establishment institutions and views on sexual permissiveness, but no significant difference is observed in the weight accorded to different child-rearing values. With the exception of attitudes towards sexual permissiveness, where there has been some liberalisation, there has been no significant change over the nine-year period between the two surveys.

There are, however, substantial variations by both age and education for all five indicators, which do point to the possibility of a

TABLE 5.17 *Political and social conservatism: Ireland and Europe compared*

	Ireland	European average
Our present society must be valiantly defended against all subversive forces	20%	18%
Political reform is moving too rapidly	19%	30%
Confidence in establishment institutions	2.8	2.5
Emphasis on traditional child-rearing values	2.3	2.2
Sexual permissiveness	2.8	4.0

longer-term decline in conservative values. At the very least it appears that modernising influences such as education are producing sharper sub-cultural variations within the broad umbrella of Irish political culture (Coakley, 1993). The results for age are set out in table 5.18 and those for education in table 5.19.

With regard to age, the important differences that emerge involve contrasts with those under thirty, those aged between thirty and sixty, and those aged sixty or over. If we allow for the possibility that the pattern observed among the younger age group might well be a life-cycle phenomenon that will not be sustained throughout the life course, one might be inclined to conclude that the extent of change is of a rather modest scale. Arguing against this are the substantial differences we observe across educational groups. While over one in four of those without educational qualifications are concerned with defending society against subversive forces, and with the fact that political reform is moving too rapidly, these concerns diminish with greater education, and the comparable figure for those with third-level education is approximately one in twenty-five. Similarly, the higher one's level of education the more likely one is to take a more permissive line in relation to sexual morality, to place less emphasis on traditional child rearing values, and to have less confidence in establishment institutions.

'Authoritarianism'?

Whether or not authoritarian dispositions are strongly in evidence might be expected to be a rather important question for understanding the complexion and style of democratic politics. As we noted earlier, we are interested in authoritarianism in the sense of a collective disposition to defer to those in positions of authority. Commentators have tended to assume that this trait was strengthened in

TABLE 5.18 *Political and social conservatism, by age group*

	18–29	30–44	45–59	60+
Our present society must be valiantly defended against all subversive forces	7%	23%	19%	28%
Political reform is moving too rapidly	14%	20%	18%	23%
Confidence in establishment institutions	3.2	3.5	3.9	4.5
Emphasis on traditional child-rearing values	1.9	2.1	2.2	2.6
Sexual permissiveness	3.2	3.5	3.9	4.5

TABLE 5.19 *Political and social conservatism, by educational level*

	Primary Cert.	Intermediate or Group Cert.	Leaving Cert.	Third level
Our present society must be valiantly defended against all subversive forces	25	22	16	7
Political reform is moving too rapidly	28	17	14	4
Confidence in establishment institutions	4.0	3.7	3.7	3.3
Emphasis on traditional child-rearing values	2.5	2.2	1.9	1.7
Sexual permissiveness	2.1	2.4	2.9	3.6

Irish society by the religious homogeneity of the population and the correspondingly rather weak development of political liberalism until relatively recently—a feature of Irish political life that distinguishes it from mainstream European political developments.

The emergence of liberal values has been identified by some authors with the need to accommodate different religious allegiances in a society (Arblaster, 1984; Rawls, 1985) and by others with conflict between the Catholic Church and a secular independent state (Lipset and Rokkan, 1967). Neither of these types of accommodation between sets of fundamental values was necessary in Ireland. The independent state was almost completely religiously homogeneous, and neither the existence of the minority Protestant population nor the presence of a majority Protestant population in Northern Ireland was sufficient to exert the liberalising influences and secularisation of state institutions that other religiously mixed societies had had to adopt (Whyte, 1980, 1–24). Furthermore, the Catholic Church had not been alienated from the population in the cause of achieving political independence—on the contrary, it was strongly identified with popular political and cultural interests.

Schmitt (1973, 54), in identifying authoritarianism as one of the central characteristics of Irish political culture, argues that it may actually have been functional in sustaining democratic government:

> Authoritarianism has in the Irish context been a beneficial component of the political culture. Democratic political procedures and institutions had been viewed as legitimate before independence. Authoritarian sentiments helped reinforce their legitimacy after the new state was founded. Furthermore, while authoritarian norms increased support for organizations and produced a willingness to accept some regulation, personalism . . . provided a mechanism for circumventing the arbitrariness and inflexibility that often accompany authoritarian institutions.

Other analysts of Irish political culture have identified traditions of uncritical acquiescence to established authority within public institutions. Chubb, for example, argues that the poor performance of the Oireachtas in legislating and in holding the Government accountable is a result not only of its being poorly organised and informed but also of the 'general acceptance by members of the dominant role of the government as policy-maker' (1992, 204). The deference to hierarchy in the civil service for much of the life of the state has frequently been noted (see, for example, Barrington, 1980, 31; Chubb, 1993, 231–8). Schmitt may be correct in suggesting that the relatively uncritical attitude to authority has been a pervasive feature of political life more generally. However, we do not intend merely to repeat this characterisation of political life, nor to confine our attention to the question of whether or not authoritarianism is functional in current circumstances. We wish to explore what the evidence may be that authoritarian values are indeed a core constitutive element in Irish political culture.

We do not have the resources to undertake a broad analysis of authoritarian personality traits in this study (cf. Adorno, 1950; Altemeyer, 1988), but our indicators should provide an approximate profile of the extent of authoritarianism in the sense we have identified. We have taken three measures of authoritarianism. The first item is a measure of generalised deference to authority as reflected in agreement with the view that 'greater respect for authority would be a good thing.' The second is the item discussed earlier concerning the priority given to freedom of speech (compared with maintaining order in the country). The third item explores adherence to traditional moral values, with a view to identifying the extent of tolerance at the individual level towards alternative value positions. It measures disagreement with the statement that 'there can never be absolutely clear guidelines about what is good or bad.'

In table 5.20 the Irish profile in relation to authoritarianism is compared with the European one. In each case the values associated with authoritarianism are more strongly in evidence in Ireland than in the overall European sample. The extent of the differential varies across indicators. The least difference is observed in relation to the existence of absolutely clear guidelines about what is good and evil. Here the Irish figure is 45 per cent and the European figure 39 per cent. In relation to the importance of protecting freedom of speech, the difference is somewhat greater, with 42 per cent of Irish respondents giving it priority compared with 51 per cent of European respondents. It is in relation to generalised deference to authority that the Irish are most exceptional. While fewer than six out of ten of the European sample as a whole believe that greater respect for authority would be a good thing, this holds for over eight out of ten of the Irish respondents.

The level of authoritarianism in Ireland, on these measures, is significantly above the average European level (see also Mac Gréil, 1977, 529–30). Once again, though, there are strikingly sharp vari-

TABLE 5.20 *Authoritarianism: Ireland and Europe compared*

| | Percentage agreeing | |
	Ireland %	European average %
Greater respect for authority a good thing	83	57
Protection of free speech a priority	42	51
Absolutely clear guidelines about what is good and evil	45	39

ations by age group and level of education, as can be seen from tables 5.21 and 5.22. Only among those aged under thirty do we observe a pattern of results that could possibly be described as less authoritarian than the overall European average. An examination of the results relating to education indicates that those with Leaving Certificate or above closely resemble the overall European pattern for free speech and absolute moral guidelines. Those with less education are substantially more authoritarian. With regard to respect for authority, only those with third-level education came near to the European pattern. While the trend towards higher levels of education in Ireland is likely to lead to a decline in the values associated with authoritarianism, the foregoing results suggest that, in European terms, we are likely to remain at the less liberal end of the spectrum.

We saw earlier that Irish respondents showed rather higher levels of confidence in public institutions than the European average. We now wish to consider the degree to which the trust vested in public authorities might be interpreted as indicating a deferential and even a rather anti-democratic orientation, that is, a tendency to endorse authoritarianism in political life.

From table 5.23 we can see that, while those who attach a low priority to freedom of speech and are confident that clear moral guidelines exist are slightly more likely to have confidence in establishment institutions, the observed differences are extremely modest. Thus, while authoritarianism (as reflected by these indicators) and confidence in establishment institutions are both influenced by similar socio-demographic factors, they are rather poorly correlated. Confidence in establishment institutions is just as likely to be high among

TABLE 5.21 *Authoritarianism, by age group*

| | Percentage agreeing | | | |
	18–29 %	30–44 %	45–59 %	60+ %
Protection of free speech a priority	50	41	39	37
Absolutely clear guidelines about what is good & evil	28	39	52	63
Greater respect for authority a good thing	68	82	88	93

TABLE 5.22 *Authoritarianism, by educational level*

| | *Percentage agreeing* | | | |
	Primary Cert. or less %	Intermediate or Group Cert. %	Leaving Cert. %	Third level %
Protection of free speech a priority	34	39	50	50
Absolutely clear guidelines about what is good & evil	55	43	37	35
Greater respect for authority a good thing	88	87	79	64

those at the liberal end of the spectrum as among those displaying authoritarian characteristics. So although confidence in establishment institutions is, in aggregate, higher in Ireland than in other European countries (cf. table 5.1), this does not indicate any tendency towards authoritarianism in the sense of suspicion of or hostility to democratic politics.

The one indicator that does have a significant association with confidence in establishment institutions is that concerning whether or not greater respect for authority is desirable. Given the previous negative findings, perhaps we should not disregard the possibility that what is being observed is a reciprocal rather than a causal

TABLE 5.23 *Confidence in establishment institutions, by authoritarianism*

Free speech	Mean confidence score	Absolutely clear guidelines exist	Mean confidence score	Greater respect for authority a good thing	Mean confidence score
Not a priority	2.8	Agree	2.9	Yes	2.9
A priority	2.7	Disagree	2.7	No	2.4

relationship. By this we mean that having confidence in establishment institutions may lead one to consider an increase in respect for authority desirable, rather than vice versa. In other words, the item relating to respect for authority may be a less than ideal measure of authoritarianism. Overall, the evidence does not suggest that there are strong grounds for viewing the high levels of confidence in establishment institutions in Ireland as forming part of an authoritarian, anti-democratic syndrome.

Unemployment and authority
We considered earlier the possibility that unemployment may be associated not with an increase in political radicalism but with a more generalised disaffection with the political process and the norms underlying it. We have no evidence of actual levels of participation or abstention from voting. One way of trying to measure disaffection with the political process is to examine responses to the question about confidence in establishment institutions.

From table 5.24 we can see that the unemployed are only marginally less likely than any of the comparator groups to lack confidence in parliament or the legal system. The unemployed may have substantial reservations about the performance of the legal and political system but they do not appear to be particularly different from other citizens in this. However, they are substantially less likely to have confidence in the police than the other groups, and this is a distinctive contrast. Approximately four-fifths of employees, those aged under thirty and those in non-skilled manual occupations express confidence in the police, compared with two-thirds of the unemployed.

TABLE 5.24 *Confidence in institutions: comparison of unemployed and employees*

	Unemployed %	Employees %	Under 30 %	Non-skilled manual %
Confidence in—				
Legal system	43	47	49	41
Police	65	85	78	80
Parliament	44	45	43	47

These responses suggest that unemployed people are relatively uninvolved in the political process, but no more so than others of comparable class and background. They are more open to unconventional forms of protest. Almost one in two of them feel that there is nothing they could do to oppose an unjust law. But this level of impotence does not differ significantly from that displayed by the non-skilled manual group as a whole.

'Localism'?
One consideration relating to people's willingness to engage in political activity and the civic culture more generally is the level of organisation with which they primarily identify. Irish political culture has generally been taken to be considerably more imbued with 'localism', or orientation to one's immediate community, than the majority of advanced democratic societies, resulting in a political system in which brokerage and clientelism may flourish (Gallagher and Komito, 1992).

We cannot contribute to the literature on the role of politicians from the evidence available in the European Values Survey, but we can make some comments on respondents' patterns of identification.

We have already seen that, compared with other personal affiliations, politics plays a relatively small part in people's lives. Nevertheless, the sense of involvement in national life does seem to be important to Irish people. Table 5.25 shows that when asked how proud they were of their nationality, Irish respondents answered much more positively than the European average. Over three-quarters assert that they are very proud of their nationality, compared with a European average of slightly over one-third. While one in six of the European sample offer a negative response, this is true for less than 2 per cent of the Irish respondents. This extremely high level of national pride is relatively constant across socio-demographic groups, and there is no significant difference between the younger and older respondents.

TABLE 5.25 *Pride in nationality among those considering themselves to be Irish compared with European average*

	Ireland %	European average %
Very proud	78	38
Quite proud	21	46
Not very proud	1	11
Not at all proud	0	6

Respondents were also asked to identify the geographical locality they felt they belonged to first of all. Table 5.26 shows that any assumption that an unusually strong sense of localism pervades Irish people's perceptions is not well founded. Irish respondents were only marginally more likely to identify with locality or town than the European sample, and rather less likely to identify with a region. Perhaps most significantly, Irish respondents showed a stronger tendency to identify with the country as a whole than in the other European countries. The very small numbers identifying with Europe or the world as a whole seem to be expressing anti-nationalistic feeling as much as a positive identity: these options are chosen by more than a quarter of those who are not at all proud of their nationality, compared with about one in twenty of those who are very proud.

TABLE 5.26 *Localism versus cosmopolitanism (primary identification with geographical groups): Ireland and Europe compared*

	Group to which respondents feel they belong first		
	Ireland, 1981 %	Ireland, 1990 %	European average %
Locality or town	55	44	41
Region of country	16	14	19
Country as a whole	25	38	26
Europe	2	2	5
World as a whole	3	2	10

We are referring here, it must be remembered, to primary identification. These levels of identification are by no means mutually exclusive, as slogans such as 'Europe of the regions' illustrate (Hume, 1990). Between 1981 and 1990 there was a substantial decline in the number identifying with their locality or town, from 55 to 44 per cent, and a corresponding increase in the number identifying with the country as a whole, from 25 to 38 per cent. These trends are also reflected in variations across age groups, but the most influential factor is level of education. From table 5.27 we can see that while half those with a Primary Certificate, or less, identify with their locality or town, this drops to one in three for those with third-level education. For identification with the country as a whole, the pattern is almost exactly reversed. Thus, the general context in which more specific political values in Ireland must be situated is one of a high level of pride in Irish identity. As in the other European countries, a sense of belonging is primarily associated with one's locality or town, with close to half of the respondents opting for this response. However, the country as a whole serves increasingly as a primary point of reference, and if we take into account first and second choices, two-thirds of our respondents opt for this identification. Furthermore, among the most educated respondents, the direction of change is not from a national to a supranational perspective but from identification with one's locality to identification with the country as a whole.

TABLE 5.27 *Localism v. cosmopolitanism, by educational qualification*

| | Group to which respondents feel they belong first | | | |
	Primary Cert. or less %	Intermediate or Group Cert. %	Leaving Cert. %	Third level %
Locality or town	50	41	45	33
Region of country	13	15	13	13
Country as a whole	33	38	38	49
Europe	3	1	3	2
World as a whole	1	5	1	3

Clearly, responses to these items are dependent on context, and people will feel themselves more strongly drawn to different levels of identification in different contexts. The interplay between local identification and national concerns has been studied, for example, in the context of electoral politics. Voters make their decisions about candidates with reference to the politicians' previous record of activism at the local and constituency level—but the national focus, involving party identification in terms of national issues and policy priorities, is never absent (Mair, 1987, 61–92). We would suggest that our findings support the conclusion that localism can no longer be assumed unproblematically to be a dominant feature of Irish political culture, and that it is likely to decline further in the future.

Democratic values reconsidered

The results of our analysis indicate that Irish respondents are very similar to other Europeans in many of their attitudes to the democratic political process and participation in political life.

Irish respondents display levels of confidence in public institutions that are comparatively high in European terms, and this confidence has shown no sign of declining in recent years. They are no different from other Europeans in considering politics to be a great deal less important than family, friends, religion, or work. The overall Irish profile is similar to the European one on such matters as the level of interest in politics, the tendency to discuss politics, and the overall importance of politics in one's life. Responses to these items vary according to social class in Ireland in a manner which is very similar to the pattern in other European countries. To the extent that differences exist between the Irish and European results they are evident in women's generally lower levels of interest and involvement in most aspects of mainstream political activity. This is accounted for to a considerable degree by the lower levels of labour force participation of Irish women.

Measures of political participation show very similar results to those found among other European respondents. A substantial minority of Irish respondents feel that there is nothing they could do to influence an unjust law, but they are in no way unusual in this respect. In fact the proportion of Irish respondents who display a sense of political powerlessness is significantly below the European average. Furthermore, this sense of a capacity to intervene successfully in the political process has increased over recent decades in Ireland. The impact of education and social class on such feelings of competence is cumulative: manual workers with less than a Leaving Certificate are twice as likely to feel impotent as professional and managerial workers with third-level education.

There is no evidence, however, that the class effect on the sense of civic competence is substantially different in Ireland from that apparent in other European countries.

With regard to willingness to engage in specific forms of protest, the Irish are less likely to have engaged in conventional forms of protest activity but are no more likely to rule out such activities absolutely. The level of support for unconventional protest is relatively low, as is the case for the European sample as a whole. A willingness to engage in political protest appears to be related to notions of what is morally right and to a generalised sense of civic obligation rather than to any calculation of the probability that one's intervention will have any effect.

The unemployed are relatively detached from the political process, but no more than one might expect on the basis of their age and class profile. Neither is there evidence that unemployment per se contributes to disillusionment with the legal system or the Dáil, though unemployed respondents showed considerably lower levels of confidence in the police.

Conservatism and authoritarianism are sometimes bracketed together as kindred features of Irish political culture. To do so, we find, is misleading. The evidence does not support the view that Irish citizens are consistently more conservative than other Europeans. Only in relation to sexual permissiveness is this apparent. But the level of authoritarianism in Ireland, defined in terms of a collective disposition to defer to those in authority positions in a power hierarchy, is indeed high by European standards. Irish respondents overall accord a lower priority to freedom of speech, are more likely to think that absolute distinctions can be made in relation to what is good and evil, and are also more likely to think it desirable that authority should be given greater respect. There are clear variations in these attitudes associated with age and education, with the younger and more highly educated displaying distinctly more liberal attitudes. However, the high levels of confidence in public institutions that we report are not part of any broader authoritarian trait in political life. Confidence in public or establishment institutions is just as likely to be evinced by those with liberal political values as by those with authoritarian values.

There is no support for the notion that Irish respondents are characterised by an unusually strong sense of localism. As in other countries, people's sense of identification is primarily local but the country as a whole is increasingly becoming the main reference point, particularly among the better educated. Our indicators do not explore what motivates people's level of identification. But Irish respondents appear to share in the wider European experience of erosion of local or parochial identification and growing relevance of national and European-level political concerns.

Overall, then, we find evidence that Irish political culture shares many central features with other advanced European countries. To some extent this is an artefact of the data available to us, which does not allow us to explore some of the more distinctive facets of democratic values and political practice in Ireland. Nevertheless, we have surveyed a number of the traits that have often been taken as constitutive of Irish political culture. We have found a good deal of evidence to confirm the suggestions of other researchers (for example Coakley, 1992, 1993) that the transformation of the social structure has wrought considerable change upon Irish political attitudes. This is in a sense hardly surprising, particularly as 'traditional' features of political culture, rather than dating from time immemorial, were associated with social structures which were of relatively recent origin. There is no reason to assume that these values would necessarily survive the particular social circumstances in which they were rooted. The pattern of political values is likely to be further altered by increases in educational participation among younger age groups, by a continuing process of secularisation of Irish society, and by the integration of regional and class-based subcultures into national life through increased exposure to the mass media. We may be witnessing the 'Europeanisation' of Irish political values. Evidence of convergence with European partners on most items may throw new light on those values that remain atypical, suggesting the areas of research which deserve more detailed study in the future.

6 Values and Political Partisanship

NIAMH HARDIMAN AND CHRISTOPHER T. WHELAN

INTRODUCTION

The most familiar way in which political partisanship is analysed, in Ireland as elsewhere, is in terms of a fairly small number of demographic and sociological variables. Age, sex and educational background are among the most frequently used indicators that can help illuminate patterns of support for political parties. And people's situation in a network of allegiances and interests, whether based on social class, religious affiliation, ethnic community or other focus of collective identity, is also generally assumed to have quite a fundamental influence on the nature and strength of their political partisanship. This chapter seeks to analyse Irish political partisanship in terms of some of these principal demographic and sociological variables. We have been able, furthermore, to analyse support for parties not only in relation to respondents' current class position but also in relation to their class of origin, so we can examine the relationship between respondents' experience of social mobility and their current political partisanship. The first part of this chapter, then, profiles support for the political parties by the main demographic and class variables outlined here.

Our data makes it possible for us to analyse support for the political parties not only with reference to the conventional sociological or demographic variables but also with regard to respondents' values. The role of values in structuring political partisanship is somewhat controversial. The claim has been made, for example, that value cleavages are beginning to supplant other kinds of political cleavages altogether: 'the younger and more educated voters in advanced industrial societies are beginning to define political competition more in terms of value cleavages than class cleavages'

(Dalton et al., 1984, 453). We accept that values may indeed be a source of political divisions. But we would also suggest that it is important not to 'exaggerate the contrast between values and interests or between education and occupation' (Heath et al., 1985, 66). In the second part of this chapter, therefore, we first analyse the composition of those who hold the values under discussion in terms of age, education, and class, before going on to investigate the ways in which these value dimensions are associated with support for each of the political parties.

Our discussion of how values are related to political partisanship begins with a discussion of respondents' identification of themselves as being either on the left or on the right. People tend to have rather broad notions of what it means to be on the left or on the right, and while the terms tend to be used quite loosely, there does seem to be a generally shared agreement on what it involves on particular issues. We discovered four principal dimensions associated with political partisanship in ways that are relatively independent of one another, the details of which will be discussed later on. The first of these is a measure of economic values of a left and right character, the most conventional and, in a comparative context, the most familiar dimension. The second is a measure of attitudes towards public morality and sexual morality issues. This is not reducible to, or at all strongly associated with, the economic dimension but cuts across it. The third dimension is the measure of confidence in various establishment institutions, which is also discussed in chapter 5. The fourth dimension is a measure of 'postmaterialism'. This is a value orientation that in other European countries is strongly associated with concerns arising from the 'new political agenda', particularly environmental or 'green' issues, although it turned out to have a more diffuse meaning in the Irish context. The relationship between postmaterialist concerns and issues of an economic left-right character has been disputed; in our study postmaterialism has its own independent effect on partisanship. Each of these four value orientations has a bearing on support for political parties. We outline how these measures are constructed, then discuss what they explain about the ways in which support for parties is structured.

THE SOCIAL BASES OF POLITICAL PARTISANSHIP

Many of the seminal ideas organising the comparative European debates about the social bases of political partisanship originate with the work of Lipset and Rokkan (1967). They argued that European societies are characterised by political allegiances that emerged in the era of state formation. Comparable processes were at work throughout Europe, although the depth and impact of waves of conflict, and the interaction of the allegiances thus generated, vary widely. The 'national revolution' gave rise to two sorts of political cleavage. The first is that of centre versus periphery, where the rise to primacy of the metropolitan state marginalised other regional identities, which were often marked by linguistic or other cultural differences. The second involves a conflict between church and state, chiefly found in countries with large Catholic populations. The Industrial Revolution gave rise to two cleavages with an economic character, one involving an opposition between agrarian and urban or industrial interests, the other involving what in many countries may be the most familiar basis of political cleavage, that of employers versus employees, or middle class versus working class. This schema has proved to be very valuable indeed in mapping the cleavage structure and social bases of political partisanship throughout European societies.

The relationship between social class and party preference in Ireland is very weak by comparison with that in other western European countries. For some, as Laver (1992, 359) notes, the reaction is to see Irish politics as wholly *sui generis*, 'quite out of the European mainstream.' Whyte (1974), attempting to apply the Lipset-Rokkan cleavage framework to the Irish party system, was led to conclude that Ireland had handled each of the four conflicts in quite exceptional ways which were not amenable to analysis in comparative terms. He concluded that Ireland was a case of 'politics without social bases.'

However, there has been a growing tendency in more recent years to move towards identifying points of comparability between the Irish experience and that of other European countries. 'The key words here are "Europeanisation", "modernisation", and "secularisation" within interpretations which see Irish peculiarities as the hangover from an increasingly distant and irrelevant past' (Mair, 1992, 383). Increasing sophistication in research techniques and a more refined approach to identifying social classes has revealed a

rather greater degree of patterning than previously suspected—
'politics with some social bases' (Laver, 1987).

The distinctiveness of Ireland's experiences have been put more
firmly into a comparative context by political scientists and political
historians. Several have focused on the formative years of the state
to explain the party system, drawing on the notion that the allegiances mobilised when the mass of the electorate was enfranchised
resulted in a 'freezing' of the party system (Lipset and Rokkan,
1967). Garvin (1974, 1981), for example, has argued that Ireland is
not so much a deviant case as an extreme one. He has drawn attention to the formative role of nationalism and the location of the
entire party system within the problematic arising from relations
between 'core' and 'periphery'—where the definition of the boundaries
of the independent state was itself a contested issue. The minority
status of the Labour Party has been interpreted by some as a consequence of its failure to stand in the crucial mobilising election of 1918
(Farrell, 1969), and attention has been drawn to the difficulties it
experienced in coping with the divisive issue of nationalism
(Gallagher, 1985, 70). But given the small size of the working class
and the dominant influence of conservative Catholic values in the
early decades of the state's existence, some have suggested that its
survival in any form was not to be taken for granted (Garvin,
1981, 149).

The period during which political allegiances were fully mobilised
has been subject to scrutiny. Rather than identifying a single mobilising election that established the shape of the party system, Sinnott
(1984), among others, has identified the shaping of the party system
as a cumulative process, lasting from 1918 until 1932.

Lipset and Rokkan (1967) hypothesised that party systems became
'frozen' during the period of mass mobilisation arising from full
enfranchisement. This seems particularly credible in the Irish case in
view of the dominance of the two main parties over time. Fianna Fáil
and Fine Gael together took 85 per cent of the vote in 1982, compared with the combined total of 80 per cent achieved by Fianna Fáil
and Cumann na nGaedheal in 1932 (Mair, 1985, 8). However, during
the intervening fifty years there had been considerable flux in the
party system. New parties, such as Clann na Talmhan and Clann na
Poblachta, enjoyed some degree of success before eventually dis-
appearing. Fianna Fáil's dominance did not escape challenge, and
coalition government forced it into opposition from time to time. The
fortunes of Fine Gael fluctuated; indeed by the end of the 1940s the

party appeared to many to be in terminal decline (Mair, 1987). Moreover, although the Labour Party experienced a steady rise in its support during the 1960s, it dropped again in the 1970s.

Thus the apparent stability or freezing of the party system compared at two moments conceals a great deal of movement in between. And while the alignment of support for the three main parties seemed steady enough during the 1960s and 1970s to warrant the term 'a two-and-a-half party system' (Farrell, 1970), generalisation subsequently became more problematic. The possibility of coalition between Fine Gael and the Labour Party in 1973 meant that the long-term dominance of Fianna Fáil could no longer be taken for granted, and indeed every election after 1969 saw a change of Government. Most strikingly, during the 1980s Fianna Fáil proved unable to form a single-party majority administration. The politics of coalition formation was extended to include almost all parties in the political system.

Given that the lines of division between parties did not follow the contours familiar in other European systems, the allegiances that ensued came to be interpreted by some as the result of party identification and traditional family loyalties. Voting is seen in this view largely as an expression of identity arising from a complex process of socialisation (Laver and Marsh, 1992, 102).

But party systems are not merely the passive outcome of social cleavages and socialisation processes. Parties also respond actively to changes in their social and economic circumstances. Although the differences between the two largest parties, Fianna Fáil and Fine Gael, originated in the Civil War and the responses of their respective precursors to the establishment of the independent state, nationalist issues have long ceased to be a major divisive factor between them. The parties have altered their appeal and their policy stance to respond to a changing electorate (Mair, 1979, 1987). Success and failure within the system were not predetermined but were a consequence of party choices and strategies, one of which was certainly the successful mobilisation of national sentiment. But increasingly, in Ireland as in other democratic countries, economic performance and especially the level of unemployment has assumed a dominant position in determining political popularity (Borooah and Borooah, 1990).

Nevertheless, support for political parties was never quite as unstructured as one might expect from Whyte's (1974) summary account of it as 'politics without social bases.' Whyte based his conclusion on the fact that social factors could explain only 3 per cent of the variance in partisanship based on a contrast between support for Fianna Fáil and the combined support for Fine Gael and the Labour Party. However, much sharper variation would have been produced had Fianna Fáil been compared with either of the other main parties, or had they mainly been compared with each other. Fianna Fáil has tended to draw support from among different classes in a manner that justifies its description as a 'catch-all' party, while support for Fine Gael and the Labour Party has tended to be more sharply differentiated in class terms. The social patterning of preferences is a good deal more predictable than it would be if politics really had 'no social bases' (Laver, 1986, 196).

In pursuing the issue of the nature of the influences on political partisanship, we wish to take advantage of a number of opportunities afforded by the data available in the European Values Study. First we will look at variations in party preference by education and social class, taking class origins as well as current class into account. This analysis produces some interesting results, which help to explain the distinctive spread of support that Fianna Fáil has enjoyed and also raise the possibility that it might not be able to maintain this spread much longer. We then extend our analysis beyond the conventional socio-demographic indicators that are most commonly used to map out political partisanship to investigate the extent of value differences associated with support for different parties. We isolate a relatively small number of values that are especially good discriminators of partisanship, and we look at the ways in which they combine in influencing the allegiance of respondents to different political parties. We think we have provided some interesting new insights, not only into the composition of party support but also into the network of value commitments within which the parties compete.

Social class and party preferences
In the European Values Survey, respondents were asked, 'If there was a general election tomorrow, which party would you vote for?' Those who responded 'Don't know' were asked, 'Which party appeals to you most?' Information from both of these questions was combined to produce an indicator of party preference. It was possible to establish such a preference for 896 of our 1,000 respondents.

The social class variables employed in our analysis are those used by the Central Statistics Office. The categories are as follows:

Social class 1: Higher professional and managerial, proprietors, and farmers owning 200 acres or more.

Social class 2: Lower professional and managerial, proprietors, and farmers owning 100–199 acres.

Social class 3: Other non-manual, and farmers owning 50–99 acres.

Social class 4: Skilled manual, and farmers owning 30–49 acres.

Social class 5: Semi-skilled manual, and farmers owning less than 30 acres.

Social class 6: Unskilled manual.

Unlike the market research social grade classifications that have been employed in most analyses of voting patterns, these class categories are formed by aggregating information relating to a highly detailed set of occupational codes and by making use of information concerning employment status. Thus, the schema should offer greater possibilities of detecting whatever variation may exist in party preference associated with social class.

Farmers are assigned to a class category on the basis of farm size. However, in our subsequent analysis we will take into account the impact of being a farmer *per se.* Our overall conclusions regarding the impact of social class on political partisanship are unaffected by whether we exclude farmers or not. In fact our results show that the variation that is of interest to us is largely captured by a three-way class schema that distinguishes:

(i) professional and managerial (and farmers with 100+ acres);

(ii) intermediate non-manual and skilled manual (and farmers with 30–99 acres);

(iii) semi-skilled and unskilled manual (and farmers with less than 30 acres).

This outcome is particularly interesting in that it supports the view that there is no significant cleavage between white-collar and blue-collar employees in terms of political partisanship. Married women have been allocated to their husband's class since we do not possess the information to implement satisfactory alternative procedures.

In table 6.1 we show the distribution of party preference by this classification. Perhaps the first point to note is that our results show Fianna Fáil with an extremely high level of support, at 52 per cent. This result, however, is quite consistent with those arising from opinion polling conducted by market research companies in the second half of 1990. In comparison with a poll conducted by the Market Research Bureau of Ireland in October 1990, our results slightly overestimate the Fianna Fáil vote and slightly underestimate the Labour Party vote. The results for all other parties are almost identical. Thus our survey captures Fianna Fáil at what was for them a peak level of support. Why the fall from this level to a figure of 40 per cent in the 1992 election should have been more dramatic than previous experience of discrepancies between opinion polls and election outcomes would have suggested is unclear, and undoubtedly due primarily to political explanations.

TABLE 6.1 *Party preference, by class*

	Professional & managerial %	Intermediate non-manual & skilled manual %	Semi-skilled & unskilled manual %	Total %
Fianna Fáil	49	54	56	52
Fine Gael	31	23	14	23
Labour	6	7	13	8
Workers' Party*	1	4	6	4
Progressive Democrats	5	5	2	4
Green	5	4	3	4
Other	4	3	3	3

*The Workers' Party ceased to exist in this form in 1991; its successor parties are Democratic Left and a considerably smaller Workers' Party.

The class effects evident in table 6.1 are quite consistent with earlier election studies. Fianna Fáil shows all the marks of being a 'catch-all' party. While there is a slight tendency for Fianna Fáil support to decline as one moves up the class scale, the difference between the upper and lower figures remains a modest seven percentage points. Concentration on Fianna Fáil, however, obscures other significant class effects on party preference. Fine Gael support is over twice as high, at 31 per cent, in the professional and managerial class as in the non-skilled manual class. The Progressive Democrat vote is also relatively low among the latter class, while support for the Labour Party and Workers' Party is strongest there. One way to bring out the nature of the social class effect is to treat Fianna Fáil for the moment as *sui generis* and to look, as we do in table 6.2, at class differences in voting for Fine Gael or Progressive Democrat versus Labour Party or Workers' Party.

TABLE 6.2 *Percentage voting Fine Gael or Progressive Democrats and Labour or Workers' Party, by class*

	Professional & managerial	Intermediate manual & skilled manual	Semi-skilled & unskilled manual
	%	%	%
(A) Fine Gael/ Progressive Democrats	36	28	17
(B) Labour Party/ Workers' Party	6	11	19
(C) Odds of A v. B	6.0	2.5	0.8

Those in the professional and managerial class are six times more likely to vote for the parties of the right than those of the left, the proportions being 36 and 6 per cent, respectively. For the intermediate class this drops to 2.5:1, with the relevant proportions being 28 and 11 per cent. Finally, among the non-skilled manual respondents the odds drop to less than one, and support for the Labour Party or Workers' Party, at 19 per cent, is just slightly higher than for Fine Gael and the Progressive Democrats.

Our analysis confirms Mair's contention (1992, 393) that 'while the Irish left is far from being composed of *parties of the working class,* in that the Labour Party and the Workers' Party win only a small minority of working class support, however defined, it is nevertheless in large part composed of *working class parties.*'

While farmers have been incorporated in our class analysis in accordance with farm size, and we can find little evidence of a pure farming effect once we have taken account of other factors, the patterns of partisanship comparing farming with non-farming households are of substantial intrinsic interest. The most fruitful way in which to pursue this appears to be to focus on the status of the chief earner. In table 6.3 we distinguish between non-farm households, farm households with less than fifty acres, and those with fifty acres or more. In view of the relatively small numbers in the farming category, the party classification has been aggregated so as to distinguish between Fianna Fáil, Fine Gael, Labour Party or Workers' Party, and all others.

TABLE 6.3 *Party preference, by farm status of chief earner*

	Chief earner		
	Non-farmer	Farmer, less than 50 acres	Farmer, 50 acres or more
	%	%	%
Fianna Fáil	51	57	61
Fine Gael	23	20	34
Labour/Workers' Party	15	2	2
Others	11	21	3

Fianna Fáil support rises gradually as we move from non-farm to large-farm households, where six out of ten respondents opt for Fianna Fáil. The relative advantage of Fine Gael, though, is entirely concentrated in the larger farm category. Among this group one in three respondents is a Fine Gael supporter, whereas for all others the figures only just rise above one in five. For the left there is a straightforward contrast between farm and non-farm households, with the respective figures being 2 and 15 per cent. The other interesting feature of the table is the extent of the difference between small and large-farm households in the degree to which their support is monopolised by Fianna Fáil and Fine Gael. In the larger farm households 95 per cent of the vote is distributed between these two parties, while for the smaller farm households the figure is much lower, at 77 per cent. In the latter households there appears to be a significant minority who are disillusioned with the two major parties but who are not attracted to the left.

It has been observed that what is unusual about Irish politics is not that class has only a modest impact but that everything else has even less impact (Gallagher, 1985). By 1990 this turns out not to be entirely true. Other factors, though, have rather different kinds of effects than class. Thus, as is clear from table 6.4, urban location, by which we mean a town or city with a population of more than 2,000, makes it much less likely that one will support Fianna Fáil or Fine Gael and substantially more probable that one will opt for the Labour Party, the Workers' Party, or the Green Party. Eighty-five per cent of those in the rural areas express a preference for one of the two major parties, compared with 68 per cent in the urban areas.

For the alternative groupings the respective proportions are 9 and 21 per cent. Thus in rural areas the odds of voting for one of the Civil War parties rather than the left or Green parties is over nine to one, but in the urban areas it drops to close to three to one.

TABLE 6.4 *Party preference, by urban v. rural location*

	Urban %	Rural %
Fianna Fáil	47	58
Fine Gael	21	27
Labour	10	6
Workers' Party	7	1
Progressive Democrats	4	4
Green Party	6	2
Sinn Féin	0	1
Other	5	2

Age, education, and party preference
Looking at the profile of party support by age and education proves even more revealing. Age bears a clear relationship to partisanship, as shown in table 6.5. Neither the Fine Gael vote nor, surprisingly, the Labour Party vote varies significantly across the age groups. Younger respondents, however, are significantly less likely to vote for Fianna Fáil. Support for the party declines from over 60 per cent in the over-60 category to just over 40 per cent in the 18–29 category. On the other hand, younger respondents are more likely to support the Workers' Party and Green Party and, in the case of those under forty-five, the Progressive Democrats.

A somewhat similar pattern emerges for education, as set out in table 6.6. In this case, however, Workers' Party support shows no significant variation. The parties whose support varies strongly in relation to education and that attract the support of disproportionate numbers of the highly educated are the Green Party, independents, and, particularly, the Progressive Democrats. Twenty-three per cent of those with higher education choose such options, compared with 5 per cent of those with primary education. Correspondingly, support for Fianna Fáil declines dramatically as education increases. Six out of ten of those with a Primary Certificate or less supported

Fianna Fáil, compared with less than four out of ten of those with third-level education.

TABLE 6.5 *Party preference, by age*

	18–29 %	30–44 %	45–59 %	60+ %
Fianna Fáil	41	53	54	61
Fianna Gael	23	21	25	26
Labour	9	9	9	7
Workers' Party	8	3	4	1
Progressive Democrats	4	8	2	1
Green Party	9	4	3	1
Sinn Féin	3	1	0	1
Independents & other	3	3	4	2

TABLE 6.6 *Party preference, by education*

	Primary Cert. %	Intermediate or Group Cert. %	Leaving Cert. %	Third level %
Fianna Fáil	61	53	47	37
Fianna Gael	20	25	26	25
Labour	9	7	7	11
Workers' Party	4	4	3	4
Progressive Democrats	2	3	5	8
Green Party	1	4	7	9
Sinn Féin	1	2	2	1
Other	2	2	4	6

In order to understand adequately the effects of age and education, it is necessary to look at their joint effects. This we do in table 6.7, simplifying our analysis by distinguishing between those under and over thirty and between those with less than a Leaving Certificate and those with a Leaving Certificate or third-level education. The most striking feature of the table is the way in which age and education come together to influence the likelihood of supporting Fianna Fáil. For those with at least a Leaving Certificate, age has very little effect on the likelihood of opting for Fianna Fáil. Among those with less than a Leaving Certificate the effect of age is quite dramatic. Among those over thirty, almost two-thirds of those with less than a Leaving Certificate support Fianna Fáil, while for those under thirty it drops to one in three.

TABLE 6.7 *Party preference, by age and education*

	Less than Leaving Cert.		Leaving Cert.		Third level	
	Under 30 %	30 or over %	Under 30 %	30 or over %	Under 30 %	30 or over %
Fianna Fáil	32	62	49	47	39	35
Fine Gael	20	22	26	26	21	29
Labour	14	8	5	8	11	12
Workers' Party	15	3	5	2	5	3
Progressive Democrats	2	3	3	6	7	9
Green Party	9	1	6	7	16	3
Sinn Féin	5	1	3	1	0	1
Other	3	2	4	4	2	9

Among the young and less educated, support for the left is relatively high, with almost 30 per cent supporting the Labour Party or Workers' Party; a further 9 per cent support the Green Party, 5 per cent support Sinn Féin, and 3 per cent support independents. In fact among this group, support for Fianna Fáil and Fine Gael only slightly exceeds that for all others. For the older less-educated group, on the other hand, support for the two largest parties reaches 84 per cent. Among the younger third-level educated group, support for the Labour Party or the Workers' Party, although not as high as among the least-educated groups, is, at 16 per cent, higher than among the Leaving Certificate respondents. Thus the left receives its support among the young from those with least and those with most education, although the latter are much less favourably disposed towards the Workers' Party. The contrast between the young and the old among those with third-level education does not relate primarily to support for the left but to support for the Green Party. A mere 3 per cent of those over thirty express such a preference, but this rose to 16 per cent among those under thirty.

Our analysis shows that in addition to class effects on the choice between Fine Gael or Progressive Democrats and the Labour Party or Workers' Party, strong age and education effects exist that cannot be adequately captured by class distinctions and that do not appear to reflect conventional left-right preferences. Young, poorly educated respondents do lean towards the left-wing parties, while also displaying significant support for the Green Party. Among those with third-level education, 'defection' from the Civil War parties is just as likely to be towards the Green Party as to the traditional left, while the Progressive Democrats also enjoy not insignificant support.

The social bases of the Fianna Fáil vote

Fianna Fáil is different from any of the other parties in the level of support it attracts right across the class spectrum. There are two aspects to the formation of this cross-class appeal that have not been investigated in detail to date: the influence of education and that of social mobility. In both cases we can see evidence of why Fianna Fáil has been so successful in the past. However, both features of Fianna Fáil support would tend to point to an emerging difficulty for the party in maintaining such high levels of cross-class support.

We have seen that while social class is not a very good predictor of the probability of voting for Fianna Fáil, education has a pronounced effect. But younger people with lower levels of education are considerably less likely to support Fianna Fáil than the older less-educated respondents. If their levels of support were comparable there would be a more pronounced class alignment in the Fianna Fáil vote. It appears from the evidence of this survey that Fianna Fáil is failing to attract or to retain an element of its support that historically has been quite important: that of younger, less-educated people, especially in the lower social classes.

We also find that class origins have a substantially stronger effect on Fianna Fáil support than does current class, a relationship that is not apparent for any of the other parties. This can be seen from table 6.8. Reading across the rows of this table, we find that whatever class one has originated from, there is no very clear relationship between current class situation and support for Fianna Fáil. But looking down the columns we see that within each class at present, support for Fianna Fáil is greatest among those with the most modest class origins. This is most pronounced among those in the professional and managerial class and in the non-skilled manual class. While 40 per cent support Fianna Fáil among those who were born into the professional and managerial class and remained there, the figure is 63 per cent for those who have moved from manual working-class backgrounds into this class. Similarly, while 62 per cent of those who have been intergenerationally stable in the non-skilled manual class are Fianna Fáil supporters, the figure is only 43 per cent for those who have been downwardly mobile from the professional and managerial class. In each case those with origins in the intermediate class also occupy an intermediate position in terms of Fianna Fáil support.

TABLE 6.8   *Probability of supporting Fianna Fáil, by class origins, controlling for class*

Class origins	Professional & managerial %	Social Class Intermediate non-manual & skilled manual %	Semi-skilled & unskilled manual %
Professional & managerial	40	54	43
Intermediate non-manual & skilled manual	53	52	52
Semi-skilled & unskilled manual	63	58	62

Fianna Fáil has thus been particularly successful in retaining the allegiance of people who have been upwardly socially mobile. Up to quite recently, education was not a prerequisite of upward social mobility in Ireland (Hout, 1989; Breen and Whelan, 1993). Rates of participation in education beyond the compulsory minimum age were relatively low until after the introduction of free secondary education in 1967. Yet during the 1960s and 1970s, economic growth and faster industrial and social development meant that the social structure changed quite rapidly, creating many new opportunities for upward mobility (Breen et al., 1990; Whelan et al., 1992). The transformation of the social structure continues in much the same direction, with a decline in agricultural and less skilled manual occupations and a growth in professional and managerial and more highly skilled industrial occupations. But the rate of change is likely to be less dramatic for the foreseeable future and the opportunities for upward mobility consequent on structural change relatively fewer. In addition, opportunities for upward social mobility are likely to depend to a greater extent in future on the possession of minimum levels of educational qualifications. There are two reasons for this. One is that the kinds of jobs where opportunities tend to be available increasingly require some sort of technical competence. The second is quite simply that, as the general level of educational participation increases, the entry requirements for various kinds of employment are correspondingly driven upwards.

Upward social mobility is likely to be strongly associated with higher rather than lower educational qualifications. It would appear, on the basis of trends to date, that the upwardly socially mobile in future are less likely to support Fianna Fáil than in the past. Furthermore, for those with low levels of educational qualifications, immobility is now much more likely to be associated with unemployment and less likely to involve employment in traditional occupations. One consequence of this is the much lower level of support for Fianna Fáil among poorly qualified younger respondents. Two of the pools of support that had previously been favourable to Fianna Fáil are now considerably less likely to continue to be so.

It must, of course, be noted that we are in no sense making a prediction about an ineluctable tendency. We are drawing attention rather to a shift in the basis and composition of support for Fianna Fáil. Support for Fianna Fáil may have grown more contingent in the categories we have identified, among groups who may once have shown considerable party loyalty and little defection to other parties. But that support could still be recovered through a change in party strategy and policy orientation. Support for a political party is not socially determined, but represents an interplay between the disposition towards a party among a particular social group and the policies and priorities adopted by the party in order to elicit the support of that group.

To a significant degree, as Mair (1992) has argued, the weakness of the left in Ireland has to be explained not in terms of sociological conditions such as the peculiarities of the class structure or some failure of class awareness but in more directly political terms. The political strategies of the parties of the left have long been constrained by the massive success enjoyed by Fianna Fáil. From its earliest years, Fianna Fáil succeeded in mobilising a coalition of support that spanned not only diverse social classes but also diverse value positions. It has accomplished profound changes in its ideological orientation towards economic policy without sacrificing electoral support (Bew, Hazelkorn, and Patterson, 1989). Furthermore, Fianna Fáil has, 'for ideological reasons, as well as more pragmatic partisan and electoral reasons sought to stress the need for the nation to be united—socially as well as territorially' (Mair, 1992, 406). Fianna Fáil has stressed the need to achieve economic growth with a minimum of conflict. This vision extends beyond Fianna Fáil and imbues the political culture more generally, making it antipathetic towards the expression of distributive and other conflicts in party politics.

We turn now to explore some of the value orientations that shape people's political partisanship, and examine how they inter-relate in the choice of one's preferred party. Again we stress that these relationships represent broad associations at work beneath the flux of the political process. They cannot automatically be used to 'read off' the level of support for parties at any particular moment. Neither can the relationship between values and parties be taken as deterministic associations. They are not immutable. The relationship between values and party support could change in response to parties' own strategies. The pattern of value orientations itself could alter over time. We are thus charting a framework for understanding rather than a fixed calculus of associations.

VALUE ORIENTATIONS AND POLITICAL PARTISANSHIP

Ireland may lack clear-cut social cleavages of the sort that, with whatever qualifications, readily account for party allegiances in other European countries. Yet support for parties is in fact a good deal more structured than this might suggest. In addition to the socio-demographic variables already discussed, we have analysed five dimensions of value orientation that have emerged as particularly useful in explaining political partisanship. Each of these adds something extra to the explanation: they are not simply reducible to one another, though they are somewhat associated with one another. They are as follows:

(1)   left versus right self-placement;
(2)   left versus right on economic issues;
(3)   liberalism on issues of sexual morality;

(4)   confidence in establishment institutions;
(5)   postmaterialism.

Left-right self-placement

The first dimension is the respondents' self-placement on a left-right scale. The European Values Survey in 1990 posed the following question, with no further elaboration: 'In political matters, people talk of "the Left" and "the Right". How would you place your views on this scale, generally speaking?' Respondents, therefore, interpreted the question in whatever way they wished. They were presented with a ten-point scale running from left to right: in table 6.9, 10 represents extreme left and 1 represents extreme right.

TABLE 6.9 *Distribution of self-assignment to the left or right: comparison of Irish and European distributions*

		Ireland %	European average %
Left	10	1	4
	9	1	4
	8	4	13
	7	6	13
	6	30	29
	5	25	14
	4	10	10
	3	12	8
	2	7	2
Right	1	5	3
Left average score		5	6

We compare the distribution of the Irish responses with those of the European sample as a whole. The Irish are distinctly less left-wing. If we take scores of 6 to 10 as constituting the left-wing half of the spectrum, 42 per cent of the Irish respondents can be classified as on the left, compared with 63 per cent of Europeans. Furthermore, the Irish responses are very much concentrated in the centre, with 55 per cent of them opting for categories 5 and 6; they also show a much greater tendency to opt for a position just right of centre. This is consistent with the findings from the 1981 European

Values Survey, where a plurality of Irish respondents identified themselves as 'slightly to the right of centre' (Fogarty et al., 1984). Irish participants in the 1990 survey also have a tendency to opt for the more extreme right-wing categories more often than the European average: 23 per cent of them, compared with 13 per cent of the European sample. Their tendency to avoid the corresponding left-wing categories is more pronounced: only 7 per cent of Irish respondents, compared with 21 per cent of the European group as a whole, are found in these categories.

In subsequent analyses, to facilitate presentation of our results, we have dichotomised the left-right self-assignment scale. The substantive conclusions we present, though, are not affected by whether we employ this dichotomy or the full range of scores.

Table 6.10 shows that self-assignment to the left varies sharply by age group, with over half of those under thirty placing themselves on the left, compared with just about one-third of those aged forty-five or over. Age is in fact the only substantial influence on such self-assignment, with education, social class and urban versus rural location having relatively little impact. That this variable is capturing something important is illustrated by the way it is associated with party preference, as set out in table 6.11.

TABLE 6.10 *Percentage assigning themselves to the left, by age group*

	%
18–29	54
30–44	43
45–59	36
60+	34

Only one in three Fianna Fáil supporters choose to describe themselves as on the left, a figure that is only slightly exceeded by those identifying with Fine Gael. The figure rises slightly to just above two-fifths for the Progressive Democrats. We then find that 56 per cent of Green Party supporters identify themselves as being on the left, two-thirds of Labour Party supporters, three-quarters of supporters of the Workers' Party, and nine out of ten Sinn Féin supporters. This clear pattern of progressive increase in left identification across the spread of parties suggests that there is more to be said about the values that structure support for parties.

TABLE 6.11 *Percentage assigning themselves to the left, by party preference*

	%
Sinn Féin	89
Workers' Party	74
Labour	67
Green Party	56
Progressive Democrats	42
Independent & Others	41
Fine Gael	38
Fianna Fáil	34

What constitutes 'left' and 'right'?

The most obvious next step is to enquire into what people mean when they speak of left and right. These are quite loosely defined terms and tend to be applied in quite different policy contexts. To be on the left or right has one meaning when choosing between policies on the management of the economy; but the terms are also often used on matters such as support for or opposition to legally available divorce or the degree of trust or scepticism displayed towards, for example, the judicial system. People tend to have a reasonably clear idea of what the policy options are in each case. A number of studies have confirmed empirically that the left-right dimension captures the spread of opinion across a variety of issue domains (see, for example, Sani and Sartori, 1983, 310–16). This is not to suggest that 'the variety of conflict dimensions ... can be squeezed into a single dimension without loss' (ibid., 314); but the imagery of left and right plays an important part in 'organising and simplifying a complex political reality' (Inglehart, 1984, 37; 1990, 287–8). As Inglehart (1990, 293) further notes, 'the concept is sufficiently general that as new issues arise they usually can be fitted into the framework. The specific kinds of change may vary but the question of more or less equality is usually involved whether it is social classes, nationalities, races, or sexes.' The question remains of what the dominant values are that might lead respondents to identify themselves as being on the left or on the right: what the leading values are that shape their partisan identification.

One approach to this issue is to think of policy dimensions as constituting a space within which parties might be situated. Laver and Hunt (1992) estimated the position of political parties in each western European country on a number of policy dimensions. This was achieved through a large-scale survey of party policy positions as characterised by expert informants. The informants were asked to rank a variety of policy dimensions in terms of their salience for each party. Two independent dimensions turned out to be of overwhelming importance in every case: an economic policy dimension ('taxes versus spending') and a social policy dimension (policies on matters such as abortion and laws relating to homosexual behaviour). These dimensions were the dominant ones for Ireland too. A Northern Ireland policy dimension was also rated as being highly salient. However, party positions on Northern Ireland policy are closely related to positions on the social and moral policy dimensions (Laver, 1992, 368). Laver (1992, 376) concludes that there seems to be nothing peculiar about the ideological configuration of Irish parties: 'They seem to fit very well with one of the major European party constellations—the Mediterranean model that is characterized by the confrontation between a divided left, on the one hand, and a powerful pole of populist nationalism, on the other—a constellation that is typically found among the Catholic countries of Southern Europe.' What is unusual is that about 80 per cent of the electorate is to be found supporting parties that appear to occupy the policy space involving right-wing positions on the two basic policy dimensions.

Our starting point, however, is with the voters, not the parties. We investigated the economic policy dimension and the social policy dimension and found that both are in fact quite independent of one another and do indeed produce rather different configurations of support for parties.

Besides these two, a third value orientation pertaining to left and right—confidence in establishment institutions—derives from a rather different set of concerns. We were interested in attitudes to authority, following on from our investigation of the degree of authoritarianism in political culture and evidence for the emergence of greater support for liberal values. This is not the same as the social policy dimension concerning liberalism on sexual morality. Rather it is a value orientation concerning greater or lesser degrees of support for established authorities.

We investigated one further value dimension, that of 'postmaterialism'. Rather than identifying this value orientation with the left-right scale, we investigated it because of recent claims in the literature that left-right electoral cleavages based on economic issues were likely to be in decline and that new value dimensions would replace them. Although we have already included some value orientations that are not economic in character, we found it worth while to include an item on postmaterialism. But rather than indicating that the politics of distributive conflict has been superseded, as the postmaterialist thesis would argue, we find the emergence of new value concerns alongside and intertwined with the other value dimensions. It is to the discussion of each of these value dimensions that we now turn.

Economic left-right preferences
Our measure of left and right economic values combines three items relating to egalitarianism with a further three items that relate to a preference for collective versus individual solutions.

The first of these items in the measure of *egalitarianism* involves a question about distributive justice. Respondents were asked the following hypothetical question: 'Imagine two secretaries, of the same age, doing practically the same job. One finds out that the other earns £20 a week more than she does. The better paid secretary, however, is quicker, more efficient and more reliable at her job. In your opinion, is it fair or not fair that one secretary is paid more than the other?' Those who deemed it unfair were scored 1, while all others were scored 0.

The second element of the measure of egalitarianism concerns views about ownership structure. Respondents were asked to choose between the following options:

(i) The owners should run their business and appoint the managers.
(ii) The owners and employees should participate in the selection of managers.
(iii) The state should be the owner and appoint the managers.
(iv) The employees should own the business and should elect the managers.

The first response was scored 0, and all others were scored 1.

The third element of the egalitarianism measure concerns general attitudes to distributive outcomes. Respondents were asked to indicate their position on a ten-point scale, where 10 represented the statement 'Incomes should be made more equal' and 1 represented the statement 'There should be greater incentives for individual effort.' Those scoring between 1 and 5 were coded 0, and those scoring 6 to 10 were scored 1.

The three items measuring attitudes to *individual versus collective preferences* involved the same response format and the same scoring system. The alternatives were presented as follows:

Individuals should take more responsibility for providing for themselves.

v.

The state should take more responsibility to ensure that everyone is provided for.

People who are unemployed should have to take any job available or lose their unemployment benefits.

v.

People who are unemployed should have the right to refuse a job they do not want to do.

Competition is good. It stimulates people to work hard and develop new ideas.

v.

Competition is harmful. It brings out the worst in people.

Combining these six items gives us a six-item scale running from 0 to 6 on left-wing economic values. We have labelled those with scores of between 0 and 2 as right-wing on economic values and all others as left-wing. Sixty per cent of our respondents fall into the former category and 40 per cent into the latter.

The measures available in the European Values Study are not necessarily the best for our purposes. Several of these items no longer discriminate clearly between left and right party positions in many European countries, as confidence in the state's capacity to efficiently direct economic resources has diminished and as social-democratic parties have increasingly come to accept the parameters of the market economy. Our scale has a reliability coefficient of 0.48, which is somewhat lower than we would ideally like. But by combining different questions, none of which is entirely satisfactory, we find that we increase the level of reliability of our measure. Moreover, the consequence of working with a less reliable scale is that our analysis is likely to underestimate the impact of left-wing economic values on political partisanship; the true extent of their influence is likely to be greater than our analysis shows. Laver and Hunt (1992, 48), for example, found that their measure of the economic left-right dimension, based on party policy towards public ownership of business, was seen as very important by most of their respondents. They conclude that the traditional left-right dimension 'may be more important in Ireland than many traditional accounts suggest.' In fact on our current measure, in a comparative European context, the Irish left-wing economic values scores are only marginally below the average.

What, then, determines whether or not one has left-wing economic attitudes? Social class is an important factor. Only one-quarter of the professional and managerial class score 'high' on left-wing economic values, two-fifths of the intermediate class, and over half the non-skilled manual class.

TABLE 6.12 *Left-wing economic attitudes, by educational qualification and age: percentage left*

	18–29 %	30–44 %	45–59 %	60+ %
Primary Cert. or less	86	59	46	39
Intermediate or Group Cert.	63	35	28	35
Leaving Cert.	42	37	20	17
Third-level	40	24	25	8

Age and education have more modest influences, with the young and the better educated being more likely to express such views. The effects of age and education are cumulative, as we can see from table 6.12. Within each category it is the least educated who are most left-wing; but within each education category there are very sharp age differences, with conservatism increasing dramatically with age. The combined effects produce a situation where, among those under thirty with low levels of education, nine out of ten score high on left-wing economic values, while among those over sixty with a third-level education the corresponding figure is one in twelve. The combined effects of age and education result in rather different groups displaying unexpected similarities. Those aged between forty-five and fifty-nine with a Primary Certificate or less and those aged between eighteen and twenty-nine with a Leaving Certificate have over four out of ten of their members scoring high on this dimension.

'Social policy' values: liberalism on sexual morality
To measure the degree of support for, or opposition to, matters of public morality, we used a measure of liberalism with regard to

sexual morality. Respondents were asked the extent to which, on a scale of 1 (for never) to 10 (for always), the following could be justified:

  (i)   married men or women having an affair;
 (ii)   sex under the legal age of consent;
(iii)   homosexuality;
(iv)   divorce;
 (v)   abortion.

An average of these items was taken in order to construct a measure of the extent to which respondents were liberal on issues relating to sexual morality. As discussed in chapter 5, these items are not necessarily the best indicators for our purposes, although we are more confident than in the case of left-right economic attitudes that the individual items are indeed measuring the same underlying factor. We have dichotomised this variable so that 50 per cent of our respondents fall above and 50 per cent below the cut-off point, and in our subsequent analysis we shall refer to them as the groups that are left-wing or right-wing on issues relating to sexual morality.

Social class is related to liberalism on sexual morality in a directly opposite fashion to left-wing economic values. From table 6.13 it is clear that, unlike economic values, in matters of sexual morality it is the upper class who are most likely to adopt left-wing or liberal positions. Almost two out of three of this group are found in the left-wing category, compared with four out of ten of the lowest class. The upper-class group is more likely to express liberal values on sexual morality, compared with just over four out of ten in the lowest class.

However, age produces the most dramatic variations in attitudes towards matters concerning sexual morality. As table 6.14 indicates, over two-thirds of those aged under thirty score high. The figure drops only slightly in the 30–44 age group but declines rapidly in the older categories, reaching a level of less than one in four in the over-60 category. Education has little impact among the older group, but otherwise within each age category the more educated are substantially more liberal. Thus, among those under thirty the proportion classified as scoring high on this factor rises from just over one in three of those with a Primary Certificate or less to over four-fifths of those with a third-level education. The pattern of relationships between class, age and education on this value dimension is very

TABLE 6.13 *Left-wing economic values and liberalism on sexual morality, by class*

	Economic values % left	Sexual morality % left
Professional & managerial	25	64
Intermediate non-manual & skilled manual	40	45
Non-skilled manual	54	43

much in line with research findings in other countries. Heath et al. (1985, 64–6), for example, identified a cluster of liberal values in Britain, support for which cut across the economic left-right dimension and its strong class patterning. They identified education as the basis of support for these values, while cautioning that education and class are not of course entirely separable indicators.

TABLE 6.14 *Left-wing on sexual morality, by age group (percentage scoring left)*

	Percentage scoring left
18–29	67
30–44	61
45–59	46
60+	22

Confidence in establishment institutions
This measure is profiled in more detail in chapter 5 (see table 5.1). It comprises six items that deal with satisfaction with the church, parliament, the armed forces, the police, the legal system, and the civil service. We found that the level of confidence expressed in establishment institutions varies with age and level of education but that social class has no significant effect.

The determinants of left-right self-assignment
In table 6.15 we show the relationship between each of the left-wing value dimensions and left-right self-assignment and also the

TABLE 6.15 *Relationship between left-right self-assignment and left-right values: matrix of correlations*

	Left-right self-assignment	(European values in parentheses) Liberalism in sexual morality	Left-wing economic values	Lack of confidence in establishment institutions
Left-right self-assignment				
Sexual morality	0.26 (0.27)			
Economic values	0.19 (0.29)	0.01 (0.07)		
Lack of confidence in establishment institutions	0.32 (0.27)	0.36 (0.37)	0.09 (0.11)	

manner in which these values are associated with each other. The index of association is once again a correlation coefficient where the potential range of values runs from 1 where there is perfect association to 0 where the measures are completely independent. The results show that all three value dimensions are correlated with self-assignment. The correlation for economic values is slightly lower than for the other dimensions. This is in fact the only way in which the Irish pattern deviates from the overall European results, where all dimensions have almost identical associations with self-assignment. The Irish results also mirror the European ones in that the only substantial association between the value dimensions is that involving sexual morality and confidence in establishment institutions; indeed the Irish and European correlations are almost identical. Further analysis that takes into account the simultaneous impact of the dimensions suggests that values relating to sexual morality are equally good predictors of left-right self-assignment for Ireland and the European sample as a whole. Economic values turn out to be a better predictor in the Irish case, while lack of confidence in establishment institutions is somewhat more powerful in the overall European situation. The cumulative effect of the dimensions is very similar in both cases: for Ireland they explain 15 per cent of variation in left-right self-assignment, while the European figure is 17 per cent.

The foregoing analysis suggests that what is different about Ireland is not the nature of such values, or the manner in which they are related to each other, but simply the extent to which such values are held. In table 6.16 we compare the results for Ireland and Europe. With the exception of the self-assignment measure there is no obvious or natural cut-off point that distinguishes left from right. There is obviously then a degree of arbitrariness in the manner in which the labels 'left' and 'right' are assigned. This does not, however, invalidate the comparisons across the groups. From table 6.16 we can see that, as we have already shown, Irish respondents are less likely to assign themselves to the left. In addition it is apparent that, to the extent that this tendency is related to the values under discussion, it cannot be explained by differences in economic values. It is due, rather, to the fact that the Irish respondents are significantly less likely to hold liberal values in relation to sexual morality or to express lack of confidence in establishment institutions.

TABLE 6.16 *Extent of left-wing values: Ireland and Europe compared*

	Ireland %	Europe %
Self-assignment	42	60
Economic values	40	43
Sexual morality	50	75
Lack of confidence in establishment institutions	25	43

Postmaterialism
The final value orientation we investigate, with a view to using it to analyse political partisanship, is that of postmaterialism. This, it has been argued, is a value dimension that transcends the values associated with the economic left-right divide and gradually displaces them as the key determinants of political partisanship.

The term 'postmaterialism' is most closely associated with the work of Inglehart (1977, 1990), who argues that there is a long-run tendency for the pursuit of self-interest to reach a point of diminishing returns, and a corresponding tendency for other values to assume a more prominent role in shaping electoral behaviour. Inglehart argues that a cluster of socio-economic changes have given rise to these developments, including rising levels of education, the changing occupational structure, and the development of mass communication networks. But of particular importance in his view is the unprecedented prosperity enjoyed by western countries during the decade following the Second World War. The experience of material affluence by postwar generations, he argues, has socialised them into a different set of value orientations. These younger citizens are said to be freer to develop an interest in 'higher-order' issues, that is issues other than those related to production and distribution. Postmaterialist or 'quality of life' issues therefore come to the fore. Out of these value concerns are born the new social movements such as environmentalism, the women's movement, nuclear disarmament, and opposition to civil nuclear power (cf. Dalton, 1988).

Inglehart's work has been subject to extensive discussion and criticism (for example Marsh, 1977; Flanagan, 1982, 1987). First of all, it is far from clear that distributive conflict (always materialist in his view) will decline in the politics of the industrial societies in the predicted manner. Postmaterialist values are thought never to be motivated by self-interest, and materialist or distributive issues are thought always to be. This means that concern for an unpolluted and crime-free environment is by definition altruistic because post-materialist; distributive issues, including the politics of welfare state provision, are excluded from consideration as quality-of-life issues by the same definitional fiat. Secondly, the motivation for the transition from materialist values to postmaterialist is questionable. In his earlier work Inglehart (1977) relied on a distinctly crude theory of a hierarchy of needs. Younger people, having grown up in a climate of greater relative affluence than their parents, are assumed to be open to what he thinks of as higher-order motivations. However, progression from material wants to self-expressive needs is unlikely to be so easily compartmentalised. Moreover there is no empirical evidence for the distinctive socialising effects of 'formative affluence'. Inglehart has not taken adequate account of the advent of mass unemployment since the 1970s in his theory of motivation; his measures of post-materialism show no decline, although his theory would predict one. Thirdly, the independent role of education in inculcating more liberal values, quite apart from theories of motivation or socialisation, is not properly controlled for in Inglehart's analyses. Finally, the indicators of postmaterialism themselves are crude, involving as they do a forced choice between a short list of so-called materialist and post-materialist items.

Nevertheless it is undeniable that a variety of new normative concerns have arisen that are loosely grouped with more traditional

liberal values and that are not strongly located in the class structure (Heath et al., 1985, 64–6; 1991, 85–101, 186–99). Inglehart's
indicators have been incorporated into the European Values Survey, and, despite the shortcomings both of the theory and the
indicators, we have analysed the relevance of postmaterialism for
the determination of political partisanship, and we have indeed
found results worthy of discussion as a consequence.

Inglehart originally used the following question to identify postmaterialist citizens: 'There is a lot of talk these days about what
the course of this country should be for the next ten years. Which
one of these do you, yourself, consider most important? And which
would be the next most important?—

(i)   maintaining order in the nation;
(ii) giving people more say in important political decisions;
(iii) fighting rising prices;
(iv) protecting freedom of speech.'

The first and third responses were deemed to indicate materialist
values, the second and fourth postmaterialist. We can see that this
question is likely to be subject to fluctuating levels of reliability, even
as a crude measure of an opposition between value orientations, as
it is likely to vary with the salience of inflation in the economy.

Inglehart himself (1990, 131) has expanded the original four
items to improve the measurement of postmaterialism. The additional set of items is as follows:

A.
(i)   maintaining a high rate of economic growth;
(ii) making sure that this country has strong defence forces;
(iii) seeing that the people have more say in how things get
      decided at work and in their communities;
(iv) trying to make our cities and countryside more beautiful.
B.
(i)   maintaining a stable economy;
(ii) progress towards a less impersonal, more humane society;
(iii) the fight against crime;
(iv) progress towards a society where ideas are more important
      than money.

However, whether we work with the original question or the
expanded set of options, when we employ the suggested scoring

scheme we are unable to construct a satisfactory index. This holds true whether the criterion applied is consistency of responses across the different items or the existence of cross-national or socio-demographic variation consistent with theoretical assumptions underlying the measure.

We have therefore adopted a simpler scoring system, which does at least produce modest correlations between classifications based on each of the individual sets, although still leaving us with a level of reliability a great deal lower than we would like. We have concentrated simply on the respondents' first choice and have given a score of 1 when they choose either of the following postmaterialist-oriented items:

   (i) 'Seeing that the people have more say in how things get decided at work and in their communities' or 'Trying to make our cities and countryside more beautiful.'
  (ii) 'Giving people more say in important government decisions' or 'Protecting freedom of speech.'
 (iii) 'Progress towards a less impersonal, more humane society' or 'Progress towards a society where ideas are more important than money.'

This gives us a measure of postmaterialism running from 0 to 3. In fact, however, we consistently find that the most interesting contrasts are between those with scores of 3 and all others, i.e. between those who are 'consistently postmaterialist' and all others.

On this dichotomous measure, 11 per cent of the Irish sample emerge as 'postmaterialist', compared with 17 per cent of the European sample as a whole. The highest figure, of 22 per cent, is observed in the Netherlands, with West Germany, Italy and Belgium clustered at around 19 per cent. Figures even lower than the Republic of Ireland's are those for Northern Ireland, with 8 per cent, and Portugal, where the lowest figure of 5 per cent is observed.

We also observe, as is clear from table 6.17, a clear relationship between age and postmaterialism. Seventeen per cent of those aged under thirty fall into the postmaterialist category, but this gradually falls to 7 per cent among those aged forty-five or over.

It is necessary to consider whether the age effect provides unqualified support for Inglehart's theoretical formulation. Inglehart's approach (1990, 68–9) is based on two key hypotheses, a scarcity hypotheses and a socialisation hypothesis. The former, he notes, is

TABLE 6.17 *Postmaterialism, by age group and educational qualification*

	Less than Leaving Cert. %	Leaving Cert. %	Third level %	Total %
18–29	13	14	27	17
30–44	7	14	21	11
45+	6	10	14	7
Total	7	13	22	

similar to the principle of diminishing marginal utility in economic theory. Prolonged periods of high prosperity are expected to encourage the spread of postmaterialist values. However, it is exposure to such an environment in pre-adulthood that is seen to be crucial, on the assumption that the basic human personality structure tends to crystallise before adulthood. The hypothesis, as Inglehart (1990, 71) notes, implies 'that the unprecedented prosperity prevailing from the late 1940s until the early 1970s has led to the substantial growth in the proportion of postmaterialists among the public in advanced industrial societies.'

While any conclusion depends on the particular indicators chosen and precisely which age range is taken as the crucial pre-adult period, it would seem difficult to argue unequivocally that the 18–29 cohort were exposed to a more secure economic environment than the 30–44 cohort, or that whatever differences may have existed were as great as those between the latter and those aged 45 and over. The possibility certainly seems to exist that other influences, such as exposure to 'postmaterialist' ideas through the media and the independent influence of education, may be playing a significant role.

The evidence presented in table 6.17 supports the argument for the independent influence of education. Variation by educational level is sharp, rising from 7 per cent for those with less than a Leaving Certificate to almost double that for those with such a qualification and over treble for those with a third-level qualification. Education has this impact despite the complete absence of a class relationship. Furthermore, there is a general trend for the level of postmaterialism to rise with increased education within each age category. The cumulative effect of age and education is shown by the fact that while a mere 6 per cent of those aged forty-five or over with less than a Leaving Certificate can be classified as postmaterialist, this figure rises to 27 per cent for those aged under thirty with third-level education. That education is not simply serving as a proxy for a relatively prosperous pre-adult environment is shown by the fact that class origin is only weakly related to postmaterialism. It is also worth noting that observed urban versus rural differences are extremely modest. We therefore find much stronger support for age and education as predictors of post-materialist values than any experience of 'formative affluence' (cf. also Burklin, 1985, 1987).

In table 6.18 we have shown the trend across age groups for Ireland and the Netherlands. The overall European comparison provides a rather similar picture, but we have chosen the Netherlands to illustrate the point we wish to make, because it is the country with the highest level of postmaterialism. The largest difference between the countries, whether measured as an absolute percentage difference or as a ratio, occurs in the 30–44 age group. The smallest difference is observed in the youngest age group. Once again it seems more plausible to accord an independent role to educational expansion and the dissemination of ideas from the core to the periphery.

In order to explore further the meaning of our measure of postmaterialism, in table 6.19 we look at its relationship to the left-right dimensions discussed earlier. For both the European sample as a whole and the Irish respondents, the postmaterialism indicator is consistently associated with a left-wing position on the other dimensions, although in the Irish case the correlations are slightly lower. While the correlations are sufficiently low to justify retaining the postmaterialism measure as a separate dimension, it does seem to form part of a syndrome of left-wing concerns.

TABLE 6.18 *Postmaterialism, by age group: Ireland and Netherlands compared*

| | Percentage postmaterialist | |
	Ireland %	Netherlands %
18–29	17	25
30–44	11	29
45+	7	15

TABLE 6.19 *Relationship of postmaterialism to left-right dimensions*

	Correlation matrix	
	Ireland	European average
Left self-assignment	0.16	0.20
Left-wing economic values	0.08	0.16
Liberalism on sexual morality	0.12	0.21
Lack of confidence in establishment institutions	0.14	0.18

TABLE 6.20 *Support for civil rights and environmental movement, by 'postmaterialism'*

	Percentage strongly approving	
	Postmaterialist	All others
Ecology movement or nature movement	57	49
Anti-nuclear movement	58	50
Disarmament movement	58	48
Human rights movement	69	61
Women's movement	49	35
Anti-apartheid movement	71	54

We extend our analysis by looking at the relationship between the measure we have constructed and responses to a range of questions that *a priori* might be thought to be tapping postmaterialist values. In table 6.20 we show the pattern of support for the women's movement, for environmental and civil rights movements, and other social movements. In each case those who are classified as postmaterialist are more favourable. The differences range from between eight and ten percentage points for the ecology and anti-nuclear movements to between thirteen and eighteen points for the women's movement and the anti-apartheid movement. Almost three out of ten postmaterialists support all six movements, compared with one in six of all others.

Similarly, there are consistent differences in quality-of-life preferences between the two groups. As table 6.21 shows, postmaterialists place less emphasis on work and material possessions and are less likely to feel that a greater emphasis on technology would be beneficial. They are also twice as likely, as we can see from table 6.22, to express strong agreement with the idea of forgoing part of their income or accepting an increase in taxes if such actions contribute to the environment, and to reject the view that environmental problems are an inevitable consequence of combating unemployment.

TABLE 6.21 *Style of life items, by postmaterialism*

	Percentage agreeing	
	Postmaterialist %	Other %
Work very important	58	66
Leisure very important	38	31
Less emphasis on money & material possessions good	82	72
More emphasis on technology good	49	63
Decrease in importance of work in our lives good	36	21

Finally, we should note that postmaterialists are somewhat less likely to argue that there can never be absolutely clear guidelines about what is good and evil, and are twice as likely as all others to believe that greater respect for authority is a bad thing.

Thus the measure of 'postmaterialism' we have employed is associated with a questioning stance in relation to the benefits of growth and technology. It appears to reflect the belief that, both in relation to individual or personal concerns and to overall social organisation, conventional priorities need to be changed. It should be obvious from our discussion that, in the Irish case, we are hesitant to apply the label 'postmaterialist'. For our younger, better-educated respondents this label may not be entirely inappropriate. For their less-educated counterparts, who in recent years have been exposed to high levels of unemployment and involuntary emigration, it may be misleading.

What seems to be involved in the overall orientation is a critical stance towards authority in general and questioning of conventional ways of defining and pursuing social and economic issues. It appears likely that for many Irish respondents such an orientation arises

TABLE 6.22 *Willingness to bear costs in order to protect environment, by postmaterialism*

| | Percentage strongly agreeing | |
	Postmaterialist %	Other %
Would give part of my income if I were certain that the money would be used to prevent environmental pollution	22	13
Would agree to an increase in taxes if the extra money is used to prevent environmental pollution	13	7
Reject the view that if we want to combat unemployment we shall in this country just have to accept environmental problems	28	16

not from a transcendence of material preoccupations but from a certain disillusionment with the notion that economic growth will necessarily translate into an improvement in their own circumstances or the quality of life in the communities in which they live.

In this regard it is striking that we have found that the unemployed do not differ significantly from employees on the postmaterialism measure. The unemployed are less likely than employees to give priority to maintaining a high level of economic growth, the respective figures being 47 and 56 per cent. It is also true that the non-skilled working class place less emphasis on growth than other classes; here the relevant figures are 45 and 60 per cent. In Ireland these figures seem more likely to reflect a certain disillusionment with the politics of growth and a sense of the limited relationship between growth and reduction in unemployment levels, rather than indicating a fixed hierarchy of needs.

What the results do seem to suggest is a desire among the unemployed to have more control over their lives and to protect their self-esteem. Thus 41 per cent of the unemployed give priority to 'seeing that people have more say about how things are done at their jobs and in their communities,' compared with 35 per cent of employees. This finding is consistent with the results for younger working-class people. It is among the young lower-working-class groups that having such a say is given its greatest priority. Among this group the proportion choosing this option is 46 per cent, which is thirteen points higher than any of the other groups. Indeed, among this group the percentage choosing the 'influence' option exceeds that choosing 'economic growth'. That what we are observing here is not simply an age effect is shown by the fact that no such effect exists outside the non-skilled working class.

The unemployed are also more likely than employees to give priority to 'giving people more say in important government decisions,' the respective figures being 44 and 34 per cent. Similarly, they place greater emphasis on 'progress towards a society in which ideas count more than money,' with the figures for unemployed and employees being 13 and 8 per cent, respectively. Once again support is provided for the view that this final finding should be interpreted in terms of economic disillusionment rather than disdain for more materialist preoccupations, by the manner in which the outcome is affected by class and age. From table 6.23 we can see that it is the young lower-working-class respondents who are most likely to choose 'progress towards a society in which ideas count more than money' and least likely to choose 'economic stability'; the respective proportions are 15 and 38 per cent, giving a ratio of 2.5:1. For none of the other sub-groups does this ratio fall below 5:1. It is only in the contrast between giving a priority to 'giving people more say in important government decisions' versus 'fighting rising prices' that an age effect between class groups emerges that is in any way consistent with a straightforward postmaterialist interpretation. In this instance those aged less than thirty are twice as likely to emphasise participation, while those over thirty are marginally more likely to give priority to fighting rising prices. In the Irish case, insofar as our measure of postmaterialism is tapping attitudes other than those captured by the other left-wing value dimensions, it appears more likely to be due to the exclusion of certain groups from the benefits of economic development rather than to the tendency to take such benefits for granted. In conclusion, therefore, we can say that the group of our respondents whom we have classified as postmaterialists are indeed anxious to put 'new' issues, such as sex roles and human rights and environment, on the political agenda. But they are not primarily identifiable as 'greens', whether understood as supporting the Green Party or as according the highest priority to environmental issues. What is more significant is their critical approach to conventional authority and their concern that all political issues should be addressed in ways that involve new forms of political involvement. These concerns can gain expression across a whole variety of issues. Postmaterialist concerns are not confined to any particular class, but they are most strongly in evidence among younger and more highly educated respondents.

TABLE 6.23 *Percentage giving priority to economic stability and progress towards a society in which ideas count more than money, by class and age*

| | Non-skilled manual class | | Other classes | |
	Under 30 %	30 or over %	Under 30 %	30 or over %
A stable economy	38	45	51	52
Progress towards a society in which ideas count more than money	15	8	10	8

Our analysis reveals that postmaterialists tend to identify with the political left but that postmaterialist values are not synonymous with economic left-right values. As we noted earlier in relation to liberalism on sexual morality and confidence in establishment institutions, the age and education effects are the most significant in structuring the postmaterialist dimension.

A number of political sociologists have suggested that the left-right distinction in western democracies may be envisaged as having two cross-cutting axes, the traditional economic left-right division based on social class position and a newer 'liberal' or 'postmaterialist' division less clearly rooted in the class structure but associated with age and educational attainment (Lipset, 1983, 510–11; Inglehart, 1990, 193, 287–8; Harding et al., 1986, 107). Our evidence bears out this analysis and confirms that the values of Irish respondents appear to be structured in a manner very similar to that identified in other European countries. The main difference in the Irish case, as in the case of the left defined in terms of economic values, is the smaller numbers in the postmaterialist category.

Political partisanship: left-wing economic values and liberalism on sexual morality

In the discussion that follows, we first explore the two principal dimensions that have traditionally been thought to structure political partisanship, i.e. left-right economic attitudes and liberalism on sexual morality. We shall then discuss attitudes to authority and postmaterialism.

From table 6.24 we can see that just over one-third of supporters of Fianna Fáil, Fine Gael, the Progressive Democrats and the Green Party have high scores on economic left-wing values. Fianna Fáil is slightly more left-wing than Fine Gael. Almost three-quarters of supporters of the Labour Party, the Workers' Party and Sinn Féin are located on the left.

TABLE 6.24 *Composition of party support in terms of left-wing economic attitudes and liberalism on sexual morality*

	Percentage left-wing on economic attitudes	Percentage left-wing on issues of sexual morality
Fianna Fáil	35	42
Fine Gael	32	48
Labour	74	60
Workers' Party	74	74
Progressive Democrats	31	75
Green Party	35	76
Sinn Féin	72	55
Independent	25	61

The parties are not quite as sharply differentiated in terms of liberalism, but the differences are by no means insubstantial. Fianna Fáil has the lowest proportion of liberal supporters—42 per cent—but Fine Gael is not a great deal higher, at 48 per cent. The Labour Party has a majority of liberal supporters, at 60 per cent. The predominantly liberal parties on sexual morality, however, are the Workers' Party and, more interestingly perhaps, the Progressive Democrats and the Green Party. Supporters of the latter two parties combine right-wing economic values with liberal positions on sexual morality.

While the foregoing discussion spells out clearly differences in the value profiles of supporting each of the political parties, it does not directly address the question of the extent to which voters on the left and right support each of the parties. The data dealing with this issue are set out in table 6.25. Here we can see that while those who are on the right, in terms of economic attitudes, are more likely to support Fianna Fáil and Fine Gael, Fianna Fáil also manage to attract the support of almost half of those on the left, compared with Fine Gael's one-fifth. The sharpest contrast occurs in the case of the Labour Party and the Workers' Party, which, combined, receive support from almost one in four of those on the left but only just above one in twenty of those on the right. These figures again bring out the fact that the relative size of the left and right is the really distinctive characteristic of the political system.

In order to pursue the issue of the consequences of ideology for political partisanship, we look in table 6.26 at the combined effects of left-wing economic values and liberalism on sexual morality. Among those who are to the right on both dimensions, over six out of ten support Fianna Fáil, but this drops to less than four out of ten for those who are found on the left in both cases. A similar pattern is found for Fine Gael, although the absolute levels, at 27 and 19 per cent, are obviously different. Exactly the opposite pattern is found for the Labour Party and Workers' Party, which receive the support of 28 per cent of those who are consistently left-wing but a mere 2 per cent from those with a consistent right-wing pattern. For the Progressive Democrats and the Green Party, on the other hand, the major factor influencing their support is the liberal dimension.

While the dimensions we have identified bear a clear relationship to party partisanship, they by no means exhaust the potential range of value influences. This is illustrated by the fact that left-right self-assignment continues to have an impact even when we control for both factors. Among those who are consistently right-wing on economic and sexual morality issues, 66 per cent of those who assign themselves to the right support Fianna Fáil, compared with 53 per cent of those who assign themselves to the left. Correspondingly, among those who are consistently left-wing, 42 per cent of those who assign themselves to the left support the Labour Party or the Workers' Party, compared with 11 per cent of those who assign themselves to the right.

TABLE 6.25 *Party preference, by left-wing economic attitudes*

| | Left-wing economic values | |
| | Right | Left |
	Percentage supporting	Percentage supporting
Fianna Fáil	56	47
Fine Gael	26	19
Labour	4	16
Workers' Party	2	7
Progressive Democrats	5	3
Green Party	4	4
Sinn Féin	1	2
Independents	4	2

TABLE 6.26 *Party preference, by left-wing economic attitudes and liberalism on sexual morality*

| | Right-wing on economic values & sexual morality | Left-wing on economic values & right-wing on sexual morality | Right-wing on economic values & left-wing on sexual morality | Left-wing on economic values & left-wing on sexual morality |
	% *Supporting*	% *Supporting*	% *Supporting*	% *Supporting*
Fianna Fáil	62	56	49	37
Fine Gael	27	20	25	19
Labour	2	14	5	18
Workers' Party	0	5	3	10
Progressive Democrats	2	2	7	5
Green Party	3	1	6	6
Sinn Féin	1	2	0	3
Independents	3	2	5	2

Political partisanship: confidence in establishment institutions and postmaterialism
Both confidence in establishment institutions and postmaterialism have an impact on political partisanship, but of a kind that is somewhat different from that associated with the dimensions analysed

in the previous section. The major consequence of a left-wing position on the dimensions considered in this section is a reduction in the Fianna Fáil vote, an increase in the left-wing vote—i.e. the Labour Party and the Workers' Party—and greater support for the Green Party. From table 6.27 it is clear that postmaterialists are substantially less likely to support Fianna Fáil and, consequently, more likely to express a preference for parties of the left and for the Green Party. Among postmaterialists, support for Fianna Fáil drops to close to one-third of the group, while for all others it remains comfortably above half. On the other hand, over one-third of postmaterialists support one of the group of 'left' parties, i.e. the Labour Party, the Workers' Party, and the Green Party, compared with about one in eight of all other respondents.

TABLE 6.27 *Party preference, by 'postmaterialism' and confidence in establishment institutions*

	'Postmaterialist' % Supporting	Other % Supporting	Confidence low % Supporting	Confidence high % Supporting
Fianna Fáil	37	54	44	58
Fine Gael	22	24	21	25
Labour Party	16	7	10	7
Workers' Party	7	3	7	2
Progressive Democrats	2	4	5	4
Green Party	11	3	7	2
Sinn Féin	4	1	2	1
Independents	3	3	5	2

If we examine the odds of supporting Fianna Fáil as against parties of the left or the Green Party, Fianna Fáil enjoys an advantage of almost four to one among respondents other than postmaterialists, while among the postmaterialists the left and the Greens enjoy parity with Fianna Fáil.

A similar pattern of results can be observed in relation to the measure tapping confidence in establishment institutions. Among those with a high level of confidence in such institutions, Fianna Fáil enjoys an advantage of 5.3:1 (58 per cent to 11 per cent), while among those lacking such confidence it drops to 1.8:1 (44 per

cent to 24 per cent). The effect appears less dramatic than in the
case of postmaterialism, but it must be kept in mind that over four
out of ten respondents are located in the left-wing category on the
issue of confidence in establishment institutions, compared with just
over one in ten in the case of postmaterialism. As a consequence,
the impact of this measure on the overall distribution of preferences is substantially greater.

Left versus right and political partisanship
We can now summarise our discussion of the effects on party
preferences of all the values discussed hitherto, i.e. left-right self-
assignment, left-wing economic attitudes, liberalism on sexual morality, postmaterialism, and attitudes to establishment institutions.
The most striking contrast that becomes apparent across all the
dimensions of our left-right indicators is the ratio of support for
Fianna Fáil or Fine Gael to that of the left, defined in its broadest
terms, i.e. the Labour Party, the Workers' Party, and the Green
Party. In assessing these results we should note that the significance of a value dimension will depend on the number of
people who fall into that category as well as on the degree of its
association with political partisanship; for example, the number of
respondents in the postmaterialist category is substantially less
than the other left-wing categories. We find, though, that, as set
out in table 6.28, the probability of voting for Fianna Fáil over the
left-wing or Green parties is much lower among those who have
value orientations towards the political left than among those
whose political values are towards the right, and that this is true
across all the dimensions. The advantage enjoyed by Fianna Fáil
and Fine Gael over the left and Green parties is between two-and-
a-half and three-and-a-half times greater among those with right-
wing values. In fact these dimensions have cumulative effects on
the probability of supporting Fianna Fáil as against the left or
Green parties. We can illustrate this by showing the ratios of
support for those who are consistently to the left or to the right.

Table 6.29 shows that among those who are consistently right-
wing the ratio of support for Fianna Fáil and Fine Gael as against
the left and Green group of parties is a very significant 23.5:1. For
those who are consistently on the left the pattern of support is
reversed and the ratio is 1:3.5, i.e. they are three-and-a-half times
more likely to support the Labour Party, Workers' Party, or Green
Party. When we have taken these values into account the only

TABLE 6.28 *Fianna Fáil or Fine Gael and left-wing or Green support, by left-wing value dimensions*

	Left-right self-assignment		Left-wing economic values		Liberalism on sexual morality		Low confidence in establishment institutions		Postmaterialism	
	Left %	Right %	Left %	Right %	Left %	Right %	Left %	Right %	Left %	Right %
Fianna Fáil/ Fine Gael	65	83	66	82	67	84	65	83	58	78
Left-wing/ Green	26	9	27	10	22	11	24	11	33	14
Ratio of Fianna Fáil/ Fine Gael to Left-wing/ Green	2.5:1	9.2:1	2.4:1	8.2:1	3.0:1	7.6:1	2.7:1	7.5:1	1.8:1	6.6:1

TABLE 6.29 *Cumulative effect of lack of confidence in establishment institutions, left-right self-assignment, left-wing economic attitudes, postmaterialism and liberalism on support for Fianna Fáil and left/Green Party*

	Consistently left %	Consistently right %
Fianna Fáil/Fine Gael support	20	94
Left/Green support	70	4
Ratio of Fianna Fáil to left/ Green Party support	1:3.5	23.5:1

socio-demographic factors to continue to have an influence on support for the largest parties against support for the left are urban versus rural location and unskilled manual class situation; and these influences are of a relatively modest order.

Unemployment, left-right values, and political partisanship
As part of the recent debate concerning the 'underclass', there has been increasing concern with the consequences of unemployment

for political orientations. The suggested consequences range from apathetic disengagement from the political process to political alienation, with potentially disturbing consequence for the 'haves'.

Once again, in order to avoid misleading conclusions, we have provided a comparison of the political values of the unemployed with the three most appropriate reference groups. These are employees aged up to sixty-five, all respondents aged under thirty, and the non-skilled manual class. The conclusions we arrive at by adopting this procedure are consistent with those arising from more sophisticated statistical analysis.

In table 6.30 we provide the appropriate comparisons for each of the left-wing dimensions. The pattern is relatively straightforward. The unemployed are substantially more left-wing in terms of their tendency to assign themselves to the left, in their economic values, and in their level of confidence in establishment institutions. No significant differences are observed in relation to postmaterialism; and the unemployed, largely as a consequence of their concentration in the younger age groups, are somewhat more liberal on issues of sexual morality. When the results relating to the unemployed are put in the context of those relating to the appropriate age and class reference groups, we find that the unemployed are different in only one respect. They are substantially more likely to hold left-wing economic attitudes. Seventy-seven per cent of them hold such attitudes, compared with 37 per cent of employees. Even when we restrict our comparisons to the non-skilled manual class, a substantial difference can be observed: the figure for this group is just under 60 per cent.

In table 6.31 we examine the consequences of unemployment for patterns of political partisanship. The unemployed are less likely to support either Fianna Fáil or Fine Gael. For Fianna Fáil the respective figures for unemployed and employees are 36 and 46 per cent, while for Fine Gael they are 19 and 24 per cent. The Labour Party vote is higher among the unemployed, but not a great deal higher. It is support for the Workers' Party and the Progressive Democrats that varies most dramatically. Almost one in five of the unemployed express support for the former, compared with one in twenty for all employees. Correspondingly, 6 per cent of employees opt for the Progressive Democrats, while none of the unemployed do so. The impact of the left-wing economic values of the unemployed is clearly reflected here. The combined support of the unemployed for the Labour Party and the Workers' Party—at 33 per cent—is substantially higher than that displayed by those under thirty or by those in the lower working class.

TABLE 6.30 *Left-wing economic values: comparison of unemployed and employees*

Percentage left-wing	Unemployed %	Employees %	Under 30 %	Non-skilled manual %
Left-right self-assignment	61	41	55	57
Left-wing economic values	77	37	49	59
Liberalism on sexual morality	62	50	66	49
Lack of confidence in establishment institutions	60	50	56	52
Postmaterialism	14	16	17	14

TABLE 6.31 *Party support: comparison of unemployed and employees*

	Unemployed %	Employees %	Under 30 %	Non-skilled manual %
Fianna Fáil	36	46	41	56
Fine Gael	19	24	23	14
Labour Party	14	10	9	13
Workers' Party	19	4	8	6
Progressive Democrats	0	6	4	3
Green Party	7	6	9	3
Sinn Féin	2	2	3	2
Independents	2	4	3	3

Of course, we have no idea what the abstention rate of unemployed people may be at election time, and it may be that they are under-represented at the polls. Their low levels of subjective political effectiveness would suggest this, as would other studies showing a lower turn-out by working-class respondents and greater political apathy among the unemployed. It seems clear, however, that unemployed people evince a distinctly different profile of political partisanship from any of the groups with which they might usefully be compared.

A summary of party profiles

The evidence we have presented provides support for the growing tendency to see party political support as involving a greater degree of social structuring than had hitherto been thought to be the case. Fianna Fáil is a genuinely cross-class party. However, support for Fine Gael and the Progressive Democrats is sharply differentiated from that for the Labour Party or Workers' Party in class terms. Furthermore, while social class has no effect on Fianna Fáil support, class origins have.

The class origin effect is accounted for by the manner in which age and education interact. Older less-educated respondents predominantly support Fianna Fáil, irrespective of whether they have been upwardly mobile in class terms. The party, however, is failing to retain anything like such levels of support among younger less-educated voters. There is also a distinct possibility that as education becomes the major route to class mobility, an important source of Fianna Fáil's traditional cross-class support will be eroded. These factors present the party with major challenges.

Younger respondents are consistently less likely to support Fianna Fáil or Fine Gael. The less educated among them are the strongest supporters of the Labour Party and the Workers' Party, and support for the parties of the left is heavily concentrated in this group. Among those with third-level education, on the other hand, the combined support for the Green Party and the Progressive Democrats actually exceeds that for the left. Both Progressive Democrat and Green Party supporters tend to be younger, better educated, and urban. We must stress, though, that the support for the Green Party registered in the European Values Survey appeared to have relatively little to do with specifically environmental issues but to be related to a broader concern with a new agenda and a new style of politics.

Being located in a town or city with a population of over 2,000 makes it significantly less likely that one will support Fianna Fáil or Fine Gael. It is rural location rather than membership of a farming household that was found to be of the greatest significance (see also Marsh and Sinnott, 1993, 111). However, when we distinguish between small and large farmers, it is apparent that Fianna Fáil support rises gradually as we move from non-farm to large-farm households, whereas Fine Gael's relative advantage is concentrated entirely among large-farm households. Furthermore, over one-fifth of small-farm households are not committed to either of the two main parties, nor do they support the parties of the left.

Summarising our findings on the value dimensions we found to be significant, we can say that Fianna Fáil and Fine Gael supporters, by and large, tend to be right-wing in terms of self-assignment, economic values, views on sexual morality, confidence in establishment institutions, and postmaterialism. Examining our results in terms of Laver's discussion (1992, 373) of European party profiles, we might depict Fianna Fáil as a 'populist conservative party with a strong nationalist appeal, neither anticlerical nor particularly liberal on social affairs.' Labour Party and Workers' Party supporters are more left-wing on each dimension, displaying a social-democratic, consistently left profile. Progressive Democrat supporters are right-wing on economic values but left-wing in terms of liberalism or matters of sexual morality, displaying a pattern of values that can clearly be characterised as liberal.

Fine Gael remains something of an anomaly, since on none of our left-right dimensions does it differ in any substantial respect from Fianna Fáil. Although the class composition of its supporters is different from that of Fianna Fáil, the major difference between the parties relates to the level of electoral support each can command. The distinctiveness of Fianna Fáil lies in its ability to draw support from different social classes—and to span diverse value orientations. The nature of this achievement is illustrated further in table 6.32 by looking at the interaction between class, left-wing economic values, and political partisanship.

It is clear that a particular strength of Fianna Fáil—and the source of fundamental problems for the left—is its ability to attract support from those with left-wing economic values throughout all social classes. Thus it has a support level of 44 per cent among this group in the non-skilled manual class. This is particularly damaging to the left, because it is among this group that it enjoys its greatest advantages over other parties.

Among those with left-wing economic values, support for the left (Labour Party and Workers' Party) varies sharply by class, ranging from 14 per cent among the professional and managerial group to 30 per cent in the non-skilled manual class. For those professing right-wing economic values, on the other hand, class has no effect on level of support for the parties of the left but has a substantial impact on the distribution of support as between Fianna Fáil on the one hand and Fine Gael on the other. Fianna Fáil is remarkably successful in capturing right-wing lower-working-class support, with almost seven out of ten of this group opting for

TABLE 6.32 *Party preference, by economic values and class (percentage by column)*

	Professional & managerial		Intermediate non-manual & skilled manual		Non-skilled manual	
	Economic values		Economic values		Economic values	
	Right	Left	Right	Left	Right	Left
	Percentage support	Percentage support	Percentage support	Percentage support	Percentage support	Percentage support
Fianna Fáil	48	46	56	50	69	44
Fine Gael	34	21	24	24	14	14
Labour Party	3	14	4	11	4	21
Workers' Party	1	0	2	7	3	9
Progressive Democrats	5	6	6	2	2	3
Green Party	4	8	5	2	5	2
Sinn Féin	0	3	1	2	1	3
Independents	5	3	3	2	4	3

them. Among this group they enjoy a forty-six point advantage over Fine Gael and the Progressive Democrats; within the intermediate class its lead is a still substantial twenty-six points, but among the professional and managerial group its lead drops to nine points.

Mair (1992, 494–9) has stressed the importance of political as opposed to sociological factors in accounting for political partisanship. He stresses the success of Fianna Fáil in sustaining its governing credibility through an emphasis on social as well as territorial unity. However, Fianna Fáil's success with groups holding both right-wing and left-wing economic values, and the manner in which this varies by class, suggests that our knowledge of how party support is mobilised requires considerable refinement.

Finally, what light can our analysis shed on the implications of the dramatic shift in support towards the Labour Party in the general election of 1992? As Marsh and Sinnott (1993, 108–11) note, the dramatic advances achieved by the Labour Party were not associated either with class or generational polarisation. The Labour Party's gains among both upper-middle-class and lower-middle-class groups were actually much more impressive than gains among the working class. As Marsh and Sinnott (1993, 108) note, 'far from indicating a polarisation of Irish politics . . . the 1992 election suggests that the Labour Party had a catch-all appeal that was equivalent, albeit at a lower level, to that achieved at any stage by Fianna Fáil.' We would hesitate, therefore, to assume that the change in patterns of party support reflects an underlying polarisation in terms of values. The evidence that changes in party support 'apparently occurred on the basis of a string of particular issues' (Marsh and Sinnott, 1993, 113) is consistent with this interpretation. Rather than positing a shift in values among the electorate, we would suggest that the increase for the Labour Party is a contingent phenomenon, a consequence of voter volatility rather than a reflection of a change in value orientations.

Nevertheless, Mair (1993, 167) argues that the 1992 election deserves to be seen as a watershed, as it confirms the disruption of the postwar party alignment first seen at the election of 1989. Party competition and Government formation since 1948, he argues, was primarily a matter of Fianna Fáil versus all other parties, thus severely constraining the political strategies open to the other parties. In the elections of 1989 and 1992, Fianna Fáil for the first time accepted the logic of coalition politics. In the process, it implicitly abandoned its role as definer of all parties' strategic opportunities and became 'just another party' (Mair, 1993, 171). The consequence of this is that the 'electoral market' has become fully open, and the outcome of elections is henceforth likely to be more unpredictable. 'Parties can no longer take any voters for granted, but must compete for each and every vote' (Mair, 1993, 172).

Our analyses give grounds for believing that voter volatility is likely to become more rather than less common. We would suggest that our analysis of the configuration of values within which parties compete adds to our ability to understand the emergent terms of political debate. Apart from economic values and attitudes to liberalism on sexual morality, to which we have given most attention in this profile of parties' support, it is also worth noting the relevance of our other two value dimensions, attitudes to authority and postmaterialism. Both are more strongly related to age and education than to class, although, as we have noted, different elements of postmaterialism or 'new politics' appeal to respondents of different class backgrounds. But there appears to be a powerfully felt if rather inchoate sense of the need for a change in the dominant priorities in political life. This desire for a new approach to politics might be thought of as the 'Mary Robinson effect'. It is a value orientation that crosses the boundaries of party support (though its proponents are rather less likely to be either Fianna Fáil or Fine Gael supporters) and spans employed and unemployed alike. These voters are likely to constitute a particularly important section of the newly expanded 'electoral market' of the future.

7 Values and Psychological Well-Being

CHRISTOPHER T. WHELAN

INTRODUCTION

Inglehart (1990, 212) notes that the relationship between values and psychological well-being is a complex one. This is directly related to differences in the short-term and long-term consequences of achieving one's heart's desire. In the short run the outcome may be satisfaction or happiness, but in the long term we may come to take things for granted. 'Thus happiness is not the result of being rich, but a temporary consequence of having recently become richer.'

The distinction between short-term and long-term consequences is also related to two further paradoxes of subjective well-being. The first is that, as we have already discussed in relation to work satisfaction, people in very different objective circumstances show generally similar levels of satisfaction and happiness. The second is that satisfaction and happiness vary only a little within countries but vary a lot between countries. In what follows we will attempt to explore these issues. Before doing so, however, we will deal with the issue of measurement.

MEASURING SUBJECTIVE WELL-BEING

In the chapter on work values we emphasised the difficulties inherent in conceptualising and measuring variables such as satisfaction. Three types of measures of overall well-being were employed in the European Values Study: a *satisfaction* measure, a *happiness* measure, and a more complex *emotional experience* measure. The satisfaction measure involved a ten-point satisfaction scale where respondents were asked to indicate along a continuum ranging from 'dissatisfied' to 'satisfied' how satisfied they were with their 'life as a whole these days.'

The second measure was a happiness self-rating, where respondents were asked to indicate, 'taking all things together whether they would say they were:

(*a*) very happy,
(*b*) quite happy,
(*c*) not very happy, or
(*d*) not at all happy.'

The third measure is known as the Bradburn Affect Balance Scale (Bradburn, 1969). This scale provides a more detailed description of emotional experiences relating to subjective well-being. Respondents were asked to indicate whether during the past few weeks they had ever felt

(*a*) particularly excited or interested in something;
(*b*) so restless you couldn't sit long in a chair;
(*c*) proud because someone had complimented you on something you had done;
(*d*) very lonely or remote from other people;
(*e*) pleased about having accomplished something;
(*f*) bored;
(*g*) on top of the world or feeling that life is wonderful;
(*h*) depressed or very unhappy;
(*i*) that things were going your way;
(*j*) upset because somebody criticised you.

The response format involved a straightforward yes/no dichotomy.

An examination of the set of items that make up the scale indicates that half the items relate positive emotional experiences, such as feeling 'particularly excited or interested in something' and 'pleased about having accomplished something.' The other five items concern negative emotional experiences, such as feeling 'depressed or very unhappy' or 'very lonely or remote from other people.' The former set of items were combined to produce a scale of 'positive affect', while the latter form the components of a measure of 'negative affect'. Finally a composite index, the 'affect balance score', is created by subtracting negative scores from positive.

The available evidence suggests that satisfaction and happiness are not synonymous, the former involving a larger cognitive component and the latter having closer links to emotional experiences consequent on immediate or recent events in a person's life. However, as Inglehart (1990, 218) notes, both measures tap one's overall sense of subjective well-being rather than specific contentment. They have been shown to correlate at a level between 0.5 and 0.7 across a range of societies. In the Irish 1990 European Values Survey a correlation of 0.51 was observed, which compares with one of 0.44 for the range of countries included in our analysis. Despite the suggestion, arising from previous studies, relating to the cognition versus emotion distinction, we found that, both for the Irish respondents and the European sample as a whole, the measure of affect balance and those relating to positive and negative affect bear a slightly stronger relationship to satisfaction than happiness. As a consequence, it seems most sensible to think of our three measures as alternative indicators of overall subjective well-being and to concentrate on patterns of relationships that are consistent across the measures.

Irrespective of which measure we focus on, our results confirm those of early studies in showing Irish respondents' relatively high levels of well-being. Over nine out of ten in 1990 indicated that they were happy. These were almost equally divided between those opting for the 'very happy' and 'happy' categories. Similarly, almost eight out of ten people score above 5 on the ten-point satisfaction scale. Finally, scores on the positive affect scale are, on average, almost two points higher than on the negative affect dimension. This reflects, among other things, the fact that while six out of ten people had recently felt 'particularly excited or interested in something,' fewer than one in six had felt 'depressed or very unhappy.' The latter figure is remarkably similar to that estimated by Whelan et al. (1991) to be located above the threshold of psychological distress that is predictive of minor psychiatric disorder.

INTERNATIONAL VARIATION IN PSYCHOLOGICAL WELL-BEING

In table 7.1 we show the distribution of results relating to the range of measures of overall well-being across countries. The pattern of results is not dissimilar to that observed for 1981 (Harding et al., 1986, 183). Ireland emerges at the positive well-being end of the continuum on each of the indicators. An average satisfaction score of over 8 is observed: almost one in two respondents say they are very happy, and the positive affect score is 2.1 points above the negative affect score. In each case the degree of well-being indicated by these figures is significantly above the overall average.

TABLE 7.1 *International variations in psychological well-being*

	Average satisfaction score	Percentage happy	Average positive affect score	Average negative affect score	Average affect balance score
Netherlands	7.9	55	2.8	1.0	1.8
Republic of Ireland	8.1	47	2.9	0.8	2.1
Northern Ireland	8.1	41	2.8	0.9	1.8
Great Britain	7.7	40	2.9	1.2	1.8
Belgium	7.8	45	2.4	0.8	1.6
West Germany	7.4	20	3.2	1.6	1.7
France	7.1	29	2.3	0.8	1.5
Spain	7.3	23	1.7	0.8	0.9
Italy	7.4	17	2.0	0.8	1.3
Portugal	7.2	15	2.3	0.9	1.4
Total	7.4	24	2.5	1.2	1.4

Ireland forms part of a group of countries that display a relatively positive profile. This group includes the Netherlands, Belgium, Great Britain, and Northern Ireland. The contrasting group, which tends towards a negative pattern of responses, comprises Italy, Portugal, Spain, and France. West Germany presents rather a mixed picture, with an average score on the satisfaction measure, a low percentage 'very happy', and high scores on the positive and negative affect dimensions.

Identifying the reasons for the marked international variations is no easy task. A number of studies have shown a strong positive relationship between gross national product per capita and life satisfaction (Gallup, 1976; Inglehart, 1990). However, over half the variance among countries tends to be unexplained by economic factors. Inglehart (1990, 32) notes that when we compare levels of economic development and satisfaction, the Irish level of well-being is that of an over-achiever, while West Germany emerges as an under-achiever.

Ultimately, such differences appear to reflect enduring cultural factors that reflect the distinctive experience of the respective nationalities. Such differences appear to reflect 'cognitive cultural norms, rather than individual grief and joy' (Inglehart, 1990, 30).

There is some evidence that life satisfaction forms part of a syndrome of attitudes reflecting generally positive or negative attitudes towards the world in which one lives. In this respect interpersonal trust appears to be particularly important (Inglehart, 1990, 36–7). In the first column of table 7.2 we show the extent to which respondents in each country felt that 'most people can be trusted.' The distribution of responses across countries is broadly similar to that already described for subjective well-being. Thus the Netherlands, Ireland (North and South) and Great Britain emerge as high-trust countries, while France, Spain, Italy and Portugal are, as with subjective well-being, at the lower end of the continuum. We have set out also in table 7.2 the rank ordering of countries in terms of both interpersonal trust and happiness, in order to illustrate the tendency for the former and measures of psychological well-being to move in the same direction across countries. In six out of the ten the difference in rank is less than two, and in only one case, that of Belgium, does it exceed three.

TABLE 7.2 *International variations in interpersonal trust and happiness*

	Percentage thinking most people can be trusted	Rank order in terms of interpersonal trust	Rank order in terms of percentage very happy
Netherlands	53	1	1
Republic of Ireland	50	2	2
Northern Ireland	48	3	4
Great Britain	46	4	5
Belgium	32	8	3
West Germany	40	5	8
France	23	9	6
Spain	35	6	7
Italy	33	7	9
Portugal	20	10	10

Inglehart (1990, 43) has developed the argument that life satisfaction and interpersonal trust form part of a syndrome that is conducive to the viability of democracy. He acknowledges, though, that we do not yet have available evidence of sufficient quality to enable us to disentangle the causal linkages between political culture, economic development and democracy in a conclusive fashion.

SOCIO-DEMOGRAPHIC VARIATION IN PSYCHOLOGICAL WELL-BEING

As we have already noted, the available evidence suggests that psychological well-being tends to be surprisingly constant across socio-economic categories within countries. This provides yet another example of the need to take into account the individual's definition of the situation in accounting for satisfaction responses. It is necessary for us to attempt to understand the terms of reference within which an individual assesses his or her situation.

What are the standards against which objective circumstances are evaluated? One way of answering this question has been proposed by Campbell et al. (1976), who argue that satisfaction reflects the gap between one's aspiration level and one's perceived situation but that one's aspiration levels gradually adjust to one's circumstance. The final part of this definition is of particular importance. Concentration on the discrepancy between what is and what is desired has not generally been considered a fruitful approach, because in the absence of any realistic reference point it becomes difficult to talk meaningfully about the current context. The notion that aspiration levels gradually adjust to circumstances allows us to link this conception to a notion of satisfaction that focuses on a discrepancy between what is and what ought to be (Whelan, 1980). We are then attempting to understand satisfaction in the light of ideas of what is fair or reasonable.

The fact that there is no simple relationship between objective circumstances and feelings of deprivation and satisfaction was a central conclusion of Runciman's classic study of reference groups. He pointed (Runciman, 1966, 218) to the 'restricted and even illogical choice of reference groups, particularly in the manual stratum on matters of economic class.' For example, manual workers who were conscious of others being better off than themselves and their families tended not to perceive the discrepancies in class terms. Instead they were likely to refer to instances such as 'people on night work,' 'people without children,' and so on. Such responses demonstrate not an ignorance of inequality but the fact that some comparisons are taken very seriously while others are not. The choice of comparisons to be taken seriously arises from assessments of what is considered to be reasonable: what one has a right to expect. Such assessments, however, are not arrived at through an abstract process of evaluation but are crucially influenced by what previous experience has led one to expect.

As Inglehart (1990, 214–15) argues, if some such process of adjustment of one's aspirations to one's circumstances is in operation, 'then one would not normally find large differences between the subjective well-being of different social groups provided that those groups had reasonably stable membership, for in the long run, the aspiration levels of stable groups would have time to adapt to their respective external circumstances.' From this perspective it follows that ascriptive characteristics such as sex or religion, or relatively stable characteristics such as education or social class, might be expected to have relatively little influence. In contrast, we would expect changes in marital status, unemployment or health status to be associated with relatively large differences in subjective well-being.

In table 7.3 we set out the range of factors that we have found to have an influence on satisfaction and happiness. These are as follows:

1. Sex
2. Social class, with the major contrast involving the non-skilled manual group and all others
3. Being widowed, separated, or divorced
4. State of health
5. Unemployment
6. Life-style deprivation.

The life-style deprivation variable was defined in terms of the enforced absence of the following items:

(a) a meal with meat, chicken or fish every second day;
(b) a warm waterproof overcoat;
(c) two pairs of strong shoes;
(d) a roast meat joint or its equivalent once a week;
(e) new, not second-hand, clothes;
(f) a car;
(g) a telephone;

(*h*) being able to save some of one's income regularly; or
(*i*) experiencing persistent debt problems in relation to routine expenses.

TABLE 7.3 *Factors influencing variation in life satisfaction and happiness*

	Average life satisfaction score	Percentage very happy
Non-skilled manual	7.5	40
Other classes	8.1	44
Unemployed	6.6	24
Other	8.0	45
Life-style deprivation score:		
0	8.3	50
1	7.9	42
2	7.6	41
3+	6.8	23
State of health:		
Very good	8.3	56
Good	7.8	39
Fair	7.0	21
Poor	6.2	21
Very poor	5.2	11
Widowed, divorced, separated	6.9	29
Other	8.0	45
Women	7.9	50
Men	7.8	37

Inglehart (1990, 220–1), drawing on Euro-Barometer and World-Survey data, found that in the early 1980s women scored, if anything, a little higher on subjective well-being than men. For Ireland and Japan he found that there were more substantial differences in satisfaction and happiness in favour of women. From table 7.3 we can see that in the 1990 European Values Survey there was no significant differences in the satisfaction measure for women and men but a tendency for women to be significantly more likely to indicate that they are very happy. This is one of the few occasions on which we find our different indicators pointing to different conclusions. Overall, our results certainly support Inglehart's conclusion that despite substantial objective differences in opportunities, women are no less satisfied than men. We are anxious not to place too great a weight on the percentage difference in relation to happiness. In 1981 the difference was in the same direction but was a more modest 4 per cent. At that time the satisfaction scores for men and women were 8.0 and 7.8, respectively. The general pattern of the results is consistent with Inglehart's suggestion that higher levels of subjective well-being for women are observed in societies where the relative position of women has improved substantially in recent years.

Consistent with the aspirations-adjustment model, we find that marital status has a stronger effect on subjective well-being than sex. In particular, those respondents who are widowed, divorced or separated display significantly lower levels of satisfaction and happiness; only 29 per cent of this group indicate that they are very happy, in comparison with 45 per cent of all others. Clearly such respondents have not adjusted to their changed economic and social circumstances.

While social class is a relatively fixed characteristic, we still observe a significant impact at the lower end of the class hierarchy, with non-skilled manual workers being both less satisfied and less happy. This effect is not surprising, however, when we take into account the extent to which a position in the lower social classes is associated with higher risks of ill-health, unemployment, and life-style deprivation. The impact of such variables on psychological distress in the Irish context has been amply demonstrated (Whelan et al., 1991; Whelan, 1992, 1994). Not surprisingly, health has the most substantial effect. Life-style satisfaction scores vary from 8.3 for those in good health to 5.2 for those in very poor health. The comparable figures for those feeling very happy are 56 and 11 per cent. Unemployment also has a striking effect. The unemployed have a satisfaction score that is only 80 per cent of that of all others and a percentage figure reporting feeling very happy only slightly greater than half that of the remainder of the respondents. Life-style deprivation is also a significant predictor of subjective well-being. Those respondents who suffer an enforced lack of none of the items included in our analysis register a life satisfaction score of 8.3, and one in two of their members indicate that they are very happy. These figures decline as deprivation increases, until for those suffering an enforced lack of three or more items, life satisfaction scores are as low as 6.8, and less than one in four report themselves as being very happy.

A couple of additional factors that emerge as relevant to psychological well-being, even when allowing for the factors already discussed, are being aged sixty or over and being in full-time unpaid home duties. When account is taken of other influences, such as state of health, those aged sixty or over are more satisfied. This finding is in line with that of Inglehart (1990, 224–6), that when we allow for the disadvantages suffered by the elderly, they emerge as significantly more satisfied than others. So, perhaps rather surprisingly, do those in full-time unpaid home duties—all of whom are women. Here the effects are modest but still significant. Once again we could draw on the notion of relative improvement in comparison with their traditional situation. However, we will postpone further discussion of this finding until we have looked at the corresponding results relating to positive and negative affect.

We have already referred to the fact that previous studies have tended to find that socio-demographic background tends to play a relatively modest role in explaining psychological well-being. Inglehart (1977) used five different measures of well-being and, by taking account of age, sex, income, occupation, education, religious denomination, church attendance, political party identification, union membership and size of community and race, accounted for on average 6 per cent of the total variance. The same set of predictors (Inglehart, 1990, 214) explained 26 per cent of the variance in voting intentions, 30 per cent of the variance in political party identification, and 33 per cent of the variance in self-placement on a left-right political scale. In the Irish case a more limited set of variables dealing with age, unemployment, marital status, life-style and being in full-time duties explains 9 per cent of the satisfaction measure and 6 per cent of the happiness measure. When health status is added to the equation the respective figures rise to 16 and 9 per cent.

In relative importance, the influences on subjective well-being can be roughly ordered as follows:

1. Physical health status
2. Being aged over sixty
3. Being widowed, separated, or divorced
4. Unemployment
5. Life-style deprivation

It will be obvious that social class does not appear in this list. The reason is that, while we find consistent class differences in psychological well-being, they disappear when we control for ill-health, unemployment, and life-style deprivation. This provides further evidence that it is relatively short-term changes in our circumstances rather than relatively permanent attributes that provide the key to understanding life satisfaction.

SOCIO-DEMOGRAPHIC VARIATION IN POSITIVE AND NEGATIVE EXPERIENCES

The set of items relating to recent positive and negative feelings enable us to provide a more detailed picture than the single-item measures, the extent of well-being and distress experienced by our respondents. That these items are tapping something quite fundamental is illustrated in table 7.4 by the extent to which they vary systematically with stated health. Those in poor health are consistently less likely to have experienced positive feelings and consistently more likely to have experienced negative feelings. One in nine of those reporting themselves in very poor health had recently felt particularly excited or interested in something, compared with seven out of ten of those in very good health. Similarly, while three out of four of those who were in very good health indicated that they had in the recent past felt pleased about having accomplished something, this held true for only one in three of those with very poor health. On the other hand, while two out of three of those with poor health had recently experienced feelings of boredom, depression, or unhappiness, the former was referred to by less than one in five of those with very good health and the latter by less than one in ten. The affect balance score ranged from 2.7 for those in the favourable health situation to –1.4 for those at the other end of the continuum. The corresponding scores for positive affect are 3.3 and 0.9, and for negative affect 0.6 and 2.3.

Variation by socio-demographic characteristics tends to be somewhat less dramatic than by health status but is by no means insignificant. In table 7.5 we set out the distribution of responses to the individual items and the overall affect scores by social class, employment and marital status and the results for the respondents as a whole. The crucial distinguishing factors are location in the non-skilled manual class, unemployment, and being widowed, separated, or divorced. However, the factor that has the strongest effect tends to vary to some extent across items.

TABLE 7.4 *Variation in positive and negative feelings, by state of health*

		Very good	Good	Fair	Poor	Very poor
				State of health		
Positive feelings:						
1. Particularly excited or interested in something	(%)	70	57	38	36	11
2. Proud because someone had complimented you on something you had done	(%)	58	49	37	21	22
3. Pleased about having accomplished something	(%)	75	71	54	39	33
4. On top of the world/feeling that life is wonderful	(%)	54	37	24	14	0
5. Things were going your way	(%)	79	68	47	29	22
Negative feelings:						
6. So restless you couldn't sit long in a chair	(%)	23	27	26	50	56
7. Very lonely or remote from other people	(%)	8	13	30	43	44
8. Bored	(%)	18	22	34	40	67
9. Depressed or unhappy	(%)	8	17	25	54	67
10. Upset because someone criticised you	(%)	8	18	12	21	0
Positive affect score		3.3	2.8	2.0	1.4	0.9
Negative affect score		0.6	1.0	1.3	2.1	2.3
Affect balance score		2.7	1.8	0.7	–0.7	–1.4

The unemployed, non-skilled manual workers and those who previously had a spouse are less likely than all other respondents to have recently experienced one of the positive feelings covered in the questionnaire. Those who have experienced the loss of a spouse are least likely to report that they have experienced 'pride as a consequence of someone having complimented them on something they had done' or 'feeling particularly excited or interested in something they had done.' The loss of intimacy and social support reflected in these responses hardly seems to be adequately compensated for by the fact that only one in ten of them had recently experienced being upset because somebody had criticised them. This group also displays the highest levels of loneliness and depression. Over one in three had recently felt very lonely or remote from other people,

TABLE 7.5   *Variation in positive and negative feelings, by socio-*
demographic situation

		Non-skilled manual	Unemployed	Widowed/ separated/ divorced	All respondents
Positive feelings:					
1. Particularly excited or interested in something	(%)	53	50	43	59
2. Proud because someone had complimented you on something you had done	(%)	42	41	36	50
3. Pleased about having accomplished something	(%)	59	43	54	69
4. On top of the world/feeling that life is wonderful	(%)	37	25	30	42
5. Things are going your way	(%)	57	40	41	68
Negative feelings:					
6. So restless you couldn't sit long in a chair	(%)	28	44	32	26
7. Very lonely or remote from other people	(%)	21	24	35	15
8. Bored	(%)	29	46	33	23
9. Depressed or unhappy	(%)	24	24	30	16
10. Upset because somebody criticised you	(%)	12	19	10	12
Positive affect score		2.5	2.0	2.0	2.9
Negative affect score		1.1	1.6	1.4	0.9
Affect balance score		1.4	0.4	0.7	2.0

compared with one in seven of the overall sample. Similarly, three out of ten had been depressed or unhappy, a rate almost twice the overall one.

For a number of items, those who have suffered the loss of a partner displayed the most unfavourable psychological profile. It was the unemployed, however, who showed the greatest deviations from the overall picture. There is a widespread belief in western society that paid employment is a necessity, and there is no doubt that most adults want to work in the sense of having paid employment (Warr, 1984). Of course, many people are willing to make exceptions to the view that work is necessary, most notably in the case of married women, and in particular those with young children. This ideological background provides the context in which evaluations of the impact of unemployment must take place. Jahoda (1981) has drawn on Freudian notions to argue that work is a person's strongest tie to reality. In this formulation work need not necessarily be pleasurable to be beneficial, but it has links with the environment that are crucial. Other employment roles may provide such ties, but they come together in the employed role in a particularly powerful combination.

The available evidence suggests that the principal material and psychological benefits derived from a job may be summarised as follows (Warr, 1984, 414):

1. *Money.*
2. *Raised activity level.* Employment permits the exercise and development of personal skills and the establishment and attainment of realistic goals.
3. *Variety.* Without paid employment a person's behaviour and environment are likely to be relatively restricted. This arises both directly, because of the exclusion from the work environment, and indirectly, through the withdrawal from activities because of financial restrictions.
4. *Temporal structure.* Occupational tasks and routines divide time into segments, each with its own built-in structure and goals.
5. *Social contact.* Paid employment gives access to a range of social contact and shared ideas and experiences that are not necessarily related to a work task.
6. *Personal identity.* The employed person is in general valued within society, paid work often being seen as a morally correct activity. At a more specific level, particular occupational roles can contribute in important ways to personal identity and self-perception.

Warr (1984, 425) suggests that psychological well-being is negatively affected by unemployment, because in addition to experiencing the loss of the psychological and material benefits offered by employment, the characteristics of the role of being unemployed are taken on. Unemployed people have few prescribed tasks, and those that they have are unpleasant or threatening: 'seeking financial allowances, "signing on" as unemployed, and applying for jobs where negative and consequent damage to self-esteem are likely: these are potentially distressing features of unemployment.'

The consequence in terms of both positive and negative experiences are reflected in the results set out in table 7.5. Just over four out of ten of the unemployed confirm that they had recently felt 'pleased about having accomplished something,' compared with seven out of ten of the sample as a whole; almost one in two were bored, in comparison with an overall figure of one in four; and one in five had recently been upset because somebody had criticised them.

Overall, the unemployed and those who have experienced the loss of or separation from a spouse have equally low scores on the positive affect dimension, but it is the unemployed who have the lowest affect balance scores.

The impact of life-style deprivation on psychological well-being is also striking. The relevant results are set out in table 7.6. Those suffering from an enforced lack of four or more items were three times more likely than those doing without none to be depressed or lonely, and twice as likely to be bored or restless. Similarly, they were only half as likely to have been excited by something, pleased about some accomplishment, proud because of having been complimented on something they had done, or to feel on top of the world. Their positive affect scores were half those of the most comfortable group, while their negative affect scores were twice as high. Wealth may not guarantee happiness, but grinding deprivation produces a great deal of psychological misery.

At this point we wish to look at the effect of the person's sex and being in full-time unpaid home duties on positive and negative psychological experiences. One of the most consistent findings in the epidemiological literature is that women experience higher rates of distress and disorder than men (Gove, 1972, 1978; Dohrenwend et al., 1980).

O'Hare and O'Connor (1987), focusing on treated illnesses rather than psychological distress, have drawn attention to the distinctive position in Ireland, where residence rates in psychiatric hospitals and first admissions to all forms of psychiatric treatment show higher male than female rates. This reversal, they argue, is connected with certain sex role characteristics of men in rural areas that appear to render them vulnerable to institutionalisation in psychiatric hospitals or dependent on out-patient psychiatric services once mental illness— usually schizophrenia—is diagnosed. There is also evidence that certain characteristics of women in rural areas make them less likely

TABLE 7.6 *Variation in positive and negative feelings, by life-style deprivation*

		No items	1 item	2–3 items	4 or more items
				Enforced absence of	
Positive feelings:					
1. Particularly excited or interested in something	(%)	68	58	52	38
2. Proud because someone had complimented you on something you had done	(%)	58	51	42	34
3. Pleased about having accomplished something	(%)	78	71	64	38
4. On top of the world/feeling that life is wonderful	(%)	50	44	33	24
5. Things were going your way	(%)	78	71	60	39
Negative feelings:					
6. So restless you couldn't sit long in a chair	(%)	22	27	25	42
7. Very lonely or remote from other people	(%)	9	14	21	28
8. Bored	(%)	19	21	26	37
9. Depressed or unhappy	(%)	10	15	20	35
10. Upset because somebody criticised you	(%)	13	9	10	20
Positive affect score		3.3	2.9	2.5	1.7
Negative affect score		0.7	0.8	1.0	1.6
Affect balance score		2.6	2.1	1.5	0.1

to look for, or receive, help from psychiatric services for depression. This, they argued, does not necessarily lead to the conclusion that rural women enjoy better mental health than urban women or women in other countries, rather that their learnt social responses, for example pressure of role obligations and lack of recognition of their symptoms, make them less likely to seek treatment.

Whelan et al. (1991, 26–7) found that their analysis of a national sample produced results that were consistent with the international literature in showing that women had statistically significant higher distress scores than men, although the substantive difference was relatively modest. The evidence from the European Values Study data is consistent with the previous findings, in that women have significantly higher negative affect scores, but no difference by sex is observed in positive affect scores.

Medical model explanations of differences by sex in mental health, based on the disease process, are not particularly persuasive. Sociological explanations have largely revolved around the idea that women's social roles are more stress-provoking than those of men. There is evidence that women are not pervasively more vulnerable than men, and attention is therefore directed to the different roles they occupy. Gove (1972) argued that sex differences were related to the nature of married women's roles, with marriage being considerably more beneficial to men than to women. However, subsequent research has suggested that the risk of distress for women is higher than for men, regardless of marital status (Thoits, 1986, 261).

One interesting finding that emerges from the present study is that while women in full-time home duties have negative affect scores that are no different from those for other women, they have significantly lower positive affect scores. In table 7.7 we display these differences for the individual items. On each of the items relating to positive psychological experiences women in full-time unpaid home duties fare worse than other women. The differences range from 4 to 12 per cent. This effect persists even when we control for marital status and other influences. These results are in agreement with those of Whelan et al. (1991, 118–19), in that such women had particularly high distress scores. They are consistent with interpretations that stress the negative aspects of housework, such as its unending and repetitive character and the manner in which it can prevent women from pursuing avenues to self-development (Oakley, 1984), although it is necessary to stress that women in the labour force in Ireland are a highly selected group.

We are confronted with the paradox that being in full-time unpaid home duties is associated with higher life satisfaction and happiness yet that such women are, like other women, more likely than men to experience negative psychological feelings and are less likely than all others to experience positive psychological feelings. These women are more satisfied with less. Once again, in order to explain the findings we need to refer to differing expectation and the consequence of relative improvements in recent years.

Two final factors that affect positive and negative psychological feeling also interact with a person's sex: these are retirement and unemployment of the 'chief earner'. The latter has a negative effect

TABLE 7.7 *Impact of being in full-time unpaid home duties on positive affect*

		Women in full-time unpaid home duties	All others
Particularly excited or interested in something	(%)	51	66
Proud because someone had complimented you on something	(%)	50	58
Pleased about having accomplished something	(%)	63	73
On top of the world/feeling that is wonderful	(%)	43	47
Felt that things were going your way	(%)	62	74

on the psychological variables. However, this effect is entirely accounted for by the life-style deprivation and health variables. This finding is consistent with that of Whelan et al. (1991, 95) that a husband's unemployment had no effect on the level of psychological distress experienced by his wife when allowance was made for level of life-style deprivation. Retirement turned out to have rather different consequences for women than for men. For men it is associated with a slightly stronger tendency to report positive experiences, while for women it is associated with a significantly lower tendency to respond in this fashion. It seems likely that for women the lower probability of having immediate family available to provide social support at this stage of their lives is probably a significant factor.

The approximate rank order of the variables having an influence on psychological affect balance is:

1. Health status
2. Life-style deprivation
3. Unemployment
4. Loss of or separation from spouse
5. Being in full-time unpaid home duties
6. Retirement for women

This set of variables explains 26 per cent of the variance in the affect balance score. Life-style, health status and unemployment are substantially more important than the other factors.

LIFE SATISFACTION AND PRIORITIES

In this section we seek to focus on the question of which areas of life have the greatest impact on life satisfaction. In addition to the overall questions relating to subjective well-being, our respondents were also asked to answer a number of questions relating to satisfaction with specific areas of their lives. In particular they were asked to assess:

(a) how satisfied or dissatisfied they were with their jobs;
(b) how satisfied they were with the financial situation of the household;
(c) how satisfied or dissatisfied they were with their home life.

In table 7.8 we show the relationship between each of these measures and our measures of overall life satisfaction, happiness, and affect balance. The figures in the table are correlation coefficients. The possible range of relationships runs from a correlation of 0 where the dimensions are entirely independent to 1 where the score on one dimension can be predicted perfectly from that on the other. The job satisfaction measure is of course relevant only for those in employment. Each of the component measures is positively related to each of the overall measures of subjective well-being. In addition, in each case it is life satisfaction that is most easily predicted by satisfaction with specific spheres of life. In turn, it is satisfaction with home life that has the strongest influence on each of the overall measures of well-being. Job satisfaction and satisfaction with financial situations have about equal impact.

TABLE 7.8 *Subjective well-being and satisfaction with different areas of life*

| | Correlation matrix (correlations by column) | | |
	Job satisfaction	Satisfaction with household financial situation	Satisfaction with home life
Life satisfaction	0.46	0.43	0.56
Happiness	0.28	0.28	0.38
Affect balance	0.24	0.30	0.39

In assessing the importance of satisfaction with different areas of life it is necessary to take into account the manner in which they go together. When this is done, through multivariate statistical procedures, a slightly different picture emerges. In relation to life satisfaction, satisfaction with home life emerges even more clearly as the crucial influence. However, satisfaction with financial situation is now seen to be substantially more important than job satisfaction. A similar situation holds in relation to the indicator of happiness. With regard to affect balance, however, job satisfaction emerges as slightly more important than financial situation. This is primarily a consequence of the fact that in relation to recent exposure to positive emotional experiences it emerges as equally important with satisfaction with home life.

The question arises of the extent to which such priorities can be considered constant across different groups. In pursuing his concern with postmaterialism, Inglehart (1990, 217) has directed attention to the possibility that circumstances that persist in the very long term can lead to intergenerational value changes, with the result that different domains come to be given priority. We have explored the possibility of such change by testing for variations in priorities across age groups and between those we have defined as postmaterialist and all others. No significant evidence of variation of this sort could be found. In fact the only evidence of variation in priorities to emerge involved the interaction of the sex of a person and job satisfaction. For women, job satisfaction is not a significant predictor of life satisfaction, while for men it is. It is necessary to stress, though, that job satisfaction was equally strongly related to recent exposure to positive and negative psychological experiences for men and women alike. It appears as if the relative position that paid employment occupies in their overall scheme of things leads women to discount its importance in comparison with men, even though such employment remains a crucial source of positive life experiences.

A LIFE SATISFACTION PROFILE

We have referred earlier to Inglehart's suggestion (1990, 241–6) that overall life satisfaction is part of a broad syndrome of attitudes and values that reflect whether one has relatively positive or negative attitudes towards the world in which one lives. The relationships between such values do not necessarily involve cause-and-effect sequences but are probably more usefully thought of as providing a psychological profile of satisfaction versus dissatisfaction. At this point we proceed to examine this suggestion at the level of the individual. In this respect the most interesting variable is our measure of affect balance, which takes into account positive and negative feelings.

In table 7.9 we compare the relationship between pride in one's nationality and the affect balance score. It is clear that those who are most proud of their nationality are also those most likely to report experiencing significantly more positive than negative emotional experiences. Another crucial feature of the way in which we view our world is the extent to which we trust others. In table 7.10 we show the relationship between affect balance and three different indicators of trust:

1. Degree of trust in one's family
2. Degree of trust in Irish people in general
3. Degree of trust in British people in general

In each case the more one's life is characterised by positive rather than negative psychological experiences the greater the degree of trust expressed.

TABLE 7.9 *Affect balance score, by pride in nationality*

	Average affect balance score
Very proud	2.1
Quite proud	1.7
Not very proud	1.7
Not at all proud	0.2

At the other extreme from trust is prejudice. Our respondents were asked which of a number of groups they would not like to have as neighbours. Here we focus on racial and religious discrimination and construct an index running from 0 to 5, based on responses involving the following groups:

1. People of a different race
2. Muslims
3. Immigrants or foreign workers
4. Jews
5. Hindus

TABLE 7.10 *Affect balance score, by trust responses*

	Your family Average affect balance score	Irish people in general Average affect balance score	British people in general Average affect balance score
Trust them completely	2.1	2.2	2.3
Trust them a little	1.1	2.1	2.2
Neither trust nor distrust	1.5	1.5	1.9
Do not trust them very much	–0.5	1.3	1.4
Do not trust them at all	0.0	–0.6	–0.2

The average prejudice score for Irish respondents was very close to the overall European average. From table 7.11 it is clear that extreme social and religious prejudice is associated with a high score on negative affect; but those who express such prejudice in relation to one or two of such groups do not differ from the 80 per cent of the sample who express no such prejudice. Clearly, the cause of such prejudice goes far beyond personal difficulties.

TABLE 7.11 *Negative affect score, by religious and racial prejudice*

Prejudice score	Average negative affect score
0	0.09
1	0.09
2	0.07
3	1.20
4	1.60
5	2.00

Finally, we will explore the extent to which differences in subjective well-being are associated with engagement in different areas of one's life. In table 7.12 we show the extent to which affect balance scores vary in relation to the extent to which work, family, friends, leisure, politics and religion are considered to be important. Positive affect balance is in each case associated with considering this sphere of life important. In the case of politics and religion, however, this is not the case. Here the most positive psychological state is associated with avoidance of the extreme responses of strong engagement or apathy. Finally, in relation to involvement, those who participate in voluntary organisations report a more favourable balance of positive and negative psychological experiences.

TABLE 7.12 *Affect balance score, by importance in life of different areas*

	Work	Family	Average affect balance score			
			Friends	Leisure time	Politics	Religion
Very important	2.2	2.1	2.1	2.2	1.6	1.6
Quite important	2.0	1.0	2.0	2.1	2.2	2.2
Not very important	1.1	0.7	1.0	1.4	2.1	2.1
Not at all important	0.2	1.0	−0.2	1.0	1.7	1.7

An interesting negative finding is that subjective well-being is not significantly related to religiosity; thus such factors as
    (*a*) believing that God is important in one's life,
    (*b*) thinking of oneself as a religious person,
    (*c*) belief in a personal God,
    (*d*) taking comfort and strength from religion and
    (*e*) taking some moments for prayer
do not enable us to predict subjective well-being.

PSYCHOLOGICAL WELL-BEING: AN OVERVIEW

Our starting point was a consideration of the limited effect of objective life circumstances on feelings such as satisfaction. One consequence of this is that we observe relatively modest variation within countries in psychological well-being in comparison with the very substantial differences that exist between countries. While economic development is strongly associated with life satisfaction, there are substantial factors that appear to be related to enduring cultural differences. Ireland ranks significantly higher on each of the indicators of subjective well-being than one might expect purely on the basis of economic considerations. Inglehart (1990, 246) argues that tendencies towards positive or negative norms of well-being seem 'to reflect profound differences in [a] society's perceptions of how benign or malignant the world is.' Consistent with this interpretation, we find that Ireland also ranks high on the degree of trust that is afforded to others.

The key to understanding the limited impact of objective circumstances lies in an appreciation of the manner in which aspirations gradually adjust to circumstances. More generally, we have to take into account the standards in terms of which an assessment is made. If we posit such a process of adjustment, then we are led to expect that relatively stable characteristics will have very little impact on psychological well-being, while those that reflect changes in life circumstances will play a key role. In general, this is what we do find. Health status, unemployment, being separated or divorced and life-style deprivation are the major factors determining satisfaction, happiness, and exposure to positive and negative psychological experiences.

Certain relatively fixed characteristics do have an effect. In the case of social class this arises entirely from its relationship to unemployment and life-style deprivation. Overall we find relatively little differences between men and women, whether married or single. Women in full-time home duties display higher levels of life satisfaction and happiness than other women but are significantly less likely to report recent positive experience arising from achievement or affirmation. This finding, and the fact that women generally are at least as satisfied as men despite enjoying less advantage, may be accounted for by the relative improvement in the status of women in recent years.

The spheres of life that are critical in determining overall psychological well-being are one's job, one's financial situation, and one's home life satisfaction. Each of these areas is associated with overall well-being. Home life is the most important, followed by financial situation, and finally one's job. Job satisfaction does play a more substantial part in relation to exposure to recent positive psychological expenses.

We could find no evidence of any intergenerational shift in value priorities involving the assignment of different weights to, for instance, satisfaction with the financial situation of the household vis-à-vis satisfaction with one's home life as a whole. The only significant variation observed was that job satisfaction was of less importance in relation to life satisfaction for women, even though it continued to be as good a predictor, as for men, of recent exposure to negative and positive psychological experiences. This finding is consistent with the results reported in chapter 4 on work values, suggesting that women are less committed to work as a central life goal.

Subjective well-being tends to go together with a high degree of pride in one's nationality and with a tendency to trust others. However, it is of relatively limited importance in helping us understand racial and ethnic prejudice.

Positive engagement with family and friends and with work and leisure is, not surprisingly, associated with a positive affect balance. In the case of religion and politics, however, it is those who occupy the middle ground who display the most positive profile.

As we have already pointed out in the chapter on work values, conceptualising and measuring notions such as satisfaction raises a variety of problems. We have proceeded by using a number of measures, none of which provides an entirely adequate indicator of subjective well-being. However, by concentrating primarily on results that hold irrespective of the particular measure being employed, we feel it has been possible to gain a reasonable, if partial, understanding of the processes involved.

8 Irish Social Values: Traditional or Modern?

CHRISTOPHER T. WHELAN

CONVERGENCE AND DIVERGENCE

At the outset we stressed that we would not attempt to offer a general theory of value change. The cultural consequences of the particular Irish experience of modernisation cannot be understood in terms of a logic of development in which the Irish value profile inexorably moves nearer to that typical of more 'advanced' societies. This is so not only because the particular path we have trod is distinctive but because we have the opportunity to accept, reject or modify the images offered to us by more developed societies.

Any attempt to understand contemporary value systems requires that we take history seriously and locate such values in the context of institutional stability and change. It also requires that we take into account not only development but failures of development, whether they are reflected, as they were traditionally in Ireland, in emigration or, as more recently, in unemployment.

The density, complexity and elusiveness of cultural values and their uncertain relationship with economic development are illustrated in the findings we have presented, particularly those relating to religion, politics, and marriage and the family.

CATHOLICISM REDEFINED

While Ireland to a significant extent has remained insulated from secularisation influences, the variations in religious practice and attitudes associated with age, education and urban location do provide clear evidence of the impact of modernisation influences. Religious practice, however, has also been affected by the current level of unemployment. Furthermore, while church attendance has declined over time at both the top and bottom of the class hierarchy, religious values continue to occupy a central position.

The Catholic Church in Ireland is facing a decline in confidence in its ability to provide satisfactory answers to social and moral questions. It must also confront the increasing tendency for members of its flock to assert the right to think for themselves on matters of private sexual morality. Such trends are also occurring in the general context of a declining tendency among people to adhere to absolutist moral positions.

The profile we observe, though, does not involve a general disenchantment with Catholicism or an inclination to adopt alternative belief systems. What appears to be involved is a redefinition of what is involved in being a Catholic. Whether or not the changes that are taking place involve a process of secularisation will probably remain a question of debate. What is clear, though, is that the current pattern of religious and moral values is distinctively Irish and shows no clear signs of becoming less so.

POLITICS AND TRADITION

A great deal of research relating to Irish political culture has focused on the persistence of a pre-industrial and rather anti-democratic style. Descriptions of political life have focused on lack of civic competence, localism, and authoritarianism. We have found a great deal of evidence that the transformation of the social structure in recent decades has brought considerable change in political values. Irish political culture now shares central features with other advanced European societies. Such change we have noted is hardly surprising, since the traditional features of Irish political culture did not date from time immemorial but derived from features of pre-industrial society that were themselves of relatively recent origin.

Our analysis of political partisanship involves one further step away from the notion of Irish politics as wholly *sui generis* and towards identifying points of comparability between the Irish experience and that of other countries. The evidence we have presented provides support for the growing tendency to see party politics as involving a greater degree of social structuring than had hitherto been thought to be the case.

Our findings point, among other things, to a shift in the basis and composition of support for Fianna Fáil. We have been at pains to stress, however, that the measurement of values cannot be employed to 'read off' levels of party support or to make predictions about ineluctable tendencies. A great deal else intervenes in people's evaluations of political parties. These other factors include the strategies of parties, which in turn are to a significant extent shaped by their understanding of changing value systems among the electorate. What has been offered is a framework for evaluation rather than a calculus of associations.

Our analysis has shown that, in addition to familiar dimensions relating to economic values and sexual morality, other values relating to confidence in establishment institutions and postmaterialism have a significant impact on party support. These values appear to connect to a powerfully felt, if rather inchoate, sense of the need for change. The relationship between value change and recent shift in electoral support, however, is far from straightforward. Our own assessment is that such shifts appear to reflect voter volatility as much as any clearly discernible sea-change in Irish politics. This is an issue that requires a great deal of further study. What is clear, though, is that political parties can rely less and less on traditional bases of support and must adjust to an expanded 'electoral market'.

SEXUAL MORALITY, MARRIAGE, AND THE FAMILY

Perhaps more than any other area, that of sexuality, marriage and the family confronts us with the paradoxical nature of Irish values. On the one hand the results of recent referendums involving the prohibition of divorce and the installation of an anti-abortion clause in the Constitution reflect an adherence to traditional conservative values. Alongside this, however, births outside marriage have reached a level of 18 per cent of all births.

There is no evidence that values relating to the 'politics of the family' are consistently more traditional than those in more economically advanced societies. There have been striking changes in some areas, coupled with strenuous adherence to traditional values in other areas along with considerable flux and uncertainty in others. Irish values are distinctly conservative in relation to abortion and sexual freedom. In relation to married women's participation in the labour market and certain forms of unmarried parenthood, Irish views are quite typical of liberal European patterns.

Values in this area follow a course that is difficult to predict and that does not conform to any orthodox notion of modernisation. While it may be helpful to describe individual values in terms of how 'backward' or 'advanced' they are, modernisation theory provides no infallible guide to where we are heading. The concept has value in guiding us through the maze, but in this and other areas we should not be surprised if the overall package reflects Ireland's own distinctive, angular variants of modern values rather than progressive movement towards a standard modern end-point.

References

Adams, J. (1963), 'Towards an understanding of inequity',
  Journal of Abnormal and Social Psychology, vol. 67, 422–36.
Adorno, T., et al. (1950), *The Authoritarian Personality,*
  New York: Harper.
Almond, G., and Verba, S. (1965), *The Civic Culture:*
  Political Attitudes and Democracy in Five Nations, Princeton:
  Princeton University Press.
Arling, G. (1976), 'The elderly widow and her family, neighbours
  and friends', *Journal of Marriage and the Family,* vol. 38, 757–68.
Barnes, S., and Kaase, M. (eds.) (1979), *Political Action: Mass*
  Participation in Five Western Democracies, London: Sage.
Barrington, T. (1980), *The Administrative System,* Dublin:
  Institute of Public Administration.
Barrington, T. (1982), 'Whatever happened to Irish government?'
  in F. Litton (ed.), *Unequal Achievement: the Irish Experience,*
  1957–1982, Dublin: Institute of Public Administration.
Bendix, R. (1967), 'Tradition and modernity reconsidered',
  Comparative Studies in Society and History, vol. 9, 292–346.
Berger, P. (1973), *The Social Reality of Religion,* Harmondsworth
  (Middlesex): Penguin.
Bew, P., Hazelkorn, E., and Patterson, H. (1989), *The Dynamics*
  of Irish Politics, London: Lawrence and Wishart.
Blackwell, J. (1989), *Women in the Labour Force,* Dublin:
  Employment Equality Agency.
Borooah, V., and Borooah, V. (1990), 'Economic performance
  and political popularity in the Republic of Ireland', *Public*
  Choice, vol. 67, 65–79.
Breen, R., and Whelan, C. (1993), 'From ascription to achievement?:
  origins, education and entry to the labour force in the Republic

of Ireland during the twentieth century', *Acta Sociologica,* vol. 36 (1), 3–17.

Breen, R., and Whelan, C. (1994), 'Social class, class origins and political partisanship in the Republic of Ireland', *European Journal of Political Research,* vol. 25.

Breen, R., and Whelan, C. (forthcoming), 'Gender and Class Mobility: Evidence from the Republic of Ireland', Sociology.

Breen, R., Hannan, D., Rottman, D., and Whelan, C. (1990), *Understanding Contemporary Ireland: State, Class and Development in the Republic of Ireland,* London: Macmillan.

Brittan, S. (1977) *The Economic Contradictions of Democracy,* London: Temple Smith.

Brody H. (1973), *Inishkillane,* London: Penguin.

Burklin, W. (1985), 'The split between the established and non-established left in Germany', *European Journal of Political Research,* vol. 13, 283–93.

Burklin, W. (1987), 'Governing left parties frustrating the radical non-established left: the rise and inevitable decline of the Greens', *European Sociological Review,* vol. 3, 109–26.

Burns T., and Stalker, G. (1966), *The Management of Innovation,* London: Tavistock.

Callan, T., and Farrell, B. (1992), *Women's Participation in the Irish Labour Market,* Dublin: National Economic and Social Council.

Callan, T., Nolan, B., and Whelan, C. (1993), 'Resources, deprivation and the measurement of poverty', *Journal of Social Policy,* vol. 22 (2), 141–72.

Campbell, A., Converse, P., and Rodgers, W. (1976), *The Quality of Life,* New York: Russell Sage.

Carty, R. (1981), *Party and Parish Pump: Electoral Politics in Ireland,* Ontario: Wilfrid Laurier.

Cheal, D. (1983), 'Intergenerational family transfers', *Journal of Marriage and the Family,* vol. 45 (4), 805–13.

Chubb, B. (1962), 'Going about persecuting civil servants: the role of the Irish parliamentary representative', *Political Studies,* vol. 11 (3), 272–86.

Chubb, B. (1982; 1992), *The Government and Politics of Ireland,* London: Longman.

Chubb, B. (1991), *The Politics of the Irish Constitution,* Dublin: Institute of Public Administration.

Clancy, P. (1992), 'Continuity and change in Irish demographic patterns' in P. Clancy, M. Kelly, J. Wiatr, and R. Zoltaniecki (eds.), *Ireland and Poland: Comparative Perspectives,* Dublin: Department of Sociology: University College.

Coakley, J. (1993), 'Society and culture' in J. Coakley and M. Gallagher (eds.), *Politics in the Republic of Ireland* (second edition), Dublin: Folens and PSAI.

Cohler, B. (1983), 'Autonomy and interdependence in the family of adulthood: a psychological perspective', *Gerontologist,* vol. 23 (1), 33–9.

Coleman, D. (1992), 'The demographic transition in Ireland in international context' in J. Goldthorpe and C. Whelan (eds.), *The Development of Industrial Society in Ireland,* Oxford: Oxford University Press.

Connidis, J. (1983), 'Living arrangement choices of older respondents assessing qualitative results with qualitative data', *Canadian Journal of Sociology,* vol. 8 (4), 359–75.

Covey, H. (1981), 'A reconceptualisation of continuity theory', *Gerontologist,* vol. 21, 628–33.

Dalton, R., and Kuechler, M. (eds.) (1988), *Challenging the Political Order: New Social and Political Movements in Western Democracies,* Cambridge: Polity Press.

Dalton, R., Flanagan, C., and Beck, P. (eds.) (1984), *Electoral Change in Advanced Industrial Democracies: Realignment or Dealignment?* Princeton: Princeton University Press.

Daly, M. (1978), 'Women, work and trade unionism' in M. MacCurtain and D. Ó Colráin (eds.), *Women in Irish Society: the Historical Dimension,* Dublin: Arlen House.

Daly, M., and O'Connor, J. (1984), *The World of the Elderly: the Rural Experience,* Dublin: National Council for the Aged.

Dobbelaere, K. (1981), 'Secularisation: a multi-dimensional concept', *Current Sociology,* vol. 29, 3–213.

Dobbelaere, K. (1985), 'Secularisation theories and sociological paradigms: a reformulation of the private-public dichotomy and the problem of societal integration', *Sociological Analysis,* vol. 46, 377–87.

Dobbelaere, K. (1987), 'Some trends in European sociology of religion: the secularisation debate', *Sociological Analysis,* vol. 48, 107–37.

Dobbelaere, K. (1989), 'The secularisation of society?: some methodological suggestions' in J. Hadden and A. Shupe (eds.), *Secularisation and Fundamentalism Reconsidered: Religion and the Political Order,* New York: Paragon.

Dohrenwend, B., Shrout, P., Egri, G., and Mendelsoun, F. (1980), 'Measures of nonspecific psychological distress and other dimensions of psychopathology in the general population', *Archives of General Psychiatry,* vol. 37, 1229–36.

Dowd, J., and La Rossa, R. (1982), 'Primary group contact and elderly morale: an exchange power analysis', *Sociology and Social Research,* vol. 66 (2), 184–97.

Dulles, A. (1976), *Models of the Church: a Critical Assessment of the Church in All Its Aspects,* Dublin: Gill and Macmillan.

Ester, P., Halman, L., and de Moor, R. (1993), *The Individualizing Society: Value Changes in Europe and North America,* Tilburg: Tilburg University Press.

Erikson, R., and Goldthorpe, J. (1992), *The Constant Flux: a Study of Class Mobility in Industrial Societies,* Oxford: Clarendon.

Farrell, B. (1970), 'Labour and the Irish party political system: a suggested approach to analysis', *Economic and Social Review,* vol. 1 (4), 477–502.

Flanagan, N., and Richardson, V. (1992), *Unmarried Mothers: a Social Profile,* Dublin: University College and National Maternity Hospital.

Fogarty, M., Ryan, L., and Lee, J. (1984), *Irish Values and Attitudes: the Irish Report of the European Value Systems Study,* Dublin: Dominican Publications.

Fox, A. (1976), *The Meaning of Work* (Occupational Categories and Cultures, 1. People and Work), Milton Keynes: Open University.

Fulton, J. (1991), *The Tragedy of Belief: Division, Politics and Religion in Ireland,* Oxford: Clarendon.

Galbraith, J. (1992), *The Culture of Contentment,* Sinclair Stevenson.

Gallagher, M. (1985), *Political Parties in the Republic of Ireland,* Dublin: Gill and Macmillan.

Gallagher, M., and Komito, L. (1993), 'Dáil deputies and their constituency work' in J. Coakley and M. Gallagher (eds.), *Politics in the Republic of Ireland* (second edition), Dublin: Folens and PSAI Press.

Gallie, D. (1988), 'Employment, Unemployment and Social Stratification' in D. Gallie (ed.), *Employment in Britain,* London: Basil Blackwell.

Gallup, G. (1976), 'Human needs and satisfaction: a global survey', *Public Opinion Quarterly,* vol. 41, 459–67.

Garvin, T. (1981), *The Evolution of Irish Nationalist Politics,* Dublin: Gill and Macmillan.

Giddens, A. (1990), *The Consequences of Modernity,* London: Basil Blackwell.

Goldthorpe, J. (1992), 'The theory of industrialism and the Irish case' in J. Goldthorpe and C. Whelan (eds.), *The Development of Industrial Society in Ireland,* Oxford: Oxford University Press.

Goldthorpe, J., and Whelan, C. (eds.) (1992), *The Development of Industrial Society in Ireland,* Oxford: Oxford University Press.

Goldthorpe J., Lockwood, D., Bechofer, F., and Platt, J. (1969), *The Affluent Worker in the Class Structure,* Cambridge: Cambridge University Press.

Gordon, M. (1977), 'Primary group differentiation in Ireland', *Social Forces,* vol. 55, 239–48.

Gove, W. (1972), 'The relationship between sex roles, marital status and mental illness', *Social Forces,* vol. 51, 34–44.

Gove, W. (1978), 'Sex differences in mental illness among adult men and women', *Social Science and Medicine,* vol. 12B, 187–98.

Greeley, A. (1992), 'Religion in Britain, Ireland and the USA' in R. Jowell, L. Brook, G. Prior, and B. Taylor (eds.), *British Social Attitudes: the Ninth Report,* Aldershot: Partmouth.

Hadden, J., and Shupe, A. (eds.) (1985), *Prophetic Religions and Politics,* New York: Paragon House.

Hakim, C. (1991), 'Grateful slaves and self-made women: fact and fantasy in women's work orientations', *European Sociological Review,* vol. 7 (2), 101–21.

Hakim, C. (1993), 'The myth of rising female unemployment', *Work Employment and Society,* vol. 7 (1), 97–120.

Halman, L., and de Moor, R. (1991), *Information Bulletin: EVSSG,* Tilburg: Institute for Social Research, Tilburg University.

Hammond, P. (ed.) (1985), *The Sacred in a Secular Age,* Berkeley, Los Angeles and London: University of California Press.

Hannan, D., and Commins, P. (1992), 'The significance of small-scale landholders in Ireland's socio-economic transformation' in J. Goldthorpe and C. Whelan (eds.), *The Development of Industrial Society in Ireland,* Oxford: Oxford University Press.

Hannan, D., Breen, R., Murray, B., Watson, D., Hardiman, N., and O'Higgins, K. (1983), *Schooling and Sex Roles: Sex Differences in Subject Provision and Student Choice in Irish Post-Primary Schools,* Dublin: Economic and Social Research Institute.

Hazelkorn, E. (1986), 'Class, clientelism and the political process in the republic of Ireland' in P. Clancy, S. Drury, K. Lynch, and W. O'Dowd (eds.), *Ireland: a Sociological Profile,* Dublin: Institute of Public Administration.

Healy, S., and Reynolds, B. (1992), 'Participation: a values perspective' in S. Healy and B. Reynolds, *Power, Participation and Exclusion,* Dublin: Justice Commission, Conference of Major Religious Superiors.

Heath, A. (1992), 'The attitudes of the underclass' in D. Smith (ed.), *Understanding the Underclass,* London: Policy Studies Institute.

Heath, A., and Topf, R. (1987), 'Political culture' in R. Jowell, S. Witherspoon, and L. Brook (eds.), *British Social Attitudes: Fifth Report,* Aldershot: Gower.

Heath, A., Jowell, R., and Curtice, J. (1985), *How Britain Votes,* Oxford: Pergamon.

Heath, A., Curtice, J., Jowell, R., Evans, G., Field, J., and Witherspoon, S. (1991), *Understanding Political Change,* Oxford: Pergamon.

Hechter, M. (1975), *Internal Colonialism: the Celtic Fringe in British National Development, 1536–1966,* London: Routledge and Kegan Paul.

Hornsby-Smith, M. (1987), *Roman Catholics in England: Studies in Social Structure Since the Second World War,* Cambridge: Cambridge University Press.

Hornsby-Smith, M. (1989), *The Changing Parish: a Study of Parishes, Priests and Parishioners after Vatican II,* London: Routledge.

Hornsby-Smith, M. (1991), *Roman Catholic Beliefs in England: Customary Religion and Transformations of Religious Authority,* Cambridge: Cambridge University Press.

Hornsby-Smith, M. (1992a), 'A recent transformation in English Catholicism: evidence of secularization?' in S. Bruce (ed.), *Secularization: Recent Trends in Theory and Data,* Oxford: Oxford University Press.

Hornsby-Smith, M. (1992b), 'Social and religious transformation in Ireland: a case of secularisation' in J. Goldthorpe and C. Whelan (eds.), *The Development of Industrial Society in Ireland,* Oxford: Oxford University Press.

Hout, M. (1989), *Following in Father's Footsteps: Social Mobility in Ireland,* London: Harvard University Press.

Hume, J. (1990), 'Europe of the regions' in R. Kearney (ed.), *Across the Frontiers: Ireland in the 1990s,* Dublin: Wolfhound.

Inglehart, R. (1977), *The Silent Revolution: Changing Values and Political Style among Western Publics,* Princeton: Princeton University Press.

Inglehart, R. (1984), 'The changing structure of political cleavages in western society' in R. Dalton, S. Flanagan, and P. Beck (eds.), *Electoral Change in Advanced Industrial Democracies: Realignment or Dealignment?* Princeton: Princeton University Press.

Inglehart, R. (1990), *Culture Shift in Advanced Industrial Society,* Princeton: Princeton University Press.

Inglis, T. (1987), *Moral Monopoly: the Catholic Church in Modern Irish Society,* Dublin: Gill and Macmillan.

Jahoda, M. (1982), *Work, Employment and Unemployment: a Social Psychological Analysis,* London: Cambridge University Press.

Jencks, C., and Peterson, P. (eds.) (1991), *The Urban Underclass,* Washington: Brookings Institute.

Jonung, C., and Persson, I. (1993), 'Women and market work: the misleading tale of participation rates in international comparisons', *Work, Employment and Society,* vol. 7 (2), 259–74.

Kelley, J., Evans, M., and Hayes, B. (1991), *Family Values and Labour Force Participation: Ireland in International Perspective,* Canberra: Department of Sociology, Institute of Advanced Studies, Australian National University.

Kennedy, F. (1989), *Family, Economy and Government in Ireland,* Dublin: Economic and Social Research Institute.

Kennedy, K., Giblin, T., and McHugh, D. (1980), *The Economic Development of Ireland in the Twentieth Century,* London: Routledge.

Kennelly, B., and Ward, E. (1993), 'The abortion referendums' in M. Gallagher and M. Laver (eds.), *How Ireland Voted, 1992,* Dublin: Folens and PSAI Press.

Kirby, P. (1984), *Is Irish Catholicism Dying?* Cork: Mercier Press.

Lang, A., and Brody, E. (1983) 'Characteristics of middle-aged daughters and help to their elderly mothers,' *Journal of Marriage and the Family,* vol. 45, 193–202.

Larkin, E. (1972), 'The devotional revolution in Ireland, 1850–75', *American Historical Review,* vol. 77.

Laver, M. (1987), 'Measuring patterns of party support in Ireland', *Economic and Social Review,* vol. 18, 95–100.

Laver, M. (1992), 'Are Irish parties peculiar?' in J. Goldthorpe and C. Whelan (eds), *The Development of Industrial Society in Ireland,* Oxford: Oxford University Press.

Laver, M., and Hunt, W. (1992), *Policy and Party Competition,* New York: Routledge.

Lee, J. (1973), *The Modernisation of Irish Society,* Dublin: Gill and Macmillan.

Lee, J. (1989), *Ireland, 1912–1985: Politics and Society,* Cambridge: Cambridge University Press.

Lijphart, A. (1980), 'The structure of inference' in G. Almond and S. Verba (eds.), *The Civic Culture Revisited,* Boston: Little, Brown.

Lipset, S., and Rokkan, S. (1967), 'Cleavage structures, party systems, and voter alignments: an introduction' in S. Lipset and S. Rokkan (eds.), *Party Systems and Voter Alignments,* New York: Free Press.

Luckmann, T. (1970), *The Invisible Religion: the Problem of Religion in Modern Society,* London: Collier Macmillan.

Mac Gréil, M. (1977), *Prejudice and Tolerance in Ireland,* Dublin: College of Industrial Relations.

Mac Gréil, M. (1991), *Religious Practice and Attitudes in Ireland,* Maynooth: Survey and Research Units, Department of Social Studies, St Patrick's College.

McKenna, A. (1988), *Child Care and Equal Opportunities,* Dublin: Employment Equality Agency.

McLellan, G. (1992), 'The enlightenment project revisited' in S. Hall, D. Held, and T. McGrew, *Modernity and its Future,* Cambridge: Polity Press.

McRedmond, L. (1980), 'The church in Ireland' in J. Cummings and P. Burns (eds.), *The Church Now: an Inquiry into the Present State of the Catholic Church in Britain and Ireland,* Dublin: Gill and Macmillan.

Mahon, E. (1991), *Motherhood, Work and Equal Opportunity: a Case Study of Irish Civil Servants* (First Report of the Third Community on Women's Rights), Dublin: Stationery Office.

Mair, P. (1979), 'The autonomy of the political: the development of the Irish party system', *Comparative Politics,* vol. 11, 445–65.

Mair, P. (1987), '*The Changing Irish Party System: Organisation, Ideology and Party Competition,* London: Francis Pinter.

Mair, P. (1992), 'Explaining the absence of class politics in Ireland' in J. Goldthorpe and C. Whelan (eds.), *The Development of Industrial Society in Ireland,* Oxford: Oxford University Press.

Mann, M. (1973), *Consciousness and Action among the Western Working Class,* London: Macmillan.

Marsh, A., and Kaase, M. (1979), 'Measuring political action' in S. Barnes and M. Kaase (eds.), *Political Action: Mass Participation in Five Western Democracies,* London: Sage.

Marsh, H. (1977), *Protest and Political Consciousness,* London: Sage.

Marsh, M., and Sinnott, R. (1993), 'The voters: stability and change' in M. Gallagher and M. Laver (eds.), *How Ireland Voted 1992,* Dublin: Folens and PSAI Press.

Martin, D. (1965), 'Towards eliminating the concept of secularization' in J. Gould (ed.), *Penguin Survey of the Social Sciences,* Harmondsworth (Middlesex): Penguin.

Martin, D. (1969), *The Religious and the Secular: Studies in Secularization,* London: Routledge and Kegan Paul.

Martin, D. (1978), *A General Theory of Secularization,* Oxford: Blackwell.

Martin, D. (1991), 'The secularization issue', *British Journal of Sociology,* vol. 42 (3), 465–74.

Mjøset, L. (1992), *The Irish Economy in a Comparative Institutional Perspective,* Dublin: National Economic and Social Council.

Moore, J. (1975), 'The Catholic priesthood' in M. Hill (ed.), *A Sociological Yearbook of Religion in Britain,* London: SCM.

Murphy, J. (1975), *Ireland in the Twentieth Century,* Dublin: Gill and Macmillan.

Nic Giolla Phádraig, M. (1988), 'Ireland: the exception that proves two rules' in T. Gannon (ed.), *World Catholicism in Transition,* New York: Macmillan.

Nic Giolla Phádraig, M. (1992), 'Religious practice and secularisation' in P. Clancy, M. Kelly, J. Wiatr, and R. Zoltaniecki (eds.), *Ireland and Poland: Comparative Perspectives,* Dublin: Department of Sociology: University College.

Oakley, A. (1974), *The Sociology of Housework,* Oxford: Martin Robertson.

O'Connor, J., Smyth, E., and Whelan, B. (1988), *Caring for the Elderly. Part I: A Study of Carers at Home and in the Community* (Report no. 18), Dublin: National Council for the Aged.

O'Hare, A., and O'Connor, A. (1987), 'Gender differences in treated mental illness in the republic of Ireland' in C. Curtin, P. Jackson, P. O'Connor, and B. O'Connor (eds.), *Gender in Irish Society,* Galway: Galway University Press.

Pateman, C. (1980), 'The civic culture: a philosophic critique' in G. Almond and S. Verba (eds.), *The Civic Culture Revisited,* Boston: Little, Brown.

Peillon, M. (1982), *Contemporary Irish Society: an Introduction,* Dublin: Gill and Macmillan.

Pyle, L. (1990), *The State and Women in the Economy: Lessons from Sex Discrimination in the Republic of Ireland,* Albany: State University of New York Press.

Raven, J., and Whelan, C. (1976), 'Irish adults' perceptions of their civic institutions and their role in relation to them' in J. Raven, C. Whelan, P. Pfretschner, and D. Borock, *Political Culture in Ireland: the Views of Two Generations,* Dublin: Institute of Public Administration.

Rempel, J. (1985), 'Childless elderly: what are they missing? *Journal of Marriage and the Family,* vol. 47 (2), 343–8.

Rose, R. (ed.) (1980), *Challenge to Governance: Studies in Overloaded Politics,* London: Sage.

Runciman W. (1966), *Relative Deprivation and Social Justice,* London: Routledge.

Sacks, P. (1976), *The Donegal Mafia: an Irish Political Machine,* New Haven: Yale University Press.

Sani, G., and Sartori, G. (1983), 'Polarisation, fragmentation, and competition in western democracies' in H. Daalder and P. Mair (eds.), *Western European Party Systems,* London: Sage.

Schlozman, L., and Verba, S. (1979), *Injury to Insult: Unemployment, Class and Political Response,* Cambridge (Massachusetts): Harvard University Press.

Schmitt, D. (1973), *The Irony of Democracy: the Impact of Political Culture on Administrative and Political Development in Ireland,* Lexington: Lexington Books.

Schmitter, P. (1981), 'Interest, intermediation and regime governability' in S. Berger (ed.), *Organizing Interests in Western Europe,* Cambridge: Cambridge University Press.

Scott, J. (1990), 'Women and the family' in R. Jowell, S. Witherspoon, and L. Brook (eds.), *British Social Attitudes: the Seventh Report,* Aldershot: Gower.

Shanas, E. (1973), 'Family kin networks and ageing in cross-cultural perspective', *Journal of Marriage and the Family,* vol. 35 (3), 505–11.

Sinnott, R. (1984), 'Interpretations of the Irish party system', *European Journal of Political Research,* vol. 12, 289–307.

Stark, R., and Bainbridge, W. (1985), *The Future of Religion,* London: University of California Press.

Stoller, E. (1982), 'Sources of support for the elderly during illness', *Health and Social Work,* no. 7, 111–22.

Sussman, M. (1965), 'Relationships of adult children with their parents in the United States' in E. Shanan and G. Streib (eds.), *Social Structure and the Family: Generational Relations*, Englewood Cliffs: Prentice-Hall.

Thoits, P. (1986), 'Multiple identities', *American Sociological Review*, vol. 51 (2), 259–72.

Tobin, S., and Kulys, E. (1981), 'The family in the institutionalisation of the elderly', *Journal of Social Issues*, vol. 37 (3), 145–57.

Topf, R. (1989), 'Political change and political culture in Britain, 1959–1987' in J. Gibbins (ed.), *Contemporary Political Culture*, London: Sage.

Troll, L., Miller, S., and Atchley, R. (1979), *Families in Later Life*, Belmont (California): Wadsworth.

Verba, S., and Nie, N. (1972), *Participation in America: Political Democracy and Social Equality*, Chicago: Chicago University Press.

Verba, S., Nie, N., and Kim, J. (1978), *Participation and Political Equality: a Seven-Nation Comparison*, Cambridge: Cambridge University Press.

Wallis, R., and Bruce, S. (1992), 'Secularization: the orthodox model' in S. Bruce (ed.), *Religion and Modernization*, Oxford: Oxford University Press.

Weafer, J. (1986a), 'The Irish laity: some findings of the 1984 national survey', *Doctrine and Life*, vol. 36, 247–53.

Weafer, J. (1986b), 'Change and continuity in Irish religion, 1974–1984', *Doctrine and Life*, 36, 507–17.

Whelan, B., and Vaughan, R. (1982), *The Economic and Social Circumstances of the Elderly* (General Research Series, no. 110), Dublin: Economic and Social Research Institute.

Whelan, C. (1980), *Employment Conditions and Job Satisfaction: the Distribution, Perception and Evaluation of Job Rewards* (General Research Series, no. 101), Dublin: Economic and Social Research Institute.

Whelan, C. (1992), 'The role of income, life-style deprivation and financial strain in mediating the impact of unemployment on psychological distress: evidence from the republic of Ireland', *Journal of Occupational and Organisational Psychology*, vol. 65, 331–44.

Whelan, C. (1993), 'Unemployment, Marginalisation and Social Exclusion' (Paper presented to inaugural session of National Economic and Social Forum, Dublin).

Whelan, C. (1994), 'Social class, unemployment and psychological distress', *European Sociological Review,* 11, 1, 49–61.

Whelan, C., and Whelan, B. (1984), *Social Mobility in the Republic of Ireland: a Comparative Perspective,* Dublin: Economic and Social Research Institute.

Whelan, C., and Whelan, B. (1988), *The Transition to Retirement,* Dublin: Economic and Social Research Institute.

Whelan, C., Hannan, D., and Creighton, S. (1991), *Unemployment, Poverty and Psychological Distress,* Dublin: Economic and Social Research Institute.

Whelan C., Breen, R., and Whelan, B. (1992), 'Industrialisation, class formation and social mobility in Ireland' in J. Goldthorpe and C. Whelan (eds.), *The Development of Industrial Society in Ireland,* Oxford: Oxford University Press.

Whyte, J. (1974), 'Ireland: politics without social bases' in R. Rose (ed.), *Electoral Behaviour: a Comparative Handbook,* New York: Free Press.

Whyte, J. (1980), *Church and State in Modern Ireland, 1923–1979* (second edition), Dublin: Gill and Macmillan.

Wilson, B. (1982), *Religion in Sociological Perspective,* Oxford: Oxford University Press.

Wilson, B. (1985), 'Secularization: the inherited model' in P. Hammond (ed.), *The Sacred in a Secular Age,* Berkeley: University of California Press.

Winter, M. (1973), *Mission or Maintenance: a Study in New Pastoral Structures,* London: Darton, Longman and Todd.

Zander, A. (1993), 'Changing work values' in P. Ester, L. Halman, and R. de Moor (eds.), *The Individualizing Society: Value Changes in Europe and North America*, Tilburg: Tilburg University Press.